Information Pr

Student's Book

Elaine Mullins

Third edition

To Ronald, Lorraine and Andrew

PITMAN PUBLISHING
128 Long Acre, London WC2E 9AN

A Division of Longman Group UK Limited

© Elaine Mullins 1985, 1988
© Longman Group UK Limited 1992

First published in Great Britain 1985
Third Edition 1992
Reprinted 1993, 1994

British Library Cataloguing in Publication Data
Mullins, Elaine
Information processing.–3rd ed.
Student's book
1. Word processing
I. Title
652'.5

ISBN 0 273 03818 4

All rights reserved; no part of this publication may be reproduced, stored in a retrieval system, or transmitted in any form, or by any means, electronic, mechanical, photocopying, recording, or otherwise without either the prior written permission of the Publishers or a licence permitting restricted copying in the United Kingdom issued by the Copyright Licensing Agency Ltd, 90 Tottenham Court Road, London W1P 9HE. This book may not be lent, resold, hired out or otherwise disposed of by way of trade in any form of binding or cover other than that in which it is published, without the prior consent of the Publishers.

Typeset by MHL Typesetting Ltd, Coventry
Printed in England by Clays Ltd, St Ives plc

Contents

9 The people factor 153

10 The electronic office 178

List of illustrations

Acknowledgements

I especially thank my family for their support so willingly given during the writing of this book.

The author and publishers would also like to thank the following for permission to reproduce copyright material:

Apple Computer (UK) Ltd
APEX
ATEP UK Ltd
Binder Hamlyn
British Telecom
Commission of the European Communities (source: Office for Official Publications of the European Communities)
Dictaphone
Electronic Information Technology Ltd
Gen Audio & Data Communications Ltd
Hewlett-Packard Ltd
IBM (UK) Ltd
IBR Microcomputer Ltd
INMAC (UK) Ltd
International Systems and Applications
Jones + Brother
Lexisystems Ltd
3M United Kingdom plc
Manpower Services Commission
NEC Telecommunications Europe Co Ltd
Olivetti
Pitman Examinations Institute for permission to use their past examination questions
Prestel
Project Office Furniture
Racal-Milgo Ltd
Shape Advertising and Publicity Ltd
Twinlock plc
WordPerfect United Kingdom

Preface to the third edition

The opportunity has been taken in this third edition to make some major changes to *Information Processing* in keeping with developments in computer hardware, software, training and usage. Certain Sections in the book have been rearranged and expanded, so that related information can be kept together for easy reference. For example, *Networks* are now covered completely in Section 2. The new **EC Directive** on health and safety requirements for work with display screen equipment is included in Section 9, Unit 34. Two new Sections have been added: Section 5 now deals exclusively with *Computer operation,* and in particular with DOS. Section 7 covers *Presentation of information*. This Section includes an extensive Unit on *Desktop Publishing* and the use of *fonts* and *graphics* in documents.

In short, the practical element in the book has been increased and is based on experience of what is required of computer users in today's working environment.

Elaine Mullins

Introduction

This book is written particularly for those of you planning an office career and who will come face to face with a host of new technology and new methods of processing information. You will be expected to work with computers and a wide range of other electronic equipment used in the processing and communication of information. You will need to be able to switch from one piece of equipment to another as the job demands. Clerical staff, therefore, could be described more accurately as 'office technologists'. As such, you should be able to use the equipment intelligently, sometimes selecting a particular piece of equipment to carry out a specific process more efficiently. For example, using a facsimile machine to send a drawing from one office to another if a true copy is urgently required. At other times it will be necessary to view several pieces of equipment as a complete system, so that they function in an integrated way, processing a job effectively and efficiently from start to finish. New office technology has reduced job specialism and you need to aim to be flexible, adaptable and versatile. It is not sufficient, say, for a secretary merely to know how to operate a particular word processor. Secretaries should be able to transfer the skills acquired on one word processor to another. They should also know how to use a computer generally for the retrieval and transference of information.

How to use this book effectively

1 Computer technology has spawned a new language. As you proceed through the book, you are introduced to this new language easily and naturally. A simple explanation accompanies each new computer term used. Knowing and understanding computer terminology is essential, as you will find that much of it is used in business. Therefore, take particular note of the new words and learn their meanings. At the end of each section, you will be asked to explain these *key terms* in your own words. Try to do just that. If in any doubt, refer to the *Glossary* where you will find an explanation of each term (the terms are listed alphabetically). You might prefer to return to the appropriate page within the section you have just completed, so that the term can be read again in context.

2 As an aid to revision, each section is immediately *summarised in 15 main points*. The summaries will also be helpful as a quick reference/reminder both during the course and later in the work situation.

3 After the summary at the end of each section, you will find a *Knowledge Check*. The questions are quick to answer and fun to do. Write the answers in pencil first (unless you are really confident that you are correct). When you have checked them, either with your tutor or with the answers on the following page, then go over them using a pen or biro. Do all the questions first before looking up the answers. It is essential that you have the correct answers written in, as the Knowledge Check will form part of your revision notes too, and can also be used later as a quick reference in the work situation.

4 A set of *additional questions* follows each Knowledge Check. These are discussion-type questions which require written answers of roughly two sides of A4 paper. Your teacher might set some of these questions for homework or you might do them when preparing for the more advanced formal information/word processing examinations.

5 Each section ends with assignments for you to do, which your tutor will check. These will indicate to both you and your tutor just how well you know and understand the principles of information processing presented in each section and your ability to put your knowledge to practical use.

I believe that you will find this book useful in the office as well because it provides not only information on the electronic equipment you will encounter, but also on the *procedures* for using computerised equipment. It will be a handy reference book for an 'office technologist' to keep on his/her work desk.

1 The why, what and how of information processing

UNIT 1 Why do we need information processing?

Increasing information

Did you know that about 10 million people in the UK are office workers? That is almost half of the total working population of around 22 million. These millions of office workers concentrate their efforts daily on the handling of ever-increasing amounts of information.

Communication technology

Because of satellites, television, telex and a host of other communication technology, we are now better informed about what goes on not only in our own country but in other countries as well. This same technology has made available to organisations information to which they would not have had immediate access before. A business organisation cannot afford to ignore this wealth of information, for fear that its competitors will be extracting vital facts and using the information to advantage. If a company is to remain competitive, and indeed in business, it must be able to harness and organise the vast amounts of available information for effective use, ie to enable its management to make informed decisions. For example, as a result of information that there is impending political unrest in the country of origin, a decision may be taken to buy extra quantities of a commodity or negotiate supplies from other areas.

Useful information

Obviously not all available information is useful but in order to determine what is and what is not useful it all has to be collected, sorted, evaluated and then used, stored or discarded as appropriate. These processes take time and are costly in terms of staff salaries for the labour involved. More importantly, business opportunities can be lost or disasters fail to be averted because of the slow traditional methods of processing information.

UNIT 2 What is information processing?

Input → process → output

The term 'information processing' means taking raw facts and figures and processing them by means of some activity to produce organised and useful information. All information processing systems operate in the same sequence, whether manual or mechanical, ie the sequence of *input → process → output*. Basic facts and figures are put into the system (input). These are calculated, selected or compared (processed) to produce information (output) on which actions or decisions can be taken. People are information processors. We are all constantly processing information. For example, somebody asks you what the time is. The question is your **input**. You look at your watch and read the time from it. This is the **process**. When you have done this you tell the person the time. This then is your **output**. Every system processes information in this sequence.

Information categories

The information used by a business organisation can usually be divided into three categories:

1 numbers (figures)
2 graphics (graphs, charts, etc)
3 text (words)

In this section we examine each type of information in turn, identify the way in which each is processed and investigate the technology available for information processing.

Data processing

In the offices of, say, a manufacturing company, figurework would include keeping records of the raw materials held (stock); records of the goods already manufactured but not yet sold (manufactured stock); records of the orders received from customers; the deliveries made and the bills sent to customers (invoices). Additionally, wages and all other expenses that the company has to meet would be recorded. However, in a business it is not enough simply to keep records. All the raw facts and figures (known as **data**) must be processed, that is they must be calculated, checked, sorted and distributed to those who need to act upon them. They must then be filed so that they can be found by those who need to refer to them later. Company managers need to inspect, compare and analyse these figures and records regularly to determine whether or not the company is making a profit and to glean other useful information which will help them to decide what action to take.

Electronic data processing

Calculating machines have been used in offices for many years to cope with the adding and subtracting of figures, but until the 1940s no machine was available to handle the processing of data. Such a machine is of course a computer, which memorises, calculates and compares data, and produces selective information as required. The processing of data by computer is called 'electronic data processing' (EDP).

Government departments, as well as nationalised industries and many other organisations such as banks and insurance companies, rely on modern computers to process data quickly and efficiently. The use of computers by these large organisations ensures that the output of their volume of data is both timely and accurate.

The history of computers

Although the history of computers is brief, computer technology has developed in leaps and bounds. This has provided us on average with a new 'generation' of computers every 10 years.

The components used in 'first generation' computers were thousands of vacuum tubes — large glass tubes through which electricity passes. These fragile tubes caused many problems, the most serious of which was overheating.

In the 1950s a technological breakthrough produced the transistor. This small electronic switching device replaced the troublesome vacuum tube, with the result that 'second generation' computers were much more reliable, considerably smaller and cheaper.

Transistor manufacturers later developed a way of placing a complete circuit of components on a single piece of material. This technology became known as integrated circuits and 'third generation' computers emerged even more reliable and further reduced in size and cost.

Most people have heard of the 'silicon chip' which has made such a great impact on our society. It has also brought the 'fourth generation' of computers down to micro size. The 'chip' is made up of layers of thin silicon material sandwiched together and incorporating thousands of miniaturised components. A 'chip' is often no larger than a fingernail (Fig 1.1). The effects of the 'chip' can be seen in business, education and entertainment, and also the way in which we obtain, present and use information. Figure 1.2 illustrates the changes in computing technology.

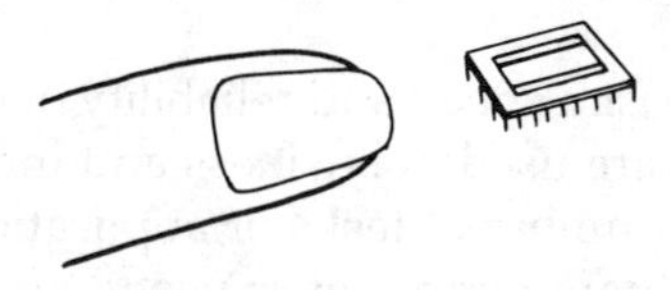

Fig 1.1
A 'chip'

Computers in data processing

While early computers were built and used purely to solve mathematical problems, each advance in the technology opened up new areas of work

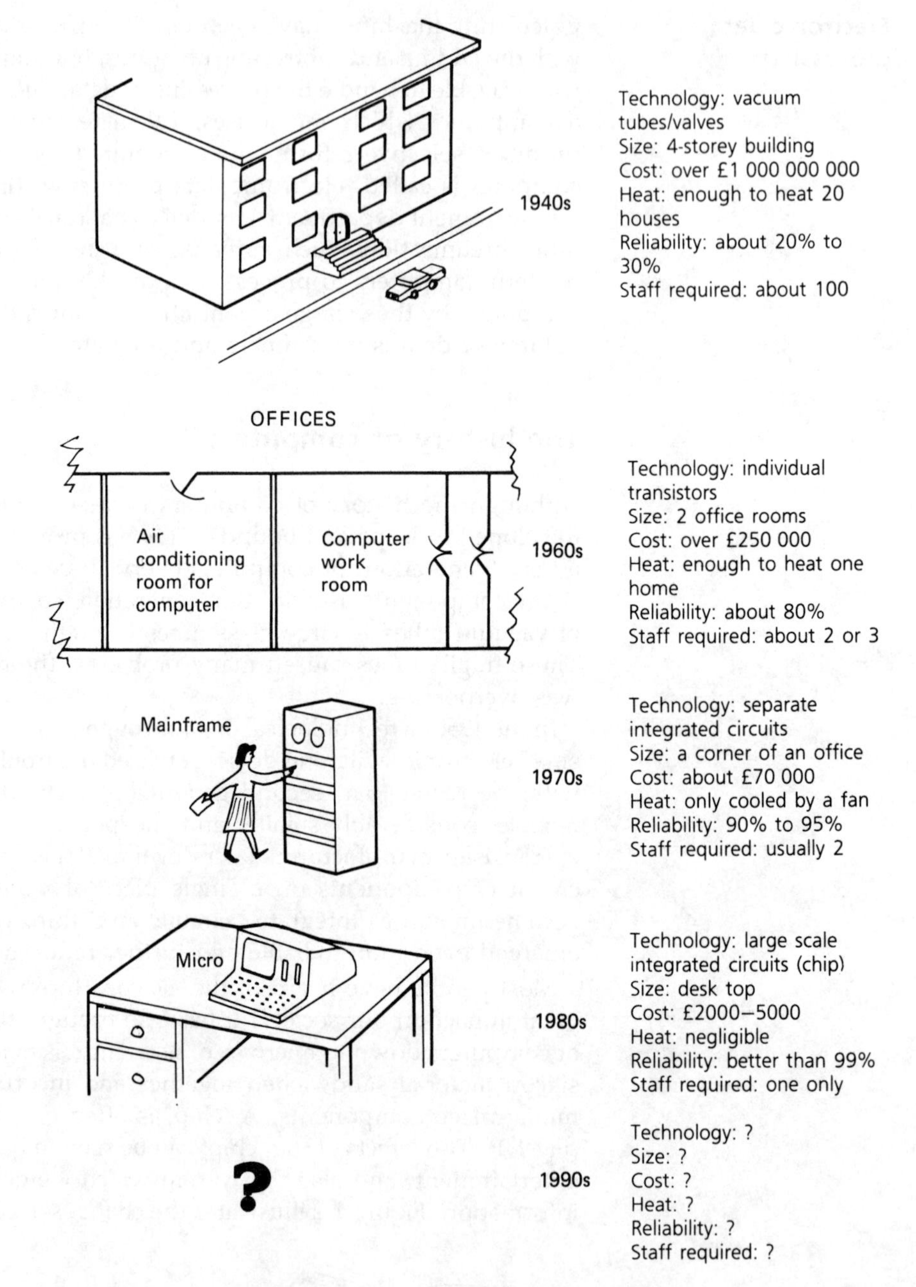

Fig 1.2
Changes in computer technology

in which the increased speed and reliability of computers proved useful. Today computers are used in business and industry for a wide range of activities and the number of tasks or applications continues to grow. In data processing, computers are most useful for repetitive operations such as stock control, payroll, accounting, etc. They can handle volumes of such work accurately and at incredible speed. Other applications are sorting data into a specified order or into selected groups (fields). Computers can also be used to manipulate their stored data to assist company management in decision making.

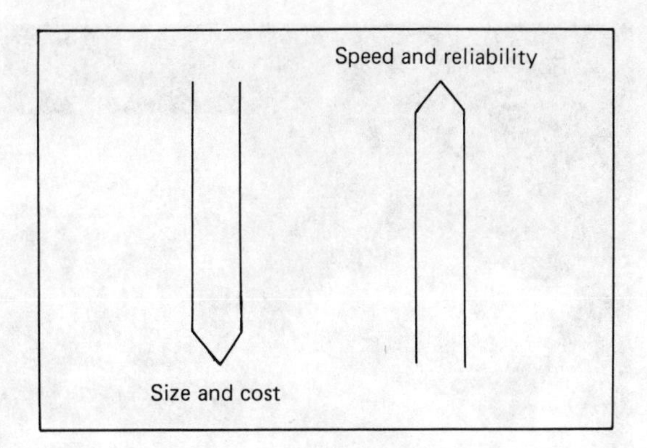

Fig 1.3
Trends resulting from computer technology

Each stage in computer development shows a marked reduction in the size and cost of a system, while there is a substantial increase in the accuracy, speed and applications. Figure 1.3 highlights the trends resulting from the changes in computer technology.

Graphics

Graphics are used in business:

1 to help evaluate and analyse data
2 as a way of presenting information to others.

Sometimes it is difficult to visualise a situation from raw numbers and a graphic picture can help clarify the information one is evaluating or analysing. For example, if a company's monthly sales figures for four different products were shown on a bar chart, an analysis could be made more quickly and easily than by reading through four separate sheets of figures. Graphics bring out the messages buried under piles of data and hidden in columns of figures. It is also an impressive way of presenting information to others. Trends and relationships can be seen at a glance from graphs and charts and comparisons can be made instantly.

Manually produced graphics

Until recently, the part played by graphics in business information was relatively small because graphic displays were produced manually. Producing graphics manually is an expensive process — not only because it takes time to draw graphs and charts, etc, but also because the usefulness of the display is shortlived. No business can thrive or even survive on out-of-date information. Manually produced graphics in business are limited in use, as hand-drawn graphics cannot be easily updated. The use of magnetic visual display boards has helped in some instances to overcome this problem but these boards are not suitable for all types of graphic displays and they are not easily transportable. Therefore, their uses too are limited.

Nonetheless, it has always been recognised that a graphic display is an interesting way of presenting information and a powerful means of projecting ideas.

Fig 1.4
Example of graphic display

Computer graphics

Recent developments in microcomputer technology have brought about an explosive interest and growth in business graphics. Computers in the 1990s have all the facilities to produce graphs, pie and bar charts, histograms and the like from data input. Provision is also made for any text, such as an explanation, to be included in the graphic display (Fig 1.4).

Unlike manually constructed graphics, computer graphic images can be changed by the touch of a key or two. New images can be created within seconds to include the most recent data received. This means that, using **computer graphics**:

1 Complex data can be transformed into easy-to-grasp graphic displays whenever needed.
2 Instant adjustments can be made to the display according to data changes.
3 The cost of producing graphic displays is considerably less than the cost of manually produced displays.

(*See also* Unit 22, *Graphics software*.)

Word processing

But information is not just a question of numbers and graphic images is it? What about words? Statistics indicate that the information used or produced by an organisation is approximately 10% graphics, 20% numbers and 70% text (ICFC – Industrial and Commercial Finance Corporation).

Internal written communications, such as reports, memos, letters and notices, are generated daily in all offices. These, together with external communications (those letters, reports, contracts, price-lists, quotations, etc written to other organisations), keep countless secretaries and typists busy at their typewriters for much of the working day. Traditionally, each piece of text is typed individually, even when the content of one letter is much the same as another. Alterations often mean that written communications have to be retyped completely. Clearly the processing of words electronically could not be neglected and of course it was not.

Development of word processing

In 1960, about the time when 'second generation' computers were in use, IBM invented an **electronic typewriter** with a memory. Text was not printed immediately on this *memory typewriter* but could be stored and corrected, then played back and printed out at about 180 words per minute (wpm). This then was the start of word processing — entry, storage, retrieval, editing and printing of text.

Computer technology

Later, word processing benefited from computer technology and the silicon chip. Computer systems, called **dedicated word processors**, were developed solely to handle the processing of text. These systems were ideally suited to rapid text editing and to handling work of a repetitive nature, such as standard paragraphs for contracts and reports, form letters and mailshots.

As microcomputers have become more powerful and sophisticated, they have also become more versatile, handling not only the processing of data, but also the processing of graphics and text. Dedicated word processors are now considered too expensive. It is far more economical to purchase one computer system which can be used for all applications than a system only for word processing. (*See also* Unit 19, *Word processing software*.)

Systems

Before we take a look at the component parts of a computing system, let us define the word 'system' in this context. This is a word which we use almost daily. We speak of the 'educational system' (the schools, the teachers, the examinations, etc); the 'central heating system' (the boiler, the pump, the radiators, and so on). Systems are made up of interacting parts that operate together to achieve a common purpose or goal. In the 'educational system' the goal is to educate students and in the 'central heating system' to heat the building. If one part of a system does not perform its function, then the whole system is affected.

Parts of a computer system

A computer system is made up of various pieces of equipment which, because they are tangible, are termed 'hardware', and programs (sets of instructions which tell the computer what to do) which, because they are intangible, are termed 'software'. The 'hardware' components are the keyboard, the monitor (visual display unit), the central processing unit (CPU), the backing store (tapes or disks) and the printer. In a computer system, the hardware and software work together to process raw data or words rapidly into useful information or accurate, well-displayed documents (Fig 1.5).

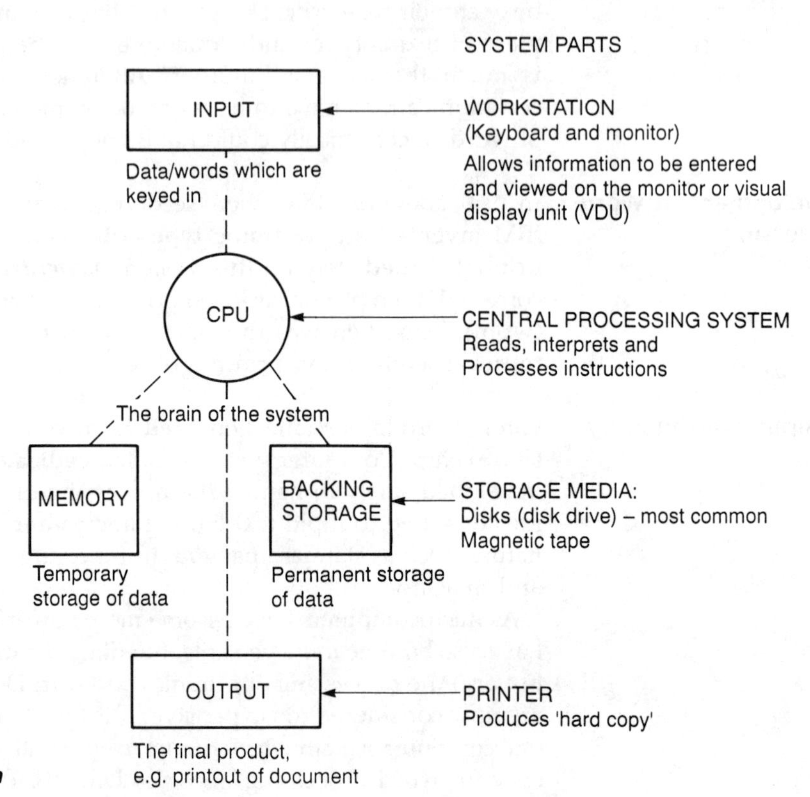

Fig 1.5
Parts of a computer system

UNIT 3 How does a computer system enter and display information?

Data is entered into a computer system using an **input device**, such as a *keyboard, mouse, scanner, touch sensitive screen*, etc. Input devices are covered in detail in Section 4, *Communication between the user and the computer system*. For now, we will look briefly at the main input device only, the **keyboard**, and examine the types of **monitor** which can be used to display information.

Keyboard

Data and instructions are **entered** or **keyed in** at the keyboard by the user. The layout of computer keyboards is based around the familiar **QWERTY** keys. This means that letter and figure keys (known as **alpha-numeric** keys) are in the same position as they are on a conventional typewriter keyboard. There is also a row of **function keys** across the top of the keyboard. These keys are used to give instructions to the system. A group of number keys (0–9), called a **numeric pad**, is positioned on the right-hand side of the keyboard. There are several other keys to be used for additional functions. The number of these keys and their layout may vary slightly on different computer keyboards.

Computer keyboards are virtually noiseless and very light to the touch. Each key is a repeater key. If a key is held down, the character or function assigned to that key will be repeated.

Visual display unit (VDU)

A VDU or **monitor** (as it is often called) is the means by which a computer system displays information. Physically, it resembles a portable television screen. When data is entered at the keyboard, it is immediately displayed on the VDU. This allows the operator to inspect the input before it is printed. Some monitors display a full A4 page of information. However, most are capable of showing only a partial page of about 25 lines vertically at a time, with a horizontal display, generally of 80 characters.

The letters, numbers and graphs that appear on the screen are made up of **pixels** (dots). The more pixels the screen displays, the clearer and sharper the image:

- A **monochrome** (one colour) monitor displays excellent quality text (720 × 350 pixels), but no graphics. To display graphics on this type of monitor, a **Hercules Graphics Card** must be added to the system.
- A **Colour Graphics Adaptor (CGA)** monitor can generate graphic images in four colours. However, the density of pixels is not very high and the display overall is only just acceptable.
- An **Enhanced Graphics Adaptor (EGA)** monitor produces far better text and graphics output. It has a pixel density twice that of a CGA (EGA 640 × 350 pixels).
- A **Video Graphics Array (VGA)** monitor has an even higher pixel resolution and can display excellent quality text and graphics in a vast number of colours.

UNIT 4 How does a computer system process information?

Central processing unit (CPU)

This is the central part of the system, to which all other component parts are connected by cable. All the devices linked to the CPU — the keyboard, monitor, printer and backing storage — are called **peripherals**. It is the function of the CPU to read, interpret and process information and instructions and control the input and output operations of the system. This is done by a computer **program** (a set of instructions which the computer can understand and which tells it what to do, step by step) which is held in the **memory** of the CPU.

The CPU contains three parts:

1 arithmetic unit (AU)
2 control unit (CU)
3 immediate access store (memory)

Arithmetic unit

The arithmetic unit carries out arithmetic processes and a section of it performs logical operations, ie makes comparisons.

Control unit

The control unit makes the computer go through the program steps in the correct sequence. It also controls other system operations.

System memory

The **system memory** is the internal storage capacity available in the CPU. Two kinds of memory exist: ***R*ead *O*nly *M*emory (ROM)** and ***R*andom *A*ccess *M*emory (RAM)**. Computer storage capacity is measured in **bytes**. A byte is a group of 8 **bits** (**b**inary dig**its**) strung together to represent a number or character. The **ROM** and the **RAM** will store thousands — even millions — of characters, referred to as **kilobytes** and **megabytes** respectively. For example, manufacturers' specifications of a system will quote: *640K memory* (that is a RAM of 640 thousand bytes or characters) or *2M memory* (a RAM of 2 million bytes or characters).

ROM (Read Only Memory)

All systems have some basic functions permanently programmed into the memory by the manufacturer, and these cannot be changed, nor are they affected if the system is switched off. This is known as the **ROM**. Without these basic control functions, the system would not be able to start up and accept other instructions or programs. The capacity of the ROM is usually quite small compared with that of the RAM.

RAM (Random Access Memory)

This is called the **RAM** because the operator has access to it and can control whatever is contained in it. RAM is memory that the computer uses to run application programs, such as word processing or stock control. Application programs are stored on a disk. When the operator wants to use a program, s/he instructs the system to load the program required. The system then *reads* the program from the disk and loads (copies) it into the RAM. When you switch off the computer, such a program will no longer remain in the RAM. This is because the RAM, unlike the ROM, does not provide permanent storage. Because the program is stored on a disk, it can be loaded into the RAM again any time that it is required. This can be done in a matter of seconds.

The storage capacity of the RAM can be quite substantial. The trend is to constantly increase the memory, as new, sophisticated programs require a vast amount of storage space. Storage capacity of the RAM is therefore an indication of the complexity of the programs which a system can handle. RAM is usually referred to simply as **memory**.

Base, extended and expanded memory

When working with today's powerful computers with megabytes of memory, it is necessary to be aware that there are three main *types* of memory. These three types are **base**, **extended** and **expanded** memory:

1 **Base memory** is the first 640 kilobytes of **RAM**. This is also known as the **conventional DOS memory**.
2 **Extended memory** is the memory addressed above 1 megabyte of **RAM**.
3 **Expanded memory** is memory outside the **base memory** which can be accessed as needed.

Temporary storage of text/data

Part of the RAM is used for storage of input text/data while the operator is working at the terminal. (Sometimes, therefore, the RAM is referred to as the **working memory**.) Changes can easily be made to the input at this stage as it will be displayed on the VDU. Storage is also available for intermediate results during processing before the final information is ready for output. Memory storage is limited, however, and remember too that it is only temporary. If you do not wish to lose your text or data when the computer is switched off, it must be saved on some permanent storage device.

UNIT 5 How does a computer system store information?

Permanent storage of information

One of the main functions of computers is that information can be stored and later retrieved and evaluated, updated or reproduced. Since the internal memory (**RAM**) is temporary, the information has to be stored on more permanent media, such as hard disks and diskettes. Disks provide **direct access** storage, which gives immediate access to any file on the disk (sometimes referred to as **random access**).

Hard disks (fixed disks)

A hard disk drive in a Personal Computer System is a sealed unit fitted in the same cabinet as the CPU. The disk is constructed of rigid platters of metal which are *fixed* and cannot be removed. Its storage capacity can be from 20 megabytes to well over 100 megabytes. When you consider that **1 Mbyte** is equal to roughly 300 pages of text, you can see that a hard disk can provide storage for a vast number of files. As it usually stores all the data, the hard disk drive is the most important drive in a personal computer system. In order for the system to distinguish between drives when information is stored or retrieved, drives are given a location address. The hard disk drive is normally referred to as *Drive C* (shown on the monitor as C:\>).

Diskette drives

It is usual for today's personal computer systems to have one hard disk drive and one diskette drive. This is because it is often necessary to move or copy information from one drive to another. A diskette drive can be either $3\frac{1}{2}$ in wide or $5\frac{1}{4}$ in wide, although the $3\frac{1}{2}$ in drive is the new standard. Some users find it useful to have two diskette drives — one of each size. This means that the system can access data stored on a diskette of either size. The first of two diskette drives (usually the one situated on top) is referred to as *Drive A* and the second as *Drive B* (shown on the monitor as A:\> and B:\> respectively).

In order to **write information to a diskette** or **read information from a diskette**, the diskette has to be inserted into a **diskette drive**. These drives are also housed in the main computer unit but there is an access slot at the front of the unit into which the operator inserts the diskette. Information can then be *read* from the diskette to appear on the monitor, or it can be sent direct to the printer. Information can also be *written* or recorded to the diskette by the operator.

Diskettes

Diskettes (or **floppy disks** as they are often called) are supplied in two sizes, $3\frac{1}{2}$ in and $5\frac{1}{4}$ in, in order to fit into the diskette drives (*see* Fig 1.6). Both disks are constructed of the same floppy plastic material, but the $3\frac{1}{2}$ in disk has a much more rigid outer case. Information is written on diskettes along concentric circles, called **tracks** or **cylinders**. Tracks are

Floppy diskettes

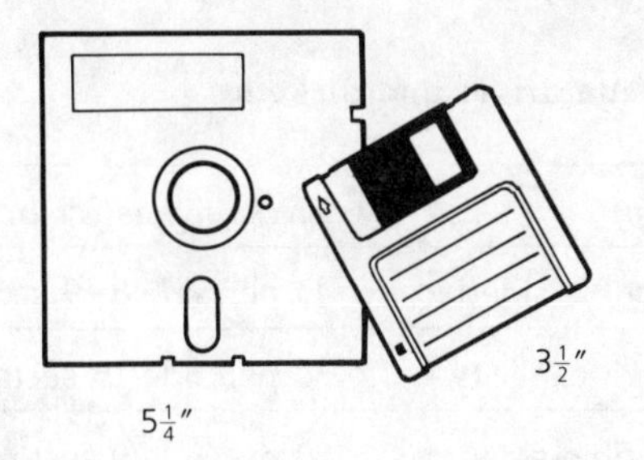

Storage capacity: Up to 2 Megabytes
Advantages: Transportable (can be removed from one system and inserted into the diskdrive of any other compatible system). Cheap form of storage.
Disadvantages: Disks need to be handled carefully.
System suited to: Personal computer systems.

Fixed disk

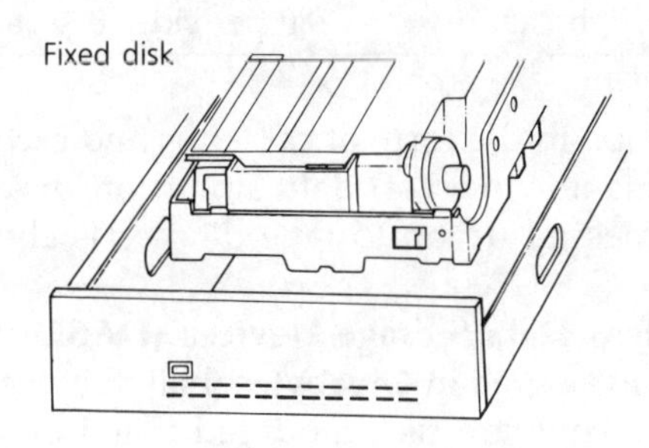

Storage capacity: Upwards from 20MB to several hundreds of megabytes.
Advantages: Vast storage capacity. Because the disk is fixed in the computer unit, it is protected.
Disadvantages: Disk is not exchangeable. If disk crashes, all data could be instantly lost.
System suited to: Personal computer systems and Local Area Network systems.

Data storage devices

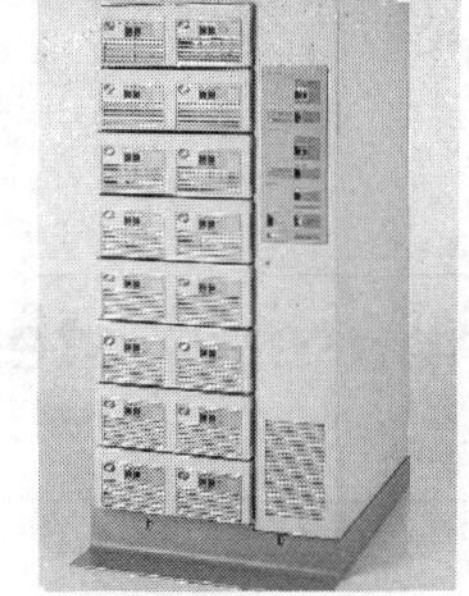

Storage capacity: Measured in Gigabytes. Up to 48 GB in a single rack.
Advantages: Capable of providing many Gigabytes of on-line storage. Very fast data transfer rate.
Disadvantages: Expensive equipment, requiring special environmental conditions.
System suited to: Mainframe computers.

Data cartridges (tape)

Storage capacity: From 2MB to about 200MB.
Advantages: Cheap tape storage for backing up hard disks.
Disadvantages: Data not so quickly accessible as on disks.
System suited to: Personal computer systems and LANs for backing up hard disks.

Fig 1.6
Magnetic storage media

then divided into **sectors** (sections). As with the RAM, space on all disks is measured in **bytes**.

Types of diskette drives and diskettes

Size	*Type*	*Tracks/sectors per track*	*Storage capacity*
$5\frac{1}{4}$ in	Double-sided	40 per side/8–9 sectors	320/360 Kbytes
$5\frac{1}{4}$ in	High-capacity	80 per side/15 sectors	1.2 Mbytes
$3\frac{1}{2}$ in	Double-sided	80 per side/9 sectors	720 Kbytes
$3\frac{1}{2}$ in	High capacity	80 per side/18 sectors	1.44 Mbytes

Magnetic tape

Magnetic tape in the form of cassettes and cartridges (Fig 1.6) is used to **back-up** (make copies of) data stored on disks. (*See also* Unit 29, *Data security*.) Backing up on to tape devices is cheap and fast.

Storage devices for mainframe computers

Direct Access Data Storage Devices (DASD) provide the high storage capacities, measured in **Gigabytes** (billion bytes), required for mainframe computers. They are rack-mounted (Fig 1.6) to save floor space.

Special software is used to handle the administration required for the vast quantities of data stored on these devices. The software also controls the allocation of space, ensuring optimum efficiency in the way information is stored.

UNIT 6 How does a computer system output information?

Printers or printing devices

A printer is an essential part of any computer system. Its function is to produce a **hard copy** (copy on paper) of the completed document. When purchasing a printer, certain factors need to be considered:

- Cost of the printer and each printed page
- Printing speed
- Quality of print
- Support for different typestyles and **fonts** (different versions of a typestyle)
- Graphics capability
- Versatility in paper handling
- Noise level

Current printers fall into two types — **impact** and **non-impact**. **Impact** means that the characters are transferred to the paper by a striking action through a carbon or inked ribbon (as a typewriter prints). An advantage of this type of printer is that it is able to handle a variety of paper, including multi-part forms. However, impact printers are very noisy. A **non-impact** printer does not use a mechanical contact between the printhead and paper. Its operation is therefore quiet, but it is less versatile in its handling of paper.

Impact printers

Daisywheel printer

This was one of the first printers available for personal computers. An impact printer, it uses a *daisywheel* type printing element. All the characters are contained on the one daisywheel, with a different character on each petal or spoke. This provides a limited character set. A different **typestyle** or **font** can be achieved by changing the daisywheel. Print quality is as good as that of an electronic typewriter, but these printers are slow (maximum of 40–50 characters per second) and noisy. Another major drawback is the daisywheel printer's inability to handle graphics. Nonetheless, because of their comparatively low cost and good print quality, there are still a fair number of these printers in use where the bulk of the work is word processing.

Dot matrix printer

The majority of printers sold for data processing are of the **dot matrix** type. These printers are cheap and fast. Moreover, they can produce graphics and many models have the facility to print in more than one typestyle and a variety of **fonts**. The printed characters are made up of a number of dots, which are formed by pins on the printhead striking against the ribbon. A printhead can have a number of pins — 9, 18 or 24. A 9-pin printer produces the poorest dot matrix print quality, but at very high speeds, suitable for standard computer output. The next step up in quality of print is the 18-pin printer, but with some reduction in speed. The output of a 24-pin printer using **letter quality** mode is considered good enough for word processing. Speed in letter quality mode is usually under 100 characters per second (**cps**) while, in **draft** mode, some printers can achieve a speed of several hundred characters per second.

Line printer

The line printer gets its name because it is able to store and print a complete line of information at a time. When a line has been printed, the paper moves up to the next print line. This is called **line feed**. During this process, another line of characters transfers from the computer to the printer buffer (temporary) store, ready for printing. Line printers are usually impact printers, with printing speeds as high as 1500 lines per minute. This type of printer is generally part of a data processing system where vast quantities of data are constantly printed out. The paper used for this type of operation would be fanfolded, with sprocket holes on either side. These holes engage in the pins on the paper feed mechanism, which can be adjusted to take paper of varying widths.

10 CPI NORMAL MODE

16 CPI CONDENSED MODE

EMPHASIZED MODE

ENLARGED MODE

NORMAL MODE

CONDENSED MODE

EMPHASIZED MODE

DOUBLE WIDTH

Fig 1.7
Dot matrix printing

Non-impact printers

Ink jet printer

Ink jet printers usually do not cost much more than dot matrix printers. The ink jet is a non-impact printer and as such does not use ribbons. Instead a fast drying ink is sprayed electrostatically onto the page to form the characters as the printhead moves along the line. The characters are not formed completely in one move, but are built up as the printhead passes back and forth across the page. This is all done quietly and rapidly so that output speed is very good. Print quality is also excellent. These printers usually have a variety of inbuilt typestyles and fonts and they have a high graphics capability. Ink jet technology lends itself to colour printing at comparatively low cost. As there is an increasing desire for colour printing, especially in the area of graphics, ink jet printers should gain in popularity.

Fig 1.8
Ink jet printer

Laser printer

This is a printer which combines laser, computer and photocopying technology to produce high-quality printed output at speeds of 4 to 15 pages per minute in near silence. These advantages, together with the current low price of this desktop page printer, are making it a popular choice in many of today's offices. The one drawback is the cost of a replacement printer cartridge, which has a life of around 4000 pages. Many laser printers have a large font selection, which can greatly enhance the look of a printed document. A high quality laser printed document can be used as original artwork by printers for a print run, thus saving on typesetting costs. Later models also have a sizeable memory, which allows for the printing of sophisticated graphics. The printer control panel will usually give the operator access to any additional features. These could be **duplex** printing (printing on both sides of the paper), selecting paper from more than one tray, page orientation (portrait or landscape), etc.

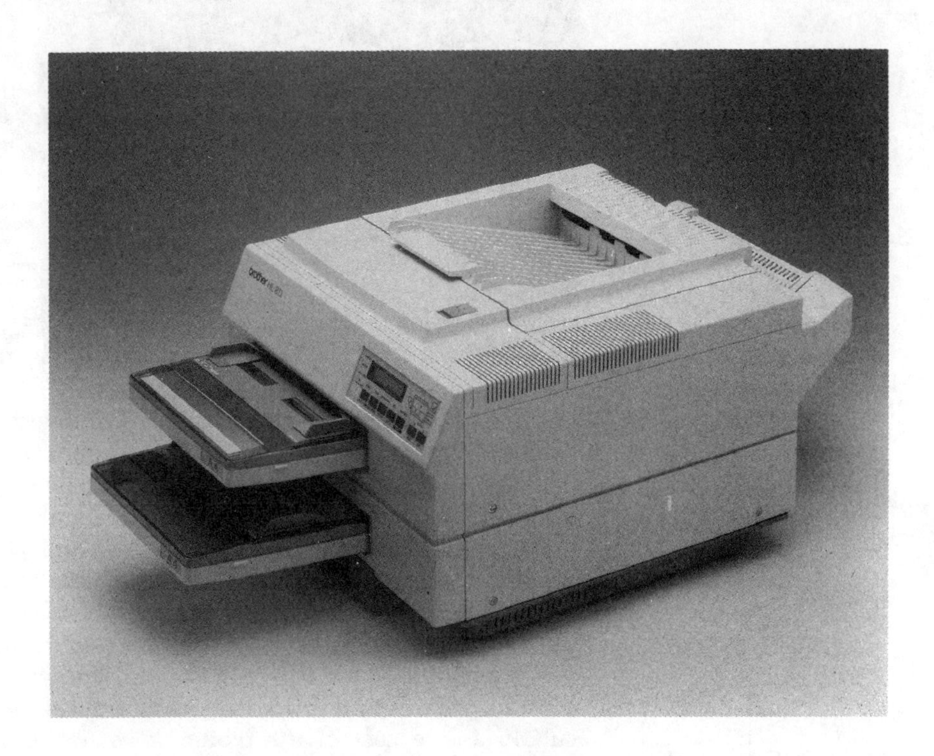

Fig 1.9
Laser printer

LED printer and LCS (Liquid Crystal Shutter) printer

Both **LED** and **LCS** printers are similar to laser printers, but with some differences in the technology. Price, speed and quality of print can also be matched to those of laser printers.

Graphics plotter

Graphics can be printed out on some of the printers used with data/word processing systems, and more manufacturers are producing printers capable of meeting all the needs of a business, ie data, text and graphics. There are also special graphics printers on the market at very low prices.

However, if presentation is important, then a graphics plotter is required, as this will increase the impact and clarity of the graphic data

Fig 1.10
Graphics plotter

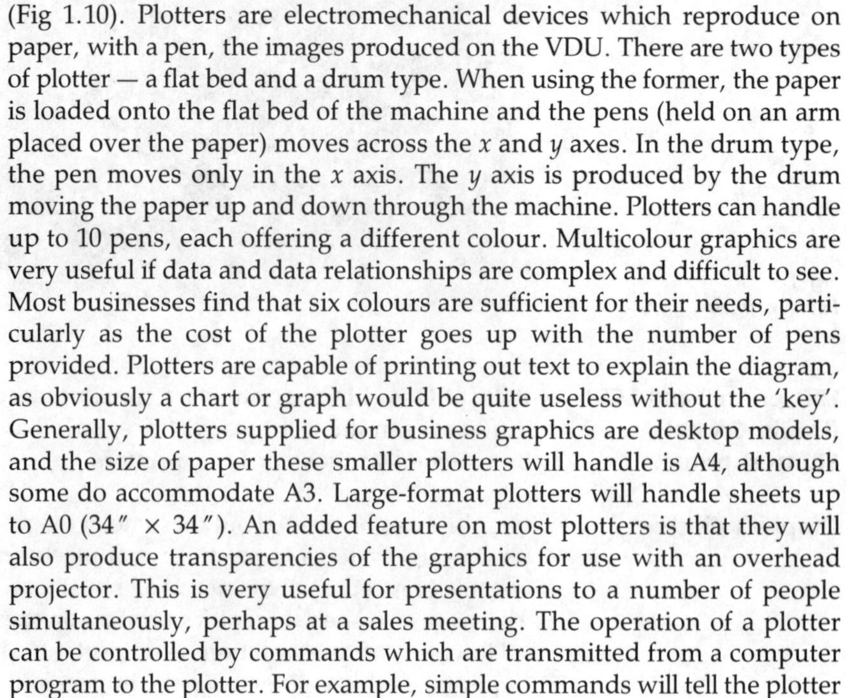

(Fig 1.10). Plotters are electromechanical devices which reproduce on paper, with a pen, the images produced on the VDU. There are two types of plotter — a flat bed and a drum type. When using the former, the paper is loaded onto the flat bed of the machine and the pens (held on an arm placed over the paper) moves across the x and y axes. In the drum type, the pen moves only in the x axis. The y axis is produced by the drum moving the paper up and down through the machine. Plotters can handle up to 10 pens, each offering a different colour. Multicolour graphics are very useful if data and data relationships are complex and difficult to see. Most businesses find that six colours are sufficient for their needs, particularly as the cost of the plotter goes up with the number of pens provided. Plotters are capable of printing out text to explain the diagram, as obviously a chart or graph would be quite useless without the 'key'. Generally, plotters supplied for business graphics are desktop models, and the size of paper these smaller plotters will handle is A4, although some do accommodate A3. Large-format plotters will handle sheets up to A0 (34″ × 34″). An added feature on most plotters is that they will also produce transparencies of the graphics for use with an overhead projector. This is very useful for presentations to a number of people simultaneously, perhaps at a sales meeting. The operation of a plotter can be controlled by commands which are transmitted from a computer program to the plotter. For example, simple commands will tell the plotter

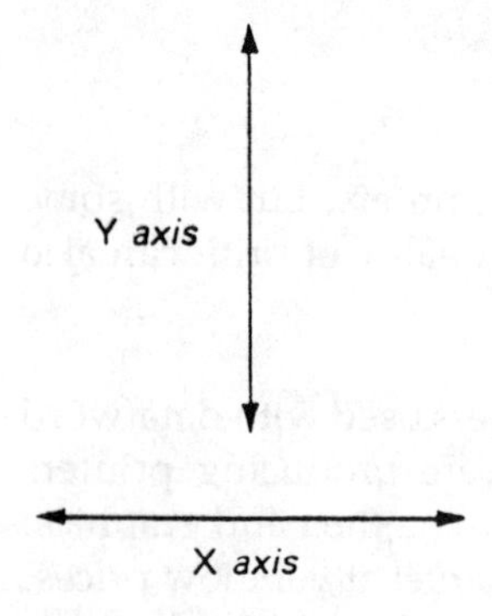

Fig 1.11
The x and y axes

which pen to select and to move it according to the data supplied. Prices of plotters have recently come down and several are priced at below £1000. It is expected that prices will fall further as the use of graphics in business increases.

Output accessories

Fanfold paper

Fanfold paper is a cheap quality continuous paper, perforated and folded in approximately A4 size sheets. It stacks neatly behind the printer and is generally used on printers connected to a data processing system. This is because the output generated is mainly for internal use and good-quality paper is therefore not required. Additionally, computers often turn out vast quantities of data in a continuous stream, and fanfold paper has several advantages when used for this type of printout. Firstly, this type of paper has sprocket holes which fit onto a tractor type paper feeder, which rotates and pulls the paper through automatically as fast as the data are printed. Secondly, data are kept in the order in which they are printed out, although the paper is perforated and sheets can be separated if required. Thirdly, fanfold paper stores easily and neatly. While computer operators are therefore freed from the chore of feeding in individual sheets of paper by hand, word processor operators all too frequently have to do just that. Obviously fanfold paper is not suitable for letters, contracts, client reports and similar correspondence, and letterheads and good quality bond paper are normally supplied in single sheets.

Sheet feeders

Cut sheet feeders are available for almost all printers. Some are built in, while others are optional. Laser printers have one or two paper trays fitted as standard, from which paper is automatically fed as required. If a more complex paper feed system is needed, eg to feed the first page of a letter, followed by continuation sheets, plus one or two copies and an envelope, then a special hopper can be attached to the printer (*see* Fig 1.12).

Fig 1.12
Special laser printer hopper for complex paper feed operations

Acoustic covers

Impact printing devices are notoriously noisy, which can be very distracting if the data/word processing system is positioned where other office work is being carried out. Acoustic hoods, covers or silencers (different manufacturers use different terms) are very effective in suppressing the noise. Covers will enclose not only the printer but the sheet feeder as well.

Hardware

We have examined a series of devices and components, all of which make up a computer system and which function together to make the system effective. All this tangible equipment, such as input and output devices, from the CPU to the storage disks, are collectively defined as **hardware**. Any part of a computer system which you can touch is therefore hardware. Programs, if you recall, are classified as **software**. The disk on which the program resides is tangible, but the program itself is not.

Summary — Key Points

1 The sequence of information processing is input → process → output.
2 Business information can be divided into words, numbers and graphics.
3 Work most suited to computerisation:
  a repetitive tasks
  b large volume tasks
  c tasks requiring high-speed processing
  d editing or updating of text/data
  e sorting and selecting information
4 A system is the grouping of related parts to achieve a common goal.
5 The component parts of a stand-alone computer system are the keyboard and VDU, the CPU, the storage media (disk and disk drive) and the printer.
6 The functions of these parts are:
  a keyboard and VDU — allow text/data to be entered, viewed and edited and operating instructions (commands) are given to the system via the keyboard
  b CPU — reads, interprets and processes instructions
  c disk and disk drive — allow for the external storage of text on storage media
  d printer — produces a hard copy of the text/data
7 The CPU contains three parts:
  a arithmetic unit
  b control unit
  c immediate access store (memory)

8 A program is a set of instructions which the computer can understand and which tells the computer what to do, step by step.
9 RAM is the working memory and application programs are loaded into the RAM.
10 Magnetic disk is the most popular form of storage media and has two advantages:
  a good storage capacity
  b random access
11 A hard disk is a sealed unit fitted in the same cabinet as the CPU.
12 The hard disk is recognised by the system as Drive C:, the first diskette drive as Drive A: and the second diskette drive as Drive B:.
13 Laser printers are most commonly used for word processing output because the quality of print is excellent, they are fast and in most companies the cost can be justified.
14 Computer graphics can transform complex data into easy-to-grasp graphic displays when needed.
15 Computer input and output devices are called *hardware*. Programs are called *software*.

Knowledge Check on Section 1

Keywords (try to explain the meaning of these terms in your own words):

Byte	Hardware	Program
Central processing unit	Input	QWERTY
Data	Memory	RAM
Disk drive	Monitor	ROM
Dot matrix	Output	System
Floppy disk	Plotter	Text
Font	Printout	Visual display unit
Hard copy		

Complete each of the following items and then check your responses either with your tutor or with the answers on page 25.

1 Match each term in the first column with its meaning from the second column:

	1	2
a ____	*1* Daisywheel	*a* A group of figure keys usually on the right of the keyboard.
____	2 Numeric pad	*b* A component part linked to the CPU.
____	3 Peripheral	*c* A printing device that contains all the characters to be printed.

b ____	*1* Duplex printing	*a*	Moving the paper up to the next print line after printing one line.
____	*2* Page orientation	*b*	Accessing text on external media in any desired order.
____	*3* Line feed	*c*	Printing on portrait or landscape paper.
____	*4* Direct access	*d*	Printing on both sides of the paper.

2 Fill in the blanks:

a Ink jet and laser printers are ____ printers.

b The CPU has basically two types of memory: ____ and ____.

c The two types of plotter available for the output of graphics are ____ and ____.

d The technology presently used in microcomputers is the ____ ____.

3 Label the following statements true or false:

a ____ All information in the random access memory (RAM) is retained when the system is switched off.

b ____ On a daisywheel printer, different typestyles can be obtained by interchanging wheels.

c ____ An ink jet printer is an impact printer.

d ____ Impact printers allow carbon copies to be taken.

e ____ High capacity disks are disks with increased storage capacity.

4 Multiple choice: select the letter that best answers the question.

1 Which of the following is not connected with backing storage? ____.

a diskette
b hard disk
c dot matrix
d cassette

2 The function of the CPU is ____.

a to provide external storage of text
b to communicate with the operator
c to read, interpret and process the information and instructions
d to provide a hard copy

3 The term used to define all input and output devices in a computer system is ____.

a monitor
b software
c peripherals
d hardware

Answers

1 **a** *1c 2a 3b*
  b *1d 2c 3a 4b*
2 **a** non-impact **b** ROM, RAM **c** flatbed, drum **d** silicon chip
3 aF bT cF dT eT
4 *1c 2c 3d*

Additional questions on Section 1

1 Explain as fully as you can what 'information processing' means.
2 Give examples of *three* different types of tasks particularly suited to computerisation (could be data and/or text processing).
3 Compare and discuss the suitability of a laser printer and a dot matrix printer as an output device for a stand-alone system.
4 Business graphics currently account for 10 per cent of business information. What effect do you think computerisation will have on this, if any? State your reasons.
5 Discuss the purpose of the RAM and how it differs from disk storage.

Assignment 1

a Load your printer with appropriate paper and get it ready for printing, making sure that it is 'on line'.
b Remove the ribbon from your printer. If it is worn, replace it with a new one. If not, replace the existing one. Check that the ribbon is replaced correctly, using the diagram in the printer manual to guide you, if necessary.

2 Configuration of computer systems

UNIT 7 Non-data sharing configurations

The inputting of data/text is still the slowest part of any computer system, dependent almost entirely on the speed at which the operator can type. If there are vast quantities of data to be entered, the CPU and the printer, both of which are capable of working at great speed, will be left idle much of the time. To use the power of the CPU and printer more effectively, and thus speed up the output of information, various arrangements (**configurations**) of computer systems are possible:

Stand-alone system

This is a term applied to a single, completely independent personal computer system, with its own CPU, disk drives and disks, monitor, keyboard and printer (Fig 2.1). If a company were to purchase just one

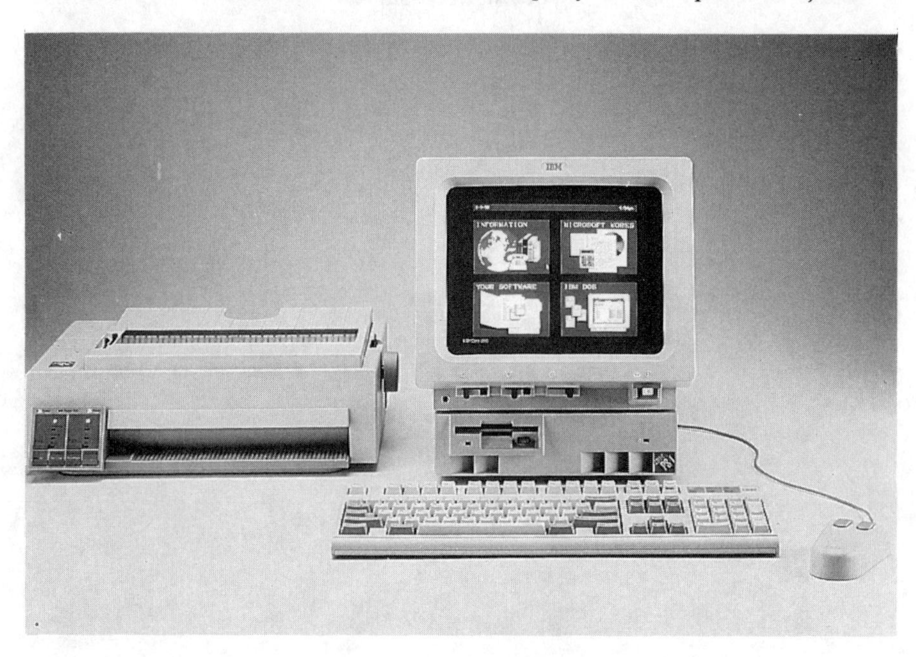

Fig 2.1
Stand-alone system

personal computer, this is the configuration it would buy. If the workload became too much for that one system to handle, the purchase of a second stand-alone system would probably be contemplated.

Shared resources

This is a configuration whereby a group of stand-alone personal computers share peripherals, such as a printer or plotter. One printer can usually cope with the output from three or four PC systems. It makes economic sense therefore for a company contemplating the purchase of a second or third computer to arrange, if possible, for certain resources to be shared between them (Fig 2.2). However, this configuration still has major limitations. The stand-alone computers cannot share information or software on their hard disks, nor can they communicate with each other. In order to do this, they need to be connected to a **network** as **workstations**.

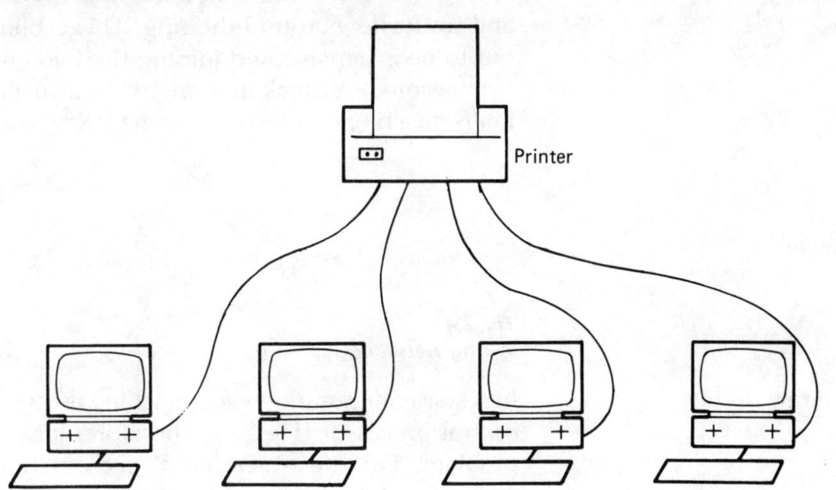

Fig 2.2
Shared resources system

UNIT 8 Networks (data sharing)

A **network** is defined as the facility to interconnect computers and peripherals so that communication and sharing of information, software and equipment can take place. A **local area network (LAN)** is the networking of computer equipment within reasonable local distances, eg *in the same room or office building.* **LAN** particularly excludes communications over distances, say, between towns, over telephone lines or microwave links. These would be covered under a **wide area network (WAN)**, also called a **long haul network**, which can span cities and countries.

Network topologies

Networks vary in layout and size. **Topology** is the term used to describe the shape of a network, the layout of the cabling and how the equipment is connected together. **Bus**, **ring**, **star** and **star-wired** are network topologies.

Bus

A bus network is cabled in a long line (Fig 2.3). Traffic (data, information, messages) passes up and down the line. The installation of this type of cabling is simple and cheap. However, locating faults can be difficult. *Ethernet* is an example of a bus network.

Fig 2.3
A bus network

Ring

A ring network is illustrated in Fig 2.4. Cable is laid in a complete ring and traffic flows round the ring. This cabling technique may well work out to be expensive and joining the two ends of the cable could prove troublesome. A break in a ring will cause all stations to fail and locating faults on a ring is not easy. *Cambridge Ring* is an example of a ring network.

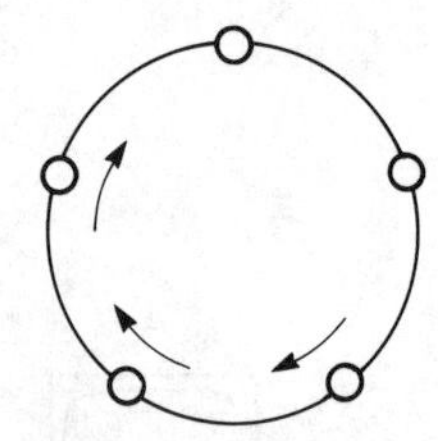

Fig 2.4
A ring network

Star

In a star configuration each machine is attached by its own cable to the central processor (Fig 2.5). Therefore, locating a fault does not cause a problem. On the other hand, each station is reliant on the central processor. *PABX* is an example of a star network.

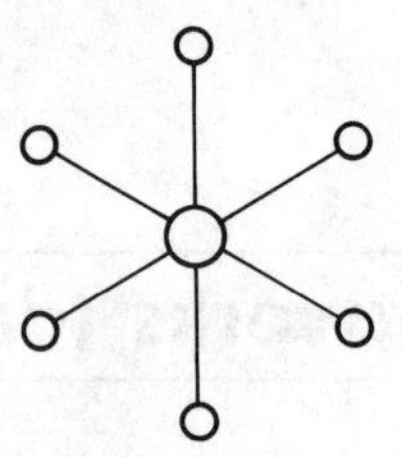

Fig 2.5
A star configuration

Star-wired ring

Each device in a star-wired ring configuration must be linked to a central **Multistation Access Unit (MAU)** by an adapter cable. Up to eight machines can be connected to each MAU. The network can be expanded by linking MAUs together (Fig 2.6). *Token ring* is an example of a star-wired network.

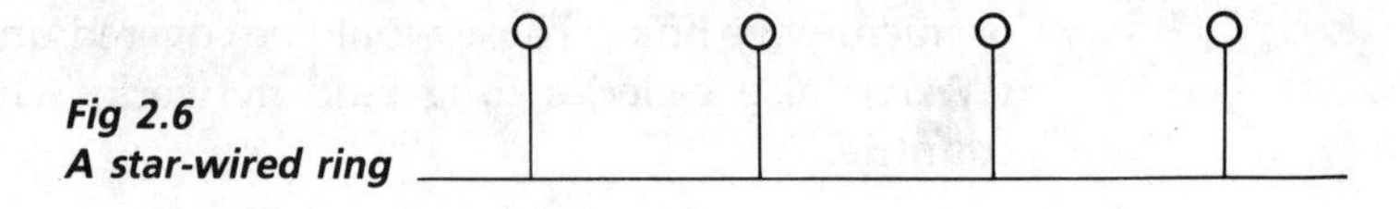

Fig 2.6
A star-wired ring

Local area networks

Basically, the hardware and software required to transform the computer equipment in a department or building into a network are:

- Network cabling system
- Network interface cards
- File server(s)
- Workstations
- Shared network printers, etc.
- Network system software

Network cabling system

Whatever the network topology, *bus, ring, star, star-wired* or variants of these, the reliability of data transmission on a LAN depends to a great extent on the quality of cabling used. Different cable types include **twisted pair**, **coaxial** and **fibre optic**. However, the same type of cable must be used throughout the network. As the cable is the lifeline to network resources, care should be taken to ensure that it does not become damaged or detached from the CPU.

Network interface cards (NIC)

All workstations must have a **network interface card** fitted to them. It is through the network interface cards that file servers and workstations communicate with each other. There are different types of **network interface cards (NICS)** and each type of NIC has its own cable requirements. Some NICS are faster than others, so the type of NIC chosen will have a bearing on the speed at which data is transmitted over the network.

File server

A **file server** can be any personal computer with a powerful processor. Its hard disk(s) will have substantial capacity to store all the software needed, as well as all data accessed or created by the attached workstations. Printers, modems and other peripherals are also connected to the file server. These resources can then be made available to any workstation on the network. A network can have more than one file server. File servers can be either dedicated or non-dedicated. A **dedicated file server** devotes *all* its attention to the network — its functions, maintenance and its users (workstations). A **non-dedicated file server** can also be used as a workstation.

Workstations

Each computer connected to a network is called a **workstation**. On the network, each workstation is assigned a unique address. Workstations can be stand-alone computers of the same make or of certain different makes. If a workstation has its own floppy or hard disk drive, it can operate independently as well as in the network.

Shared network printers, etc.

Workstations logged onto the network can use any printer or other peripheral that is attached to the network file server. If necessary, a network can have several printers attached to it. These can be parallel or serial printers.

Network system software

The main part of **network system software** is the **network operating system**. This program is loaded into the file server. Its function is to control all network resources and the processing of information on the network. Some of the standard network operating systems are *Novell Netware, Unix, Xenix* and *LAN Manager*. Additional network system software could be **support programs** and **network utility programs**. At the workstation level, operating programs such as *DOS, OS/2* or *MAC* will also be in use.

Who works on a network?

Staff who use computers in their job, on a regular or irregular basis, could find themselves working on a network if this is the configuration their department or company has decided upon. For example, in such a situation, a secretary would use a network workstation to access the word processing software and input, save and print the documents. Similarly, an accounts clerk would access the accounting software on the file server, update the ledgers and print out any report required. (*See* Fig 2.7 for examples of applications.)

These jobs would be done in much the same way if the secretary and accounts clerk were using stand-alone personal computers. However, working on a network means that certain *procedures* have to be followed. Security on a network is very strict because of the large volume of information held on the file server disk(s). Much of this information, such as personnel records and certain company transactions, would be confidential. Consequently, not everyone who uses the network can have access to all its facilities and information. Users are therefore classified into specific groups and each group has its own **rights** (network access privileges).

Fig 2.7
Different applications of the software being used in a network

Network manager/supervisor

The **network manager/supervisor** is the person responsible for the efficient operation of the network (*see* Unit 10, *Network training*). As such, the supervisor has **full rights** to any information on the network. It is the network supervisor who determines the **rights** of all other network users. S/he is able to access all utilities and change users' passwords and login names.

Network user

A user is anyone who regularly works at a workstation logged into the network and has access to its resources. If you are a regular network user, you will be able to access those directories and files to which you have rights.

Network user 'groups'

A group of users, eg secretaries in the same department, can be given **group rights** to directories and files which they will all need to access. This means that each user assigned to the group will have the same rights as the others and the same restrictions will apply to all users in the group. A user can be assigned to several groups. This way, the access requirements of all users can be met, while security is maintained.

Summary — Key Points

1. A stand-alone system is a single, completely independent personal computer system.
2. A shared resources configuration is a group of stand-alone personal computers sharing peripherals, such as a printer or plotter.
3. A shared resources configuration cannot share information.
4. Computers that are networked can communicate with each other and share information, software and equipment.
5. A local area network (LAN) is the networking of computer equipment within local distances, eg the same building.
6. A wide area network (WAN) is the networking of computer equipment over long distances, eg between cities.
7. Topology is the term used to describe the shape of the network.
8. Popular topologies are *bus*, *ring*, *star* and *star-wired*.
9. Computers connected to a network are called workstations.
10. All workstations must be fitted with a network interface card (NIC).
11. A *file server* is a personal computer with a powerful processor, to which all the workstations and printers, etc, are attached.
12. The network operating system, loaded into the file server, controls all resources and processing on the network.
13. The network manager/supervisor is responsible for the operation of the network.
14. Network users are only able to access those directories and files to which they have rights.
15. Users have to *log on* to a network and enter their password.

Knowledge Check on Section 2

Keywords (try to explain the meaning of these terms in your own words):

Bus network	Rights
Configuration	Shared resources
File server	Stand-alone
Local area network	Topology
Network groups	Wide area network
Network	Workstation

Complete each of the following items and then check your responses either with your tutor or with the answers on page 33.

1 Match each term in the first column with its meaning from the second column.

__ *1* Networked computers	*a* Allow file servers and workstations to communicate with each other.
__ *2* A dedicated file server	*b* Is the lifeline to network resources.
__ *3* The network cabling	*c* Devotes all its attention to the network.
__ *4* Network interface cards	*d* Can communicate with each other.
__ *5* Novell Netware	*e* Is a network operating system

2 List the hardware and software required for a network.

________________ ________________
________________ ________________
________________ ________________

3 Label the following statements true or false:

a ____ On a bus network traffic travels round the ring.

b ____ On a star network each machine is attached by its own cable to the central processor.

c ____ A stand-alone system has its own CPU, disk drives, disks, monitor, keyboard and printer.

d ____ Shared resources can share files and software.

4 Fill in the blanks:

a The function of the ________ ________ ________ is to control the network resources and processing of information.

b A network supervisor has ________ ________ to any information on the network.

Answers

1 *1d 2c 3b 4a 5e*

2 Network Cabling System
Network Interface Cards (NICS)
File server(s)
Workstations
Shared Network Printers, etc.
Network System Software

3 **a**F **b**T **c**T **d**F

4 **a** network operating system **b** full rights

Additional questions on Section 2

1 What would you consider are the advantages and disadvantages to a company in installing a networked system rather than computers sharing resources?
2 Discuss whether you prefer to work at a workstation on a local area network or on a stand-alone system. What do you consider the benefits to you as a network user would be?
3 The network manager or supervisor is responsible for the operation of the network. As such, what aspects of the job would you consider important?

Assignment 2

a If the systems in use at your computer centre require diskettes, establish whether they are $3\frac{1}{2}$ in or $5\frac{1}{4}$ in and whether or not they are **high capacity** diskettes.
b If you have a network system in your computer centre, try to establish its topology from the layout of the cables and the connections between terminals, and also the connection between individual terminals and the file server (main computer).
c Find out which network operating system is in use.

3 Changing over to computerised systems

In this section we will discuss how to effect a successful changeover from traditional methods of dealing with office tasks to a computerised system.

Each business has its own reasons for computerising its office functions. The most common reasons are:

1 existing systems are unable to accommodate the rate of growth
2 delays in output of information (turnaround times)
3 delays in retrieving and collating information
4 high error rate in output
5 inefficient and time-wasting procedures, often involving duplication
6 lack of information for management decision-making

Any one of the above could result in reduced company growth, loss of business, reduced profits, projection of a poor company image and the lowering of staff morale.

UNIT 9 Feasibility study for a computerised business system

Systems team

If a company is contemplating the installation of a computer system, a feasibility study will usually be carried out before any decisions are made. This is to examine any problems with the present system and to determine the needs of the company. It will also establish if computerisation would be a practicable solution to the problems. In a large organisation a 'working party' or 'systems team' might be selected from among the staff to undertake such a feasibility study. The team will generally include a fairly senior member of staff who is fully conversant with company policy and procedures. Naturally it is advisable to have someone on the team who is knowledgeable about computer systems and their capabilities. If there is no one on the staff with this expertise, an independent consultant will probably be brought in to assist. Such a person would normally be a **systems analyst**. The job of a systems analyst is to analyse the existing business system and determine what the needs are. Thereafter s/he will design an efficient computer system by specifying the hardware and software needed and outlining the procedures for the system. In a nutshell, the systems analyst should determine *what* has to be done and *how* it has to be done.

In a small firm where a single stand-alone unit will suffice, the feasibility study is just as important and should still be carried out. In such firms the owner/manager is usually involved with every aspect of the business and often, with the help of staff, will define the problem and personally complete the feasibility study.

Staff co-operation

A company's staff is its most valuable resource and one which wise management will acknowledge by fostering a good employer/employee relationship. Prime consideration must be given to employees' feelings and attitudes on changing over to a computerised system. Before a feasibility study is conducted, top management should arrange a meeting with all staff who will be affected, to inform them that such a study will be taking place and to explain the purpose of it. Staff should be told what the company hopes to achieve by implementing a computer system, and it would be sensible to point out any benefits to staff. More importantly, staff should be reassured that their jobs are secure and that adequate training will be provided. A brief description of what the study will entail is essential as the support and co-operation of staff will be required if the study is to yield accurate information. If the company's interest in computerisation is openly discussed with staff in this manner and they are given the necessary assurance, they will not feel nearly so threatened by the new system. They will undoubtedly not all be immediately in favour of it, but at least they will be given the opportunity to raise questions on any points of concern to them and management will have the opportunity to allay any fears. Not everyone enjoys changes and, particularly in the work situation where changes have all too often resulted in redundancies, there is bound to be a certain amount of hostility. The aim of good management is to inspire confidence in the organisation and in the future, and to encourage and develop a team spirit in the new venture.

Work measurement

During the feasibility study the workload of all those who will be affected by the changeover — secretaries, typists, clerks, executives and managers — will be measured over a period of, say, a month to establish the pattern, quantity and type of work done and time taken. This can be done by various methods:

1 observation at various times during the period and the making of notes
2 interviewing
3 inspection of records

4 requesting each person to keep a daily record of each and every task — even answering the telephone — and the time it takes
5 providing a questionnaire for each person to complete
6 requiring a copy to be taken of all paperwork, including revisions

It is usual to combine two of the above to obtain more accurate data.

Analysis

Once all the data has been collected, it will be organised and then analysed. From the analysis the following should emerge:

1 a breakdown of the data processing, typing and managerial administrative workload — ledgers, stock control, invoicing, multipage documents, standard letters, reports, financial projections, filing, etc
2 the busy and slack periods in the day, week and month both organisationally and departmentally
3 any duplication of functions and paperwork within the organisation
4 the frequency of re-starts and revisions
5 how work is presented for processing — handwritten, typed or dictated
6 the type of administrative work carried out by each person and the time spent on such tasks
7 average processing and turnaround time (time taken to process orders and invoices (in batches and individually), payroll, book entries, reports, letters, etc from receipt)

Systems design

The information obtained from the analysis will indicate if the installation of computers is feasible and if so the size and type of system required. Having said that, the equipment cannot be looked at in isolation. The floor space and design of the offices, the staffing and procedures are major considerations in the design of the system. There may be constraints which will also affect the design, such as company policy, union agreements, existing equipment and equipment budget.

Nevertheless, the size and type of installation will be based on the volume and type of processing needed. The systems analyst will take a systems approach. That is to say the processing needs of the entire organisation will be viewed as a whole, the input, the disk storage required and output (printers). In the design of the system, special attention will be paid to problem areas identified earlier in the study, such as bottlenecks. The overall objective will be to install a system which will not only adequately cope with the present workload, but which will allow for growth, and at the same time make optimum use of the equipment.

Equipment specification

Based on the system's design, the systems team will prepare a **hardware/software specification** and approach selected suppliers. The specification will stipulate the *essential* requirements of the system and the *desirable* ones. For example, if large amounts of data are to be processed, then a fast processing unit is an essential requirement, as is a fast printer. If mailshots are regularly sent out by the company to selected customers, then a word processing program with an easy to use mailmerge and sorting facility is essential. The desirable features will assist in making a decision if there is a choice between two or more systems. The specification will be discussed with the suppliers, who will be asked specific questions about their hardware and software. This will identify those suppliers to be invited to submit proposals for the installation. Potential suppliers should be required to demonstrate their equipment. An effective systems team will arrange for each supplier to perform the demonstration on examples of the company's own work, so as to assess and compare the capabilities of the hardware and software in meeting the company's essential requirements.

Recommendations

From all this you will realise that the systems team needs to be responsible, knowledgeable and highly organised. Their recommendations on equipment, installation, staffing and procedures should result in the most suitable and effective system possible for the company. These recommendations will normally include:

1 the hardware and software required
2 the type of installation (stand-alone personal computer systems/shared resources/networks)
3 implementation strategy (the stages of installation and implementation)
4 systemised procedures
5 staffing and training of personnel
6 future expansion

For example, if there is a constant, heavy and particularly repetitive text processing workload, as may be found in a firm of solicitors, then a networked system with laser printers, running suitable word processing software, would be considered appropriate to cope with this type of work. It might be recommended that installation be staggered, so that when the system is implemented in one department, installation for the next department takes place, and so on.

UNIT 10 Implementation: staffing and training

When changing over to a computerised system, most companies will prefer to select and train members of their existing staff rather than employ new staff as operators. There are two reasons for this:

1 Existing staff are familiar with company business, procedures and policy.
2 Employing new staff without making some of the existing staff redundant increases the wage bill, which defeats the object of implementing a computerised system.

Selecting computer staff

There are various methods of selecting staff for computer/word processing training. A systems team will generally establish criteria for the recruitment of operators. Some companies use a series of aptitude tests while others request departmental managers to recommend suitable members of their staff. It goes without saying that those considered must be willing to train in the first place. Training is an investment and companies should know what they are looking for in their future operators. If training of an operator has to be aborted because the person is found to be unsuitable, this is a waste of time and money for the company and a demoralising experience for the person involved. Therefore, staff should be carefully selected. The age of the person is of little importance, so long as s/he possesses the right qualities and skills. Most companies would like to be reasonably sure that an operator will remain with them for some time after training. Staff, on the other hand, will wish to know what their new status will be — whether they will be upgraded, downgraded or remain the same. They will also wish to know their promotion and career prospects. A natural fear might be the loss of skills through non-use (**deskilled**).

Desirable operator qualities

1 *A logical way of thinking*: this is helpful in finding the simplest way of preparing a complicated document or worksheet; in understanding and using the system's more advanced features such as sorting or merging information.
2 *An interest in machinery*: this is helpful in order to get the best out of the equipment. Such a person will not be afraid to experiment or try something new.
3 *Good concentration*: operators are often expected to produce documents compiled by a number of complex function sequences, as in the case of merging data from different files. Lack of concentration could result in a batch of letters being incorrectly addressed merely by calling up the wrong address file. Because of the power and speed of the

computers, errors such as this are magnified as the whole operation is over before it can be 'rescued'.

4 *Self-confidence*: this quality will be a great asset during training, as the person will adopt a positive approach.
5 *Common sense*: this is essential in determining what is a priority job and what can safely be left if time is limited. There are many decisions to be made in information processing and this is a desirable quality.
6 *Coolness and composure*: pressure is often put on an operator. Reports, etc are needed yesterday rather than tomorrow, which would be reasonable. Composure under such stress will not, of course, produce the report yesterday, but at least the operator will not panic and will get the job done as soon as possible. If one of the peripherals, such as the printer, appears not to work, a cool and composed operator will check the various causes, such as switches, etc systematically before sending for maintenance.

Essential computer operator skills

1 *Fast and accurate keyboarding*: although a computer is able to produce hard copies of prerecorded information at great speed, original data/text will take as long as it takes the operator to key it in. A computer's many facilities were not designed to cover up an operator's inaccuracy, but to assist good operators to be even more effective.
2 *Proofreading/checking*: this is essential to check that input is correct and accurate before it is printed out.
3 *Good language skills*: this is just as essential to a word processor operator as to a secretary. Dealing with words all day requires a good vocabulary, good spelling and a sound knowledge of punctuation (there is no software available for this yet!). The grammar of authors cannot always be relied upon and the operator should be able to recognise and correct grammatical errors.

Role of centre manager/supervisor

The success of a word/data processing centre is dependent on the effectiveness of its manager or supervisor. The role of a centre manager/supervisor is a dynamic one. It is not just a question of booking work in and out of the centre. Running the centre efficiently so that the text/information needs of the organisation are met and the centre staff are happy in their work, requires a combination of many skills and qualities.

Required manager/supervisor qualities (personal skills)

1 *Diplomacy and tact*: the manager/supervisor generally acts as intermediary between users of the centre and operators and ensures that each understands the other's requirements. These qualities are also constantly required when supervising the work of others.

2 *Coolness and composure*: a manager/supervisor must be unflappable. There will be many 'rush' jobs and occasions when the centre is under pressure. This pressure will be borne by the person in charge, who has calmly to set about organising the staff and resources effectively to cope with the 'emergency'.
3 *Self-confidence*: this quality will in turn inspire staff to have confidence in their chief. It is invaluable in discussions with management.

Required manager/supervisor skills

1 *Management skills*: this covers a wide range of skills, some personal and some general. The ability to lead a team, to ensure standards of performance, to organise the workload, to maximise the use of resources, to establish a congenial working atmosphere, to make decisions, are all vital skills.
2 *Communication skills*: a manager/supervisor is responsible for the work which leaves the centre and all work must be checked for input accuracy, and, in the case of word processing, spelling or grammatical errors which the operator might have overlooked. Obviously the centre manager must have a good command of language, which will also be necessary when communicating with operators, all those who submit work to the centre, maintenance and management, and when training new staff.
3 *Computer skills*: the person in charge must have a thorough knowledge of the system in use and be aware of the potential of the hardware and software. This will assist in assessing whether a job is possible, how long it will take to complete and how it should be planned. S/he must also possess good operating skills and be able to offer advice and support to operators when needed. Good computer skills will help in understanding operators' problems and needs.
4 *Ability to work with computer equipment*: a centre manager or supervisor should understand what makes the system function, what needs to be checked and, finally, when to send for maintenance.

Staff training

With the implementation of any system, staff training is important. With the implementation of information processing — a new technology and new procedures — staff training is critical to the success of the system. It may be that the company intends to conduct its own computer training courses. If not, then dealers who have been invited to submit a proposal for the system, and who offer computer training, should be requested to include training in their proposal. Independent computer training companies could also be approached to submit a training proposal. Any such proposal, from whichever source, should include post-training support. Training can be arranged in any one of the following ways, depending on which arrangement the company considers to be most effective, economical and convenient:

1 *In-house*: training is conducted in a training room on the company's own premises using their own training staff and their own course material. This allows for courses to be tailored to suit the company's specific requirements.
2 *In-house*: but instead of using their own permanently employed training staff, the company contracts out the training to a training agency or to independent trainers. Course material may be supplied either by the company or by those conducting the training. This again allows for courses to be tailored to suit the company's specific requirements.
3 *On site*: training is conducted by a computer dealer or computer training company, on the client's site, using the client's facilities, ie training room and computer system. Course material is supplied by those conducting the training. They are generally prepared to tailor courses and material to suit the company's specific requirements, although there might be an extra charge for this.
4 *Off-site*: training is conducted on the premises of the computer dealer or training company, using their own training facilities, training staff and material prepared by them. Courses and course material can be designed to suit specific requirements, generally for an extra charge.
5 *Scheduled courses*: courses presented by computer dealers or training companies on set dates at a fixed venue. As these courses are open to delegates from various firms/companies, it is not possible to tailor the training to any one company's needs. Although not flexible, this type of course is economical if only one person in a company requires training at a time. However, it is not the most convenient, economical or effective means of training when a number of staff in one company are to be trained.

As training is part of the implementation of the system, training of staff needs to follow as soon as possible after installation. Staff will derive the most benefit from their training if they are required to use the system and the software immediately afterwards. If there is a time lapse between training and use, much that was learned will be forgotten and enthusiasm and motivation will also have waned somewhat. However, it is not reasonable to expect staff to be fully competent in the use of the system and software immediately after training — they will need a little time to consolidate the skills learned. This can best be achieved if they are not required to work under pressure right away.

Support and follow-up training

Support should be available to all users, particularly during their first few weeks on a new system when problems and queries are likely to arise. Most companies recognise the value of having one or more members of staff trained up to technical level in the system hardware and software to assist users. Usually a **helpdesk** or **helpline** is provided, looked after by support staff. Users are therefore assured of assistance when needed. Once staff are experienced in the use of the basic functions of the system and software, training on any required advanced functions should be arranged.

Manager/supervisor and support staff training

Data/word processing centre managers/supervisors and support staff usually receive training in the operation of the equipment and software at the time of installation or even before. This helps in effecting a smooth changeover to the new system, understanding of new procedures and in getting the system operational at the earliest possible date. Centre managers/supervisors are often given additional training specific to their jobs. This will cover management skills, management of the equipment, training skills, health and safety legislation, cost implications of information processing, etc.

Network training

Special two-day or three-day courses are arranged for network managers/ supervisors. These courses introduce participants to networking in general and cover the features of the network operating system in use, for example Novell Netware. The main aim of the course is to teach managers/ supervisors how to manage a network efficiently. The network manager/ supervisor usually trains new users to use the network and its facilities, and is available to provide support to users when needed.

Management/ executive training

A few enlightened companies arrange training for management/executive staff and all those who submit work to the data/word processing centre and to other users. These are neglected groups when it comes to computer training. A demonstration of the equipment or covering the subject in general terms, as in the overworked 'familiarisation' course, is not enough. They need to know how to use the centre's facilities effectively and be aware of any procedures to be followed. An understanding of the cost implications of information processing, and a knowledge of the capability of the system and software in use, are also helpful. Last, but not least, they should be aware of the type of problems that operators might encounter during the course of the day.

UNIT 11 Implementation: procedures for an information processing system

This unit uses word processing as an example. The American National Standards Institute defines word processing as 'a transformation of ideas and information into a readable form of communication through the management of procedures, equipment and personnel'. Equipment and personnel have been dealt with and we will now look closely at procedures. First of all, what do we mean by 'procedures'? The dictionary definition is 'the regular order of doing things'. When we talk about procedures in information processing this is what is meant. If procedures are not established, the work will not flow smoothly through the system. Processing text from conception (the idea) or raw data to final distribution or storage stage involves a number of staff within an organisation, either directly or indirectly. Set rules and routines must be laid down for each person to follow if confusion and problems are to be avoided. Only with such standardised procedures will it be possible to achieve the expected increase in efficiency and productivity.

Procedures manual

Procedures are best outlined in a procedures manual. Managers, supervisors, operators and all those likely to use the system should be issued with a copy. The complete changeover to computerisation will not be implemented overnight and neither will office procedures change overnight. The procedures manual should be developed along with the implementation of the system. A systems team involved with the implementation will lay down a framework of procedures for the efficient running of the system. The procedures manual is built up within this framework. As each new application is identified, procedures for that application should be thought through and drawn up step by step. In this way staff are initiated into both the application and related procedures simultaneously. Each new application, or task, which is absorbed into the system, and the procedures for dealing with it, must be added to the procedures manual. From time to time the manual will also need to be reviewed and updated. Some of the initial procedures might not have been sufficiently well thought through or, in the light of experience, may prove to be inefficient or unworkable. It is vitally important to the effectiveness of the manual (and the system) that all copies of the manual are updated regularly. The help of operators is often welcomed in the preparation and updating of the procedures manual. As they are closely involved with the processing, they are able to make valuable contributions to the actual procedures.

Format of procedures manual (word processing is used as an example)

The standard format of the procedures manual should be simple. A popular format is the **item** format. In this layout the 'item' is listed as a side heading with a description and an explanation of the item to the right. The procedures related to that item then follow. Examples of 'items' in the application of word processing would be letters, memos, reports, etc. An example of a 'description' would be: sales letter (S1). An example of an 'explanation' would be: first letter to a new customer after receipt of initial order. An example of the 'procedures' related to such a letter would be: add customer details to customer file (word processor operator); send letter S1 to customer (word processor operator); send memo R1 to representative (word processor operator); distribution: sales manager for signature (messenger) (Fig 3.1). The language used in the manual must be clear and concise so that the procedures can be easily followed even by those new to the system.

Procedures should be introduced during the implementation stage.

Item	Description	Explanation	
Standard letter	Sales letter (S1)	First letter to a new customer after receipt of initial order	
		PROCEDURE	
	Origination:	Sales order, Copy 3	(sales clerk)
	Production:	Add customer details to customer file	(WP operator)
		Sales Letter (S1) to customer	(WP operator)
		Sales Memo (R1) to representative	(WP operator)
	Distribution:	Sales Manager for signature	(messenger)

Fig 3.1 Example of the item format used in a procedures manual for word processing

They will help to get the system up and running in an organised way as quickly as possible. The results are usually increased productivity and efficiency. Unfortunately not all companies plan their installation right down to the procedures. This has resulted in some cases in greater problems than before. What such companies have, in fact, is not a system at all but merely a collection of hardware, software and individuals operating at random. Not only are they wastefully utilising an expensive resource but disillusionment with the system is likely to occur throughout the company.

Training in procedures

If a systems team does its job well, procedures would be considered an essential part of the implementation. Staff training would not just cover the use of the hardware and software, but also the procedures involved. Let us take a look at a trainee engaged to work in an organisation's reprography department (where all the duplicating, photocopying, etc is done). Obviously s/he will be trained to operate the machinery, but just as important will be the training given in the procedures which are to be followed. There would be procedures for work coming into the department, which might include filling out a standard form with the name of the person authorising the work, the number of copies required, the due date, etc. Production procedures might include which equipment to use for different jobs, the type of paper, the layout, etc. Filing procedures might indicate where the form should be filed and/or details to be entered in a record book. Distribution might state whether completed work is to be delivered or collected.

Business system

This is not a computerised system — just a traditional business system with procedures laid down in order to control the workflow of the reprography department. This in fact sums up a *business system* — a set of procedures to accomplish a business function. Take, for example, the traditional stock control system. The function of controlling the level of stock is carried out in a very organised way, adhering strictly to the procedures of entering new stock in the appropriate column and adding

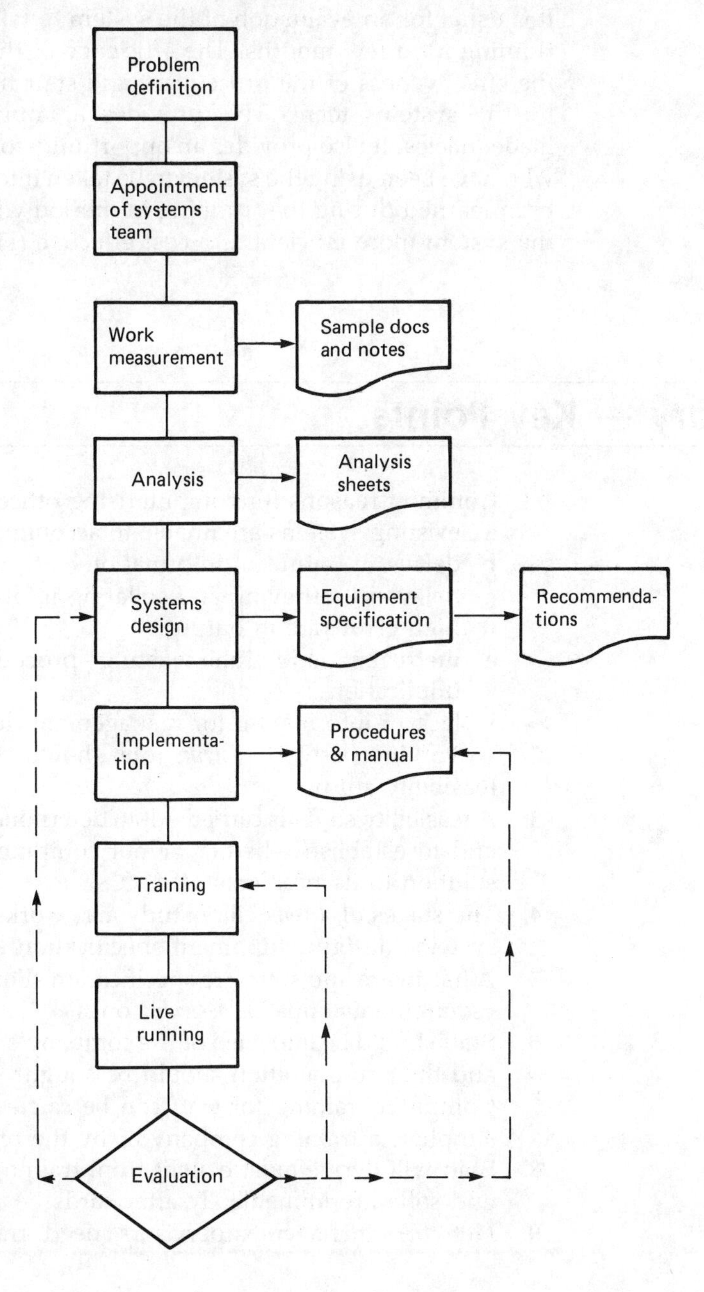

Fig 3.2
Flow chart of a feasibility study and implementation

it to the balance, to arrive at the new stock level, etc. All manual business systems are made up of sets of procedures. If we computerise a business system, some of the procedures are performed by the computer, but some will still have to be done manually. Furthermore, if we want to take advantage of the speed and capacity of a computerised system, additional or new procedures need to be devised.

Evaluation

It is usual for an evaluation of the system to take place after it has been running for a few months. The efficiency of the system, together with the effectiveness of the procedures and staff training, will be assessed by the systems team. This provides an opportunity to rectify any inadequacies. It also provides an opportunity for the suggestions of staff who have been using the system to be taken into account. A lot will have been learned during the 'running in' period which could help to make the system more efficient and cost effective (Fig 3.2).

Summary — Key Points

1 Common reasons for computerising office functions are:
   a existing systems are unable to accommodate the rate of growth
   b delays in output of information
   c delays in retrieving and collating information
   d high error rate in output
   e inefficient and time-wasting procedures, often involving duplication
   f lack of information for management decision making.
2 A working party or *systems team* should be set up to undertake a feasibility study.
3 A feasibility study is carried out to determine the needs of a company and to establish whether or not computerisation is a practicable solution to its problems.
4 The stages of a feasibility study are: work measurement; analysis; systems design; equipment specification; recommendations.
5 A hardware and software specification should stipulate the *essential* requirements and the *desirable* ones.
6 Staff should be informed of the company's intention to computerise and their co-operation should be sought.
7 Computer training for staff can be carried out by the equipment supplier, a training company or by the organisation itself.
8 Staff will derive most benefit from training if they use the system and software immediately afterwards.
9 Network managers/supervisors need training on the network

operating system and on how to manage the network efficiently.

10 Help and support should be available for staff after training.

11 Staff training and procedures are part of the implementation of the system.

12 Procedures must be established for the work to flow smoothly through the system.

13 Procedures are best outlined in a procedures manual and all staff likely to use the system should be issued with a copy.

14 A computer will perform only some of the procedures of a business system. Other procedures will still have to be carried out manually.

15 Evaluation of the efficiency of the system, together with the effectiveness of the procedures and staff training should take place after the system has been running for a few months.

Knowledge Check on Section 3

Keywords (try to explain the meaning of these terms in your own words)

Business system	Procedures manual	Systems analyst
Feasibility study	Proofread	Turnaround time
Helpdesk	Scheduled courses	Work measurement
In-house training		

Complete each of the following items and then check your responses either with your tutor or with the answers on page 49.

1 Match each term in the first column with its meaning from the second column.

a

____ *1* Feasibility study — *a* A book of rules and routines relating to the processing of text and data.

____ *2* Reprography — *b* Reproduction by means of photocopying and duplication.

____ *3* Procedures manual — *c* Research into the possibility of computerising.

b

____ *1* Equipment specification — *a* The use of techniques to establish the amount of work done and the time taken.

____ *2* Peripheral — *b* Details of the functions of which the equipment should be capable.

____ *3* Work measurement — *c* Lose a skill through non-use.

____ *4* Deskill — *d* A component connected to the CPU.

2 Label the following statements true or false.

a ____ A systems analyst should determine what has to be done and how it has to be done.

b ____ Staff should not be informed of the implementation of a computerised system until it is too late for them to do anything about it.

c ____ Support should be available to staff during the first weeks after training.

d ____ Training in computing should be given only to operators.

3 Multiple choice: select the letter that best answers the question.

1 Which of the following is undesirable in a word processor operator? ____.

a common sense
b composure
c restlessness
d self-confidence

2 Which of the following is *not* an essential skill for a word processor operator? ____.

a typing skill
b management skill
c communication skill
d proofreading skill

4 Fill in the blanks.

a ____ of the system should take place after a running in period.

b Procedures should be considered an essential part of the ____ of a system.

c A business system is a set of procedures to accomplish a ____ ____.

d A word/data processing centre needs a good ____ to control it.

e No other tasks are dealt with in a word processing centre apart from ____ ____.

Answers

1a *1c* *2b* *3a*
b *1b* *2d* *3a* *4c*
2 aT bF cT dF
3 *1c* *2b*
4 **a** evaluation **b** implementation **c** business function **d** supervisor/manager **e** text (word) processing

Additional questions on Section 3

1. Describe how a systems team would conduct a feasibility study.
2. When a company selects staff for computer training what qualities and skills do you think it should look for?
3. Describe the role of a centre manager or supervisor and discuss some of his/her responsibilities.
4. What do you consider are the benefits of producing a word processing procedures manual?
5. Why is it so important that management obtain the co-operation of staff in the implementation of computer systems and how would you suggest they go about it?

Assignment 3

a Draw up an equipment specification for a computer system for your own personal use. Keeping in mind what you would like to use the computer for, justify your specification.

b Write down everything you do today in college/school and how long each job takes you. Make this a work measurement exercise and, where possible, break each job down into units of work, noting down starting and finishing times for each unit.

4 Communication between the user and the system

In this section we examine communication between the user/operator and the system. The more simple a system (hardware and software) is to operate, the more acceptable it is to both user and management. Of prime concern to computer users/operators are the keyboard and the VDU (monitor), as these are the main tools for the job.

UNIT 12 How the operator communicates with the system

The keyboard is the operator's principal means of communicating with the system. Good keyboarding skills will help you to key in data/text quickly and accurately. Figure 4.1 shows an enhanced computer keyboard, which is standard today. Take a look at the keyboard layout below as we identify the various groups of keys and their functions.

Fig 4.1 Standard personal computer keyboard

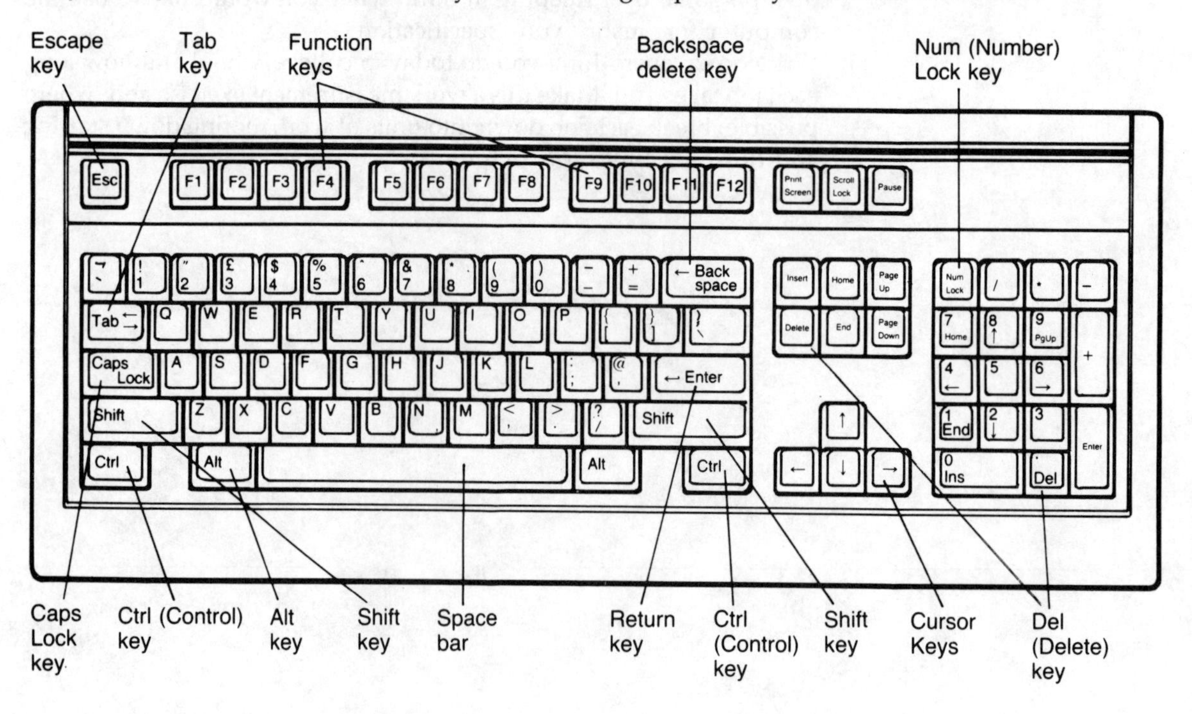

QWERTY keys

This is the largest group of keys on the keyboard, made up of all the letters of the alphabet, numbers 0–9 and punctuation marks. These keys are used to enter text and numbers. If you can type, your fingers will feel quite at home using this part of the keyboard as the arrangement of the keys is the same as on any typewriter. Just one or two little reminders: in computing, the capital letter **O** is never used for the figure **0** (**zero**), and the letter **l** is never used for the figure **one**. The **Caps Lock** only affects letters so, even when Caps Lock is **on**, you must still use the **Shift** key to produce the upper symbols on the number and punctuation keys.

The key marked **Enter** ↵ acts like a *carriage return* on a typewriter, and is often referred to as the **Return** key. A second and very important function of the Enter key is that it is frequently used to tell the computer to take action. For example, if you enter a command, the computer might not carry out your instruction until you press the Enter key.

Function keys

Usually on the very top row of the keyboard, above the QWERTY keys, are the **function keys**, marked **F1** to **F12**. These keys enable quick execution of frequently-used functions. The function that each of the keys performs depends on the application program you are using at the time, ie the type of work you are doing. For example, if you are using a spreadsheet program, then each of the function keys would perform a specific spreadsheet function (eg press **F5** to go to a specific cell). Similarly, should you be using word processing software, each function key would execute a word processing function (eg press **F5** to list all the files in the directory). It is quite usual for each function key to be allocated not just one function but two or more. Other functions are achieved by pressing the **Shift** key, or the **Alt** or **Ctrl** key, together with the function key. For example, when working with **WordPerfect** (one of the most popular word processing programs), you would hold down the **Shift** key and press **F5** to insert the date automatically. Most software packages include a **function key template** (Fig 4.2) to rest on the flat surface of the keyboard in line with the function keys. From this, the user/operator can tell at a glance which function(s) each key controls in the application software being used. Without this memory aid, a learner would have a lot more to remember! Function key templates also make it easier for users to switch from one type of application software to another.

Fig 4.2
Keyboard overlay

WordPerfect®
for IBM® Personal Computers

Column Left/Right	Home, ←/→
Compose	2
Delete to End of Ln/Pg	End/PgDn
Delete Word	Backspace
Hard Page	Enter
♦Margin Release	Tab
Pull-Down Menus	=
Screen Up/Down	–/+ (num)
Word Left/Right	←/→

74 - 10- 10

© WordPerfect Corp. 1990 TMUK/WP51XID—3/90

	F1	F2	F3	F4	F5	F6	F7	F8	F9	F10	F11	F12
Ctrl	Shell	Spell	Screen	Move	Text In/Out	Tab Align	Footnote	Font	Merge/Sort	Macro Define		
Alt	Thesaurus	Replace	Reveal Codes	Block	Mark Text	Flush Right	Columns/Table	Style	Graphics	Macro		
Shift	Setup	♦Search	Switch	♦Indent♦	Date/Outline	Centre	Print	Format	Merge Codes	Retrieve		
	Cancel	♦Search	Help	♦Indent	List	Bold	Exit	Underline	End Field	Save	Reveal Codes	Block

Cursor/navigation keys

The **cursor** can be a flashing horizontal line — or a solid rectangle ■ (both about the same size as one of the characters). In some application software, such as spreadsheets, it can be a highlighted bar ▬▬ (often referred to as the **pointer**). The **cursor** will indicate on the screen the position that the next typed character or entry will take. The group of keys to the right of the QWERTY keyboard are the **cursor movement** keys. They enable you to move around in the document, spreadsheet or file that you are working on. When doing so, you will need to keep your eye on the cursor. Touching any one of the four **arrow keys** ↑ ↓ ← → moves the cursor once in the direction indicated; holding the key down repeats the action. If you want to move from one typed word to the next, use the appropriate arrow key. Do not use the **spacebar**. The spacebar will insert blank spaces over your original characters.

Above the arrow keys are the **Page Up** and **Page Down** keys, and to the left of these are the keys marked **Home** (for moving the cursor to the top of the screen) and **End** (for the bottom of the screen, ie the last character entered).

Next to the **Home** key is the **Insert** key. Pressing this key once changes the mode from *insert* to *overtype*. To return to *insert mode*, press the **Insert** key again. This is called a **toggle key**. When in *insert mode*, you can insert as many extra characters/words as necessary. When in *overtype mode*, existing characters will be erased as the new characters are keyed in.

Pressing the **Delete** key (beside the **End** key) will delete the character immediately above the cursor and, if you hold down the **Delete** key, it will continue to delete characters to the *right* of the cursor. The **Backspace** key (above the **Enter** key) will delete characters to the *left* of the cursor.

Numeric pad

The keys located on the far right of the keyboard and numbered 0–9 have two functions. Their prime function is to be used for figure work and the numbers are therefore set out as they are on a calculator. When using this pad for figure entry, the **Num Lock** key must be **on**. Pressing the **Num Lock** key toggles it on/off.

```
Enter the number required

     1  Open file
     2  Recall file
     3  Print
     4  Index
     5  Applications
     6  Copy file
     7  Rename file
     8  Close file
```

Fig 4.3
Example of a menu

When using a computer for calculations, the **plus (+)** and **minus (−)** work as usual to indicate addition and subtraction. To indicate **multiplication**, you must use an **asterisk (*)** and to indicate **division**, you must use a **slash (/)**. These keys are located on the top row of the **numeric pad**.

When the **Num Lock** is **off**, the keys on this keypad act as **cursor keys** to navigate your way around the screen.

UNIT 13 How the system communicates with the operator

The system's way of communicating with the operator is normally via the screen (VDU).

Menus

Before entering information, the operator will need to tell the system what s/he wants to do. On some systems the operator can select the activity from the keyboard using **mnemonics** (eg typing **pp** for 'print page'). Application software is frequently **menu driven**, which means that a **menu** (a list of available activities) is displayed on the screen. The operator chooses an activity by pressing the key indicated on the menu or uses a pointing device, such as a mouse, to select the required activity. If the choice has been made from a **main menu**, a **submenu** might appear on the screen which will give the user various **options** regarding the activity selected. For example, if the activity is to **print**, the submenu might display options to print more than one copy, to number the pages, to change the pitch, say, from 10 characters to the inch to 12 characters, and so on (Fig 4.3).

Status line

The **status line** is a line of information which appears at the top or the bottom of the screen during input. The information supplied will vary from one application program to another. In word processing software, the status line will probably display the name of the file, the number of the page which is currently on the screen, and the line and column position of the cursor. As the cursor moves on the screen, the status line information alters accordingly. The operator is therefore able to tell at a glance on which page of the document s/he is working and also the exact position of the last typed character on the page (*see* Figs 4.4a and 4.4b).

Fig 4.4a
Example of a status line (word processing) at the top of the screen

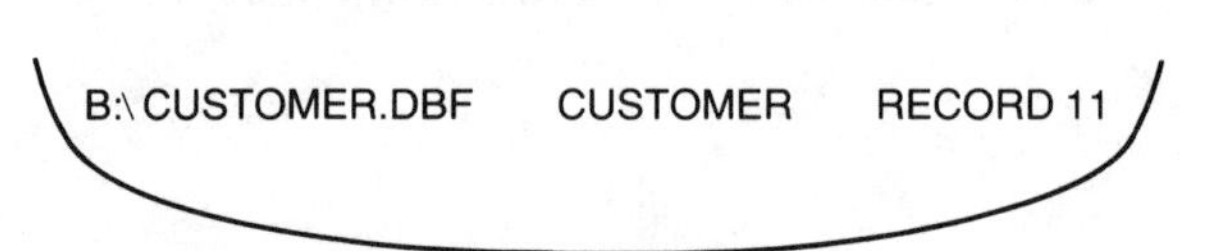

Fig 4.4b
Example of a status line (database file) at the bottom of the screen

Prompts

Prompts are the system's way of asking the operator for the information that it next requires. For example, when you start up the system, it will usually prompt you to 'ENTER NEW DATE'. In word processing, when the operator wishes to search for a particular word and touches the **search** key, a prompt such as 'SEARCH FOR WHAT?' might appear on the screen. The operator responds by keying in the appropriate word, eg CITY.

Messages

Some systems use **messages** to inform the operator that action is being taken. For example, once the instruction above (to search for CITY) has been given, the message might be SEARCHING. **Error/warning messages** also appear on the screen. If, as in our example above, an attempt has been made to locate the word CITY and it does not appear on the current page of text, a message such as CANNOT FIND ONE might appear. Similarly, a message such as INVALID ENTRY or ILLEGAL COMMAND could be displayed if the operator keys in an incorrect instruction. Messages are usually displayed at the top or the bottom of the screen.

Audible messages such as beeps are sent to the operator on some systems as a warning to indicate the end of a page or perhaps that the screen memory is full. Often audible messages indicate that an invalid instruction has been entered.

Scrolling

Because of the size of the monitor screen, only a section of the document, worksheet or data file you are working on can be displayed at any one time. The remainder is held in the system's working memory (RAM) and can be **scrolled** (moved up or down) to bring it into view when needed (*see* Fig 4.5). Although the average screen displays only 80 characters across, you do, in fact, have a wider typing line to accommodate wide accounting and financial worksheets, etc. Horizontal scrolling (using the left and right arrow keys) will bring any such extended width into view.

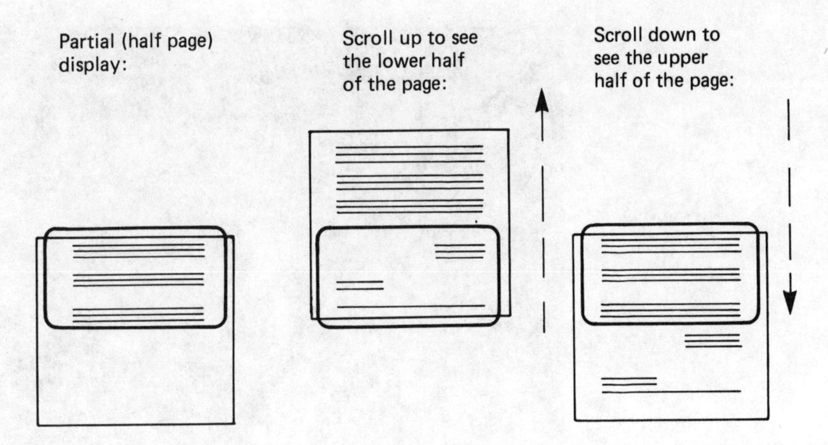

Fig 4.5
Scrolling

UNIT 14 User interface technology

The user

Because of the nature of their work, and their keyboarding skills, secretaries and data/word processor operators generally find it more efficient to use the keyboard as the only input device. However, they are not the only users of computers. Many business executives and professional people increasingly need to use computers in their day-to-day work to keep records, obtain information, calculate and analyse figures, produce reports, prepare graphic presentations, etc. These people usually are not so familiar with the keyboard and rarely have the time nor, in most cases, the inclination to learn efficient keyboarding. Their need, and the need of other inexperienced (naive) users, is for hardware and software that are easy to use; hence the growing popularity of the **mouse** and other user interface technology.

User interface technology

User interface technology is the term used for devices and methods incorporated in hardware and software which allow the user to think and act intuitively. The more the system does what the user expects, the less documentation is needed. Man–machine interface technology for this group includes various pointing and touch devices. These go some way towards overcoming the user's inability to enter instructions efficiently at the keyboard. They enable the user to use the system effectively while at the same time reducing the number of commands the user is required to remember. In short, user interface technology makes computers easier to use, and includes the following.

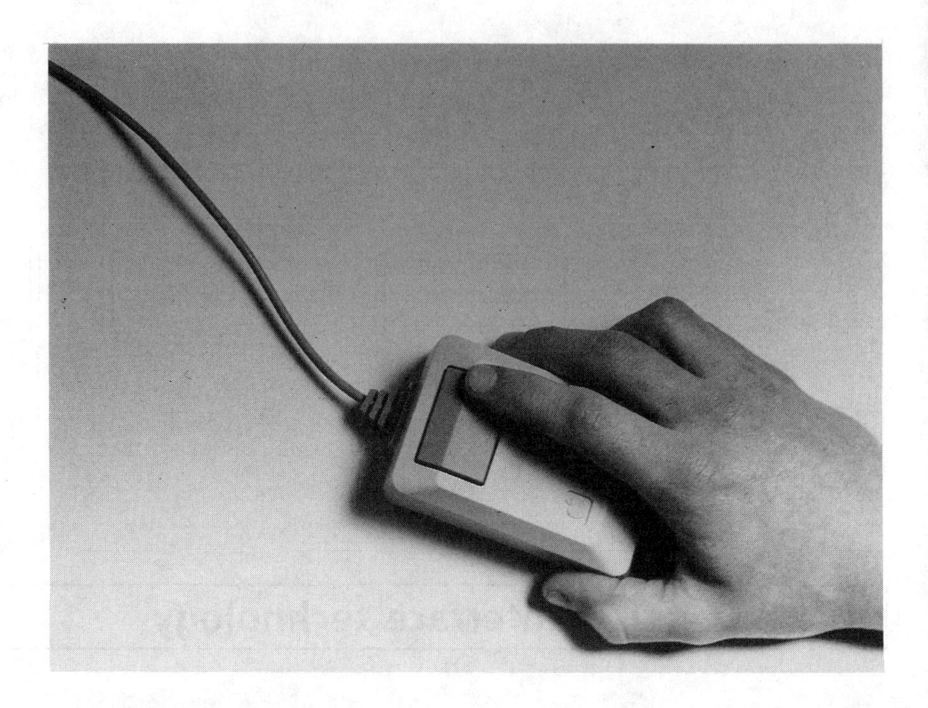

Fig 4.6
A mouse

Mouse

The mouse is so called because it resembles a child's toy mouse and is widely in use with several computers and application programs. It is a hand-held pointing device with a direction sensor. The mouse is rolled in the direction the user wishes the cursor (which might be an arrow) to be moved. The response is quick and accurate and commands can then be executed at the press of a button. In word processing it can speed up the marking of text to be moved or copied, as well as the selection of various commands. This device is often used with graphic displays. It is an aid for those who have little or no typing skill (Fig 4.6).

Touch screen

This screen is covered with transparent material which responds to the touch of a finger. This is truly an intuitive device as the finger needs no special instructions. Pointing at what we want comes naturally to us. Words can be deleted from the screen by first touching the words and then one of the touch activated labels on the screen (Fig 4.7). The same response is obtained when using other application programs such as spreadsheets and graphics. With graphics your numbers can be converted to graphs when you touch the screen.

Light pen

The light pen is a device which the user points at the screen. It can be used when the display presents a list of alternatives (a menu). The user can simply point to the activity chosen with the pen. The light pen is also frequently used with graphics. The user can draw the input on the screen with the pen. This is easier than using the keyboard to input the coordinates of a complex drawing. Pointing at the screen with a pen or the finger does have disadvantages however. The user needs to be close to the VDU and keeping the arm raised for any length of time is tiring.

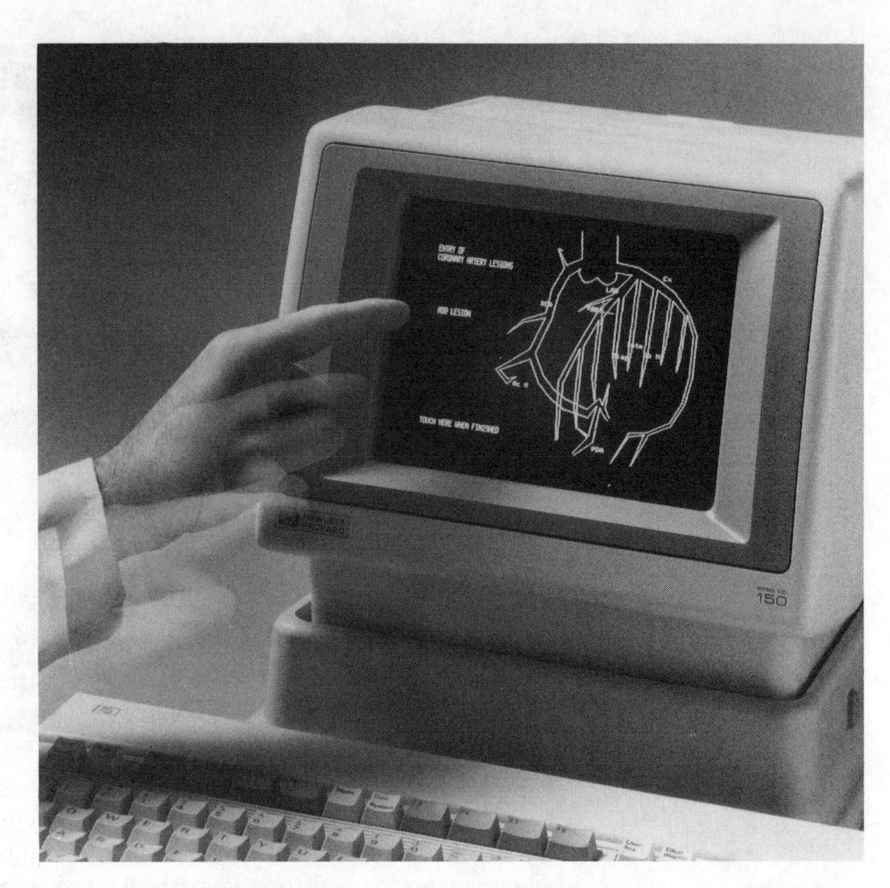

Fig 4.7
The infra-red touch screen

Touch tablet

This is yet another touch-sensitive tool which can be hand-held or used on the desk. Anything drawn on the touch tablet with the finger appears on the screen. There are also tablets which use an electric stylus instead of the finger to generate data on the screen.

Desktop metaphors — icons and windows

Based on Dr Alan Keys' idea that computers would be easier to learn to use if programs could be more like physical objects than like mathematical abstractions (*Byte Small Systems Journal*), 'desktop metaphors' refer to pictures of objects in common use in the office. Pictures or symbols are used on the screen to represent files, documents, in/out trays, etc. These symbols are called **icons**. Using one of the pointing devices mentioned earlier, the user can point to an icon on the screen and thus communicate an instruction to the system. For example, by pointing to a document and then to the filing cabinet the user indicates the instruction to file the document. It should appear to the user that the computer is physically performing the task. This is an important software development in user interface technology (Fig 4.8).

Figure 4.8 also depicts a screen resembling a desktop with multiple documents (**windows**) overlapping. Each window resembles another document or another program, eg a report document (using a word processing program) and a sales data sheet (using a spreadsheet program). The user is able to transfer information from one document to another.

Fig 4.8
Example of a screen with windows and icons

For example, in Fig 4.8 the data from the spreadsheet have been transferred to the sales report in the overlapping window. The user also has the freedom to stop work on one window and move to another window when required to work on that particular task – **multitasking**. Movements and commands can be carried out with the aid of pointing devices. Certainly windows, icons and point devices will go some of the way to enabling users to become productive more quickly and use a computer system more effectively.

Pen-based computers

Pen-based computers are currently being developed by hardware manufacturers. These are electronic pads on which you can write with a pen as you would on a sheet of paper. These machines will use a pen-based operating system, such as **PenWindows**. The system will learn to recognise your handwriting. A written *shorthand* is used to instruct the system to carry out commands, such as **Delete** or **Copy**, which would normally be entered at a keyboard. Using the pen, you will also be able to select standard commands from the **menu** on the screen. Completed documents and forms are ready for immediate printout. With a pen-based system, there is no need for a keyboard or a mouse. Such systems can easily be carried around with you to use wherever and whenever needed.

Scanners

When you get the opportunity to use a **scanner**, you will realise just how revolutionary it is. Not only can it replace the keyboard, it can also replace

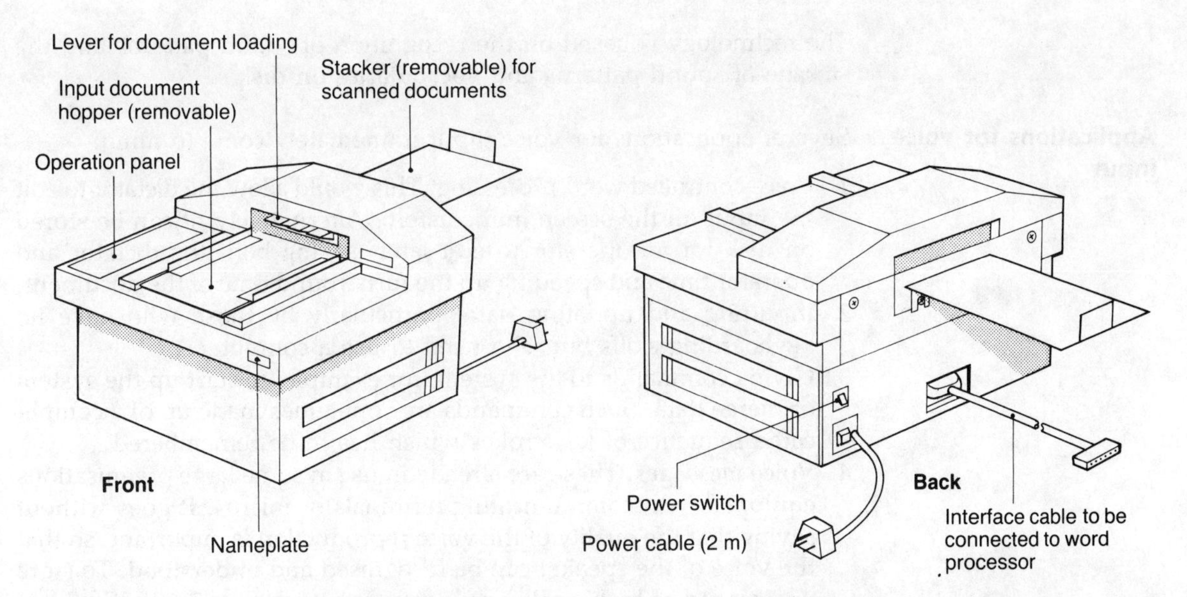

Fig 4.9
Front and rear view of a desktop scanner

the keyboard operator — that is temporarily while it is doing the inputting for you. What a **scanner** actually does is *read* printed text and automatically copy it into the computer. It does this at a speed of about 15 pages a minute, regardless of typestyle or page layout, and with virtually 100 per cent accuracy! **Scanners** can also capture pictures, photographs, graphs and drawings, which can then be inserted into company newsletters, etc. As many companies are now preparing their own in-house magazines, brochures and other publications, etc, they are finding that a scanner saves both time and money. **Scanners** are usually desktop size (Fig 4.9), but there are some hand-held models available.

Voice technology

Speech is the most natural way for people to communicate. The idea that we should ultimately communicate in this way with computers, the machines which have become more and more responsive to us, has been a popular one for some years. It does, however, involve some very advanced technology which has so far not been completely resolved. Voice recognition is proving to be the most difficult part of speech technology. Several techniques have already been developed:

1 Training the computer to recognise the voice of a specific speaker. However, a person's voice can change from one day to the next because of a cold, tiredness or some other reason.
2 Training the computer to recognise the voices of a particular group of speakers, eg all females. This is clearly more difficult because of the range within the group.
3 Training the computer to recognise isolated words, ie words spoken with long pauses between. This places a strain on the speaker.
4 Training the computer to recognise connected words, which is more natural for the speaker but more difficult for the computer to cope with.

The technology is based on the recognition of sound patterns and the storage of sound patterns and vocabularies on disk.

Applications for voice input

Several applications for voice input immediately come to mind:

1 Voice-controlled word processing. This would allow the dictator to edit the input on the screen immediately. Alternatively, it can be stored on disk for an operator to edit later, saving both the dictator and operator time and speeding up the turnaround time of the document.
2 Inputting and updating data, particularly by those who have no keyboarding skills but who need to use a computer.
3 Giving commands to the system, for example, to start up the system or merge data. Such commands are sometimes made up of a complicated sequence of keystrokes which has to be remembered.
4 Voice messages. These are already in use in some large organisations equipped with communicating terminals or micros. It goes without saying that the quality of the voice reproduction is important, so that the voice of the speaker can be recognised and understood. To store one second of high-quality speech can require from 2 to 8 Kbytes of data (*Byte Small Systems Journal*). There are clearly advantages to voice messages, eg when a document is transmitted from one machine to another and the sender appends a verbal message relating to the document. However, for independent messages the telephone could be the better choice as an immediate response can be obtained. In the event that the recipient is not in, an answering machine, fax, telex or written message sent through the system network would serve just as well. When using microcomputers, the amount of data storage required for voice messages is a factor to be considered.

There are many applications for speech technology which we can think of, not just in the office but in other areas too. Voice input is presently used in industry in situations where the user's hands are busy but input to a computerised system is required, often from a remote position. Certainly, using voice input will make a very worthwhile contribution to carrying out some tasks. Used with other applications it might not warrant the expense.

Natural language

Languages spoken by people are called **natural languages**. When we communicate with computers our instructions have to be worded in a language which the computer understands. We cannot deviate from that language structure or the computer will not be able to follow our instructions. It takes time and effort to learn computer languages such as BASIC, COBOL, PASCAL. It would be very much simpler if we could give the computer instructions in straightforward English rather than in a formal computer programming language. This type of input is particularly needed for the millions of users of today's personal computers.

Query languages

Natural language has been in use for some time with mainframe computer systems, in the form of **query languages**. These are languages which have been compiled especially for management to question the system's database. Since the purpose of a query language is to ask for and retrieve information, it has been possible to develop these languages to the point where a simple English dialogue can be carried out between the user and the system. The increased capability of personal computers has made it possible for natural language to be adapted for these systems. Although natural language still has to be entered at the keyboard, the benefits lie in the natural way in which queries to the system can be phrased. Figure 4.10 is an example of a natural language query and the same query expressed in a formal language.

Natural language:	How do Surrey reps actual sales for last month compare with estimated sales for May?
Formal language:	Print LName, 92 May Act Sales, 92 May Est Sales, 92 May Act Sales, 92 May Est Sales 92 May Act Sales - 92 May Est Sales If Region Surrey

Fig 4.10
Example of a natural language query

Summary — Key Points

1. The more simple a system is to operate, the more acceptable it is to both user and management.
2. The keyboard is the operator's principal means of communicating with the system.
3. Users with typing skills feel comfortable with the main part of the keyboard, which is the same as that of a typewriter.
4. The system communicates with the operator via the screen, displaying menus, prompts and messages.
5. Business executives and professional people who are not familiar with the keyboard increasingly need to use computers in their day-to-day work. Their need is for hardware and software with which they can interface more intuitively.
6. User interface technology is the term given to devices and methods, such as icons, windows, touch screens and the mouse, which are employed to make computers easier to use.
7. The mouse is in use with several computers and application programs

working in the windows environment. Many more such programs are being developed with a view to helping users become productive more quickly.

8 Windows allow the user to work with more than one document or application program at a time. The windows screen resembles a desktop with multiple documents (windows) overlapping.
9 Voice technology is based on the recognition of sound patterns, and the storage of sound patterns and vocabularies on disk.
10 Voice recognition is proving to be the most difficult part of speech technology.
11 Applications for voice input would be voice controlled word processing, inputting and updating of data, giving commands to the system and voice messages.
12 Language as spoken by people is called natural language.
13 Query languages are natural languages used on mainframe computers. They were developed so that managers could easily question a system's database. They have been adapted for use on personal computers.
14 A scanner is an important computer input device, particularly when a graphic image needs to be incorporated in a document.
15 Scanners can scan typed and printed pages and capture pictures, photographs, graphs and drawings and automatically transfer the contents into the computer.

Knowledge Check on Section 4

Keywords (try to explain the meaning of these terms in your own words).

BASIC	Mouse	Scanner
Cursor	Multitasking	Scrolling
Enter	Natural language	Status line
Function keys	Numeric pad	Toggle key
Icon	Prompt	Windows
Menu	Query language	
Mnemonics	QWERTY keys	

1 Complete each of the following items, then check your responses either with your tutor or with the answers on page 64. Match each term in the first column with the meaning in the second column.

a ____	*1* Navigation keys	*a* Keys which perform different functions according to the application program in use.
____	2 QWERTY keys	*b* Keys which enable movement within the document, worksheet or file.
____	3 Function keys	*c* Standard typewriter keys.

b ____	*1* Status line	*a*	Act as warnings to the operator.
____	*2* Audible messages	*b*	Brings into view text held in the working memory.
____	*3* Scrolling	*c*	Indicates the position of the cursor.
c ____	*1* Natural language	*a*	Computer input based on the sound patterns of speech.
____	*2* Query language	*b*	Computer input reading printed and typed documents.
____	*3* Voice recognition	*c*	Computer input using everyday language.
____	*4* Scanners	*d*	Computer input allowing users to question a system's database in a straightforward language.

2 Fill in the blanks:

a The mouse is ____ in the direction the user wishes the ____ to be moved.

b The touch tablet is a hand-held device and anything drawn on it appears on the ____.

c Documents which overlap others on the VDU are called ____.

d An ____ is a picture or symbol which appears on the screen to represent an office item.

e A light pen is a ____ ____ used to give commands to the system and to ____ information.

Answers

1 **a** *1b 2c 3a*
  b *1c 2a 3b*
  c *1c 2d 3a 4b*

2 **a** rolled/moved, cursor **b** screen (VDU/monitor) **c** windows **d** icon **e** pointing device, input

Additional questions on Section 4

1 Do you consider that the standard layout of a personal computer keyboard is well suited to its purpose or could it be improved upon? Give your reasons and include examples where appropriate.
2 Explain the reasons for the development of user interface technology and describe in detail three such devices/methods.
3 Do you consider voice input will make a useful contribution to computer technology? State your reasons.
4 Do you think that the increased use of scanners will threaten the jobs of VDU operators, or do you believe that there is work for both? Discuss.

Assignment 4

a Get some practice on a computer keyboard, get the feel of it and try to familiarise yourself with the layout of the keys. Use the *numeric/calculator pad* on the right with the *Num Lock* OFF and also with it ON. Notice that all the keys on the keyboard are repeater keys when held down.

b Make a *template* to fit above the function keys on your computer keyboard. Fill in the functions that each key will provide. This should relate to the application program you will be using during training, eg *WordPerfect, WordStar, SuperCalc*.

5 Computer operation

So far, we have discussed in detail computer hardware (the CPU, monitor, disk storage, printer) and only briefly mentioned software. Now it is time for you to learn something about software, which is a key element in a computer system. Software is needed to control the hardware — in fact, to tell it what to do. The two are interdependent and one cannot function without the other.

In this Section, you will also be introduced to the basics of computer operation. Everyone who uses a computer in business needs to know:

1 How to get the system started
2 How to use frequently needed operating system commands
3 How to load and use application software
4 How to end a session on the computer

UNIT 15 Software

Software can be divided into three types:

1 Programming languages
2 System software
3 Application software

Programming languages

When the same type of job has to be done repeatedly, it is a waste of time and effort to key in the same instructions at the computer keyboard each time. It is far more efficient to enter the instructions once only as a program and save it on disk for reuse when needed again. Programs are written by **programmers** in a **programming language**. A **programming language** is a particular way of coding instructions so that the computer will accept them. There are a great many different ways of instructing someone to do something, and it would be extremely difficult to get the computer to understand all the variations in everyday language. To overcome this problem, special computer languages are used. In each particular computer language, there are standard words to use and a set way of

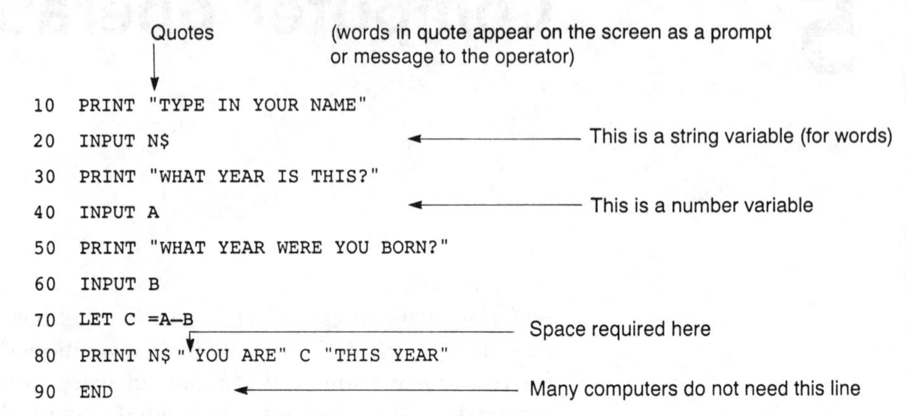

Fig 5.1
An example of a program written in BASIC

issuing the instructions. The format varies from one programming language to another. BASIC (which stands for Beginners' All-purpose Symbolic Instruction Code) is the language of microcomputers. Other programming languages suited to business-type applications are COBOL and PASCAL. Figure 5.1 is an example of a program written in BASIC. Notice the code words used and the structure of the program.

System software

Programs which control the performance of the system are referred to as system software. In this category are the following.

1 **Operating systems**.
2 **Compilers** and **interpreters**. They are used to translate programs written in a 'high-level' language (such as BASIC or COBOL), which humans can handle, into 'machine code' which computers can handle.
3 **Communication software**. This is used to transfer data from one computer to another.
4 **Diagnostic programs**. These programs enable the system to run a series of tests on itself to locate a problem with any of the system's hardware components.

Operating systems

Just as the CPU is the core of computer hardware, so the **operating system** is the core of computer software. This is a collection of programs which direct and switch information between the operator, the application software and the key computer components. There are several different operating systems. To a large extent, it is the computer's operating system which determines what application software can be used with the computer. The operating system most popular for personal computers is **DOS** (Disk Operating System). A very wide range of business software has been developed to run on **DOS**. Other operating systems growing in popularity are **Windows** and **OS/2**. These systems support **multitasking**, that is, they provide an environment where the user is able to work with more than one application program at a time.

Application software

This kind of software performs a particular type of task, ie it has been written for a specific application, such as accounting and word processing. As these are business application programs, they will probably be written in BASIC, COBOL or PASCAL. Programs can be **tailormade** (specially written) by an organisation's own programmers or by a **software house** (a company which produces software). Application software can also be bought as a **software package** from the system manufacturer and from a software house.

Packaged software

Microcomputers usually run packaged software, which is considerably cheaper than tailormade application programs. Once a master program has been written to instruct a computer to carry out a specific task, a software house produces and markets many copies of the program. Generally, these will be available to run on different makes of computer. The 'package' includes the floppy disks on which such an application program is stored and user/operator instruction manuals. Sometimes a training or tutorial disk is added to introduce operators to the program's features and functions, which each operator can then use as needed for his/her own type of work.

UNIT 16 DOS (Disk Operating System)

The **D**isk **O**perating **S**ystem (**DOS**) is stored on a **system disk**, often called the **DOS disk**. Whenever you start up your computer, you begin by loading **DOS** into the computer's memory. This is sometimes referred to as *booting up*, taken from the phrase *pull yourself up by your bootstraps* because, in essence, this is what **DOS** does. It loads *itself* from disk into the computer memory.

You will now be shown how to get the system started and how to use **DOS** commands. Startup procedures differ, depending on the type of system you have. If you work on a **network**, you will have to **logon** to get started. The procedures for logging into a network will depend on how that system has been set up. The **network supervisor** will usually instruct new users as to the procedure to follow. We will therefore confine our startup procedures to a stand-alone personal computer system. Instructions will cover:

1 A system with a hard disk and one diskette drive.
2 A system with two floppy diskette drives and no hard disk.

1 Getting started on a hard disk system

a Switch on the monitor; then turn ON the system power switch. DOS loads itself into the computer's memory from the hard/fixed disk. (It takes a few seconds to boot up.)

b If the screen displays the current date and prompts: *Enter new date*
Press **Enter** if the current date is correct. If not correct: key in today's date like this: **22-06-92** and press **Enter**.

c If the screen displays the current time and prompts: *Enter new time*
Press **Enter** if the current time is correct. If not correct: key in the time like this: **10:25** and press **Enter**.
(DOS uses a 24-hour clock, eg 1 pm = 13:00 and 2 pm = 14:00)

The screen then displays the **DOS prompt:** *C:\>*

The actual *prompt* is > and the **C:** indicates that the **hard disk**, which is addressed as the **C drive**, is now the **default drive** (drive presently in use).

The **DOS prompt** shows that DOS is ready for your commands.

2 Getting started on a dual floppy drive system with no hard disk

a With the system OFF, put the **system disk** into **Drive A** (this will be either the left drive or the top one).

1 If the drive is $5\frac{1}{4}$ in, place your thumb on the label of the floppy disk and push the disk in until it clicks into place (Fig 5.2). Close the drive door or press the button, as required.

2 If the drive is $3\frac{1}{2}$ in, slide the diskette into the drive with the arrow side up (and the arrow pointing towards the drive). Press the outer edge of the diskette until it clicks into place.

b Switch on the monitor and then turn ON the system power switch.

c When the screen displays the current date and prompts: *Enter new date*
Press **Enter** if the current date is correct. If not correct: key in today's date like this: **22-06-92** and press **Enter**.

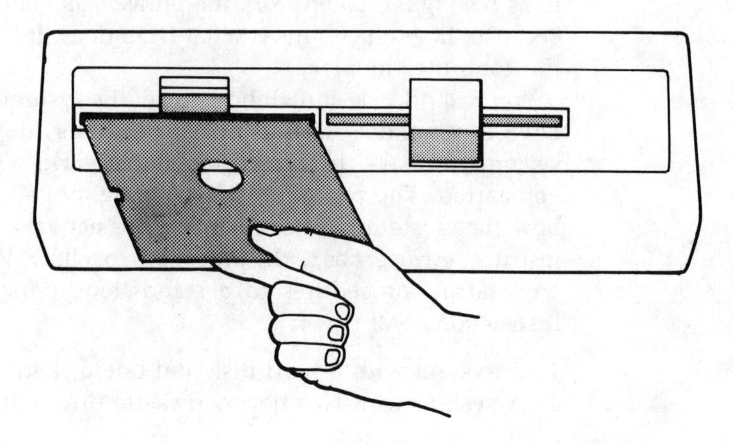

Fig 5.2
Inserting a diskette

d When the screen displays the current time and prompts: *Enter new time* Press **Enter** if the current time is correct. If not correct: key in the time like this: **10:25** and press **Enter**.

The screen displays the **DOS prompt:** *A:\>* and DOS is ready.

The DOS prompt **A:\>** means that the **A Drive** is now the **default drive**. This is because DOS was loaded from the diskette in Drive A.

Using DOS commands

As you saw from the above, whatever letter appears in the DOS prompt indicates the default drive. DOS will search the disk in that drive for any commands or filenames that you key in unless you tell it to search in another drive. You can change the default drive by typing the new drive letter followed by a colon (:). For example, to make Drive B the new default drive:

A:\>	existing prompt
A:\>B:	key in **B:** as the new default drive and press **Enter**
B:\>	new prompt appears showing Drive B as the default

We are now going to use the following DOS commands:

DIRECTORY	to display the disk directory
FORMAT	to prepare a new disk for use
COPY	to copy a file or files
TYPE	to examine the contents of a file
RENAME	to rename a file
ERASE	to erase a file or files

Note: When giving a DOS command:

1. The DOS prompt (eg A:\>) must be the last character on the screen.
2. DOS commands can be in capitals or in small letters.
3. The command word, eg FORMAT, must be followed by a **clear space**.
4. You must press the **Enter** key after typing the full command, otherwise the computer will not execute the command.

DIRECTORY command

A:\> Type **DIR** and press **Enter**

To display the **DIR**ectory of any disk in Drive B:

A:\> Type **DIR B:** and press **Enter**

You use the **DIR**ectory command to find out what files are on a disk. The **DIR**ectory displays the size of the file and the date on which you created the file or last updated it (*see* Fig 5.3). The last line of the display notes the number of files and the number of **bytes** free on the disk.

When there are several files on a disk, not all the files can be seen on the screen at one time. To display the files in a wide format across the screen:

A:\> Type **DIR/W** and press **Enter**

Explanation:
Col. 1 displays FILENAME
Col. 2 displays FILENAME EXTENSION
Col. 3 displays FILE SIZE IN BYTES
Col. 4 displays DATE FILE CREATED OR UPDATED
Col. 5 displays TIME FILE CREATED

```
COMMAND   COM   23210 3-07-92  1:43P
ANSI      SYS    1651 3-07-92  1:43P
ASSIGN    COM    1509 3-07-92  1:43P
ATTRIB    EXE   15091 3-07-92  1:43P
BACKUP    COM    5577 3-07-92  1:43P
BASIC     COM   17792 3-07-92  1:43P
BASICA    COM   27520 3-07-92  1:43P
CHKDSK    COM    9435 3-07-92  1:43P
COMP      COM    3664 3-07-92  1:43P
DISKCOMP  COM    4073 3-07-92  1:43P
DISKCOPY  COM    4329 3-07-92  1:43P
EDLIN     COM    7261 3-07-92  1:43P
FDISK     COM    8173 3-07-92  1:43P
FIND      EXE    6403 3-07-92  1:43P
FORMAT    COM    9398 3-07-92  1:43P
GRAFTABL  COM    1169 3-07-92  1:43P
GRAPHICS  COM    3111 3-07-92  1:43P
JOIN      EXE   15971 3-07-92  1:43P
KEYBFR    COM    2473 4-12-92  4:22P
KEYBGR    COM    2418 4-12-92  4:23P
KEYBIT    COM    2361 4-12-92  4:25P
KEYBSP    COM    2451 4-12-92  4:24P
KEYBUK    COM    2348 4-12-92  4:26P
Strike a key when ready....
```

Fig 5.3
Directory display

Entering the command DIR/W ↵ results in the directory being displayed in a wide format across the screen. (Note that only the filenames are displayed.)

```
A>dir/w

    Volume in drive A has no label
    Directory of A:\
COMMAND   COM ANSI      SYS ASSIGN    COM ATTRIB  EXE BACKUP    COM
BASIC     COM BASICA    COM CHKDSK    COM COMP    COM DISKCOMP  COM
DISKCOPY  COM EDLIN     COM FDISK     COM FIND    EXE FORMAT    COM
GRAFTABL  COM GRAPHICS  COM JOIN      EXE KEYBFR  COM KEYBGR    COM
KEYBIT    COM KEYBSP    COM KEYBUK    COM LABEL   COM MODE      COM
MORE      COM PRINT     COM RECOVER   COM RESTORE COM SELECT    COM
SHARE     EXE SORT      EXE SUBST     EXE SYS     COM TREE      COM
VDISK     SYS SETCLOCK  COM GETCLOCK  COM TIMER   COM AUTOEXEC  BAT
        40 File(s)     56320 bytes free
A>
```

Fig 5.4
Wide directory display

FORMAT command

Before you can use a brand new diskette, you have to **format** it. You do not format a disk each time you use it. If you format a disk with data stored on it, **format** will clear all the data off the disk. *So be careful when using this command!*

If you are using a computer with a hard disk (fixed disk) and one diskette drive, **Drive C** should be the default drive and the diskette to be formatted should be placed in **Drive A**.

1 C:\> Type **FORMAT A:** and press **Enter**
2 Insert a new disk in **Drive A** as prompted by the system
3 Press **Enter** (wait while formatting takes place)
The system prompts
Format Complete... Format another (Y/N)?
4 Type **N Enter** if you do not want to format another
Type **Y Enter** if you do and follow the prompts

If you are using a dual floppy system, the **DOS disk** (System Disk) should be in **Drive A**, which should be the default drive. The diskette to be formatted should be placed in **Drive B**.

1 A:\> Type **FORMAT B:** and press **Enter**
2 Insert a new disk in **Drive B** as prompted by the system
3 Press **Enter**

COPY command

COPY is used to make a duplicate (back up) of a file, usually on another disk. The disk you are copying *from* is called the **source disk** and the disk you are copying *to* is referred to as the **destination disk** or the **target disk**. To copy the file named **Maillist.acc** on the hard disk (C Drive) to the diskette in the A Drive:

1 C:\> Type **COPY C:MAILLIST.ACC A:** and press **Enter**

A copy of the file **Maillist.acc** now resides on both the hard disk and the diskette in the A Drive.

If you want the new copy to have a different filename, you need to type in the new filename as well, eg:

Type **COPY C:MAILLIST.ACC A:CUSTOMER.LST** and press **Enter**
If **copy** is successful, the screen displays
1 file copied

TYPE command

The **type** command is useful to check the contents of text files such as the **Autoexec.bat** file. This is a file which **DOS** looks for on startup and then carries out the commands in it. For example, the **autoexec.bat** file can contain commands to enter the date and time for you on startup and even automatically load the application program you usually work with.

C:\> Type **TYPE FILENAME** and press **Enter**
(for *filename*, substitute the name of the file you want to inspect)

RENAME command

Use the **RENAME** command to change a filename. Type the existing name first, followed by the new filename.

C:\> Type **RENAME OLDNAME NEWNAME** and press **Enter**

ERASE or DEL command

The command **ERASE** or the command **DEL** can be used to delete one or more files from a disk. After the command, simply type the filename of the file to be erased:

C:\> Type **ERASE MAILLIST.ACC** and press **Enter**

or type **DEL MAILLIST.ACC** and press **Enter**

Commands used when working on a hard disk (fixed disk)

Because hard disks can store vast numbers of files, it is sensible to group files into categories and store each group separately on the disk. Similarly, in a conventional filing system, groups of files would be placed in different sections of the filing cabinet. On a disk, these sections are called **subdirectories**, or simply **directories**, and each group of files is put into a separate subdirectory. When a new system is installed, there is only one directory on the hard disk, called the *root directory* (or the *root*), because, like a tree, the whole directory structure grows from it. The *root* is represented by a **backslash (\)**. (You will have noticed the backslash in the DOS prompt C:\>.) This indicates that you are using the hard disk and are in the root directory. Subdirectories have to be created as and when they are required.

Application software is generally installed on the system's hard disk and each program will have its own directory. For example, the files that make up the *WordPerfect 5.1* program will be stored in the *WP51* directory. The *DOS* files will be put into the *DOS* directory. There will probably be other directories for different types of work, such as a *DOCS* directory for documents, etc. However, before files can be stored in a directory, you must *make* that directory.

To make a directory

C:\> Type **MD WP51** and press **Enter**
A subdirectory for *WordPerfect 5.1* is created.

You can create as many subdirectories as you like, and also subdirectories of subdirectories (like a family tree). If you wish to use or save files in a particular directory, you must first *change* to that directory.

To change directory

If, for example, you need to move from the *root directory* to the *WP51 directory*

C:\> Type **CD WP51** and press **Enter**

C:\WP51> This is the new prompt, letting you know that you are in the *WordPerfect 5.1 directory*, which is an off-shoot of the *root directory*. (*Note: WP51* follows the **backslash**.)

To move from one subdirectory to another subdirectory, you must go via the *root directory*. For example, to change from the *WP51 directory* to the *DOS directory*:

C:\wp51> Type **CD\DOS** and press **Enter**

Inserting the **backslash** immediately *after* the command **CD** (**C**hange **D**irectory) tells the system to go first to the *root directory* and then to the *DOS directory*.

However, if the *WP51 directory* had a subdirectory branching from it called *DOCS*, you could move directly from the *WP51 directory* to the *DOCS subdirectory*. This is because *DOCS* is not a branch of the *root*, but is directly connected to the *WP51 directory*.

C:\WP51> Type **CD DOCS** and press **Enter**

C:\WP51\DOCS> The new prompt shows that you are in the *DOCS directory* and the **path** to get there. *Note:* The backslash is also used to separate directory names. As you are in the *DOCS directory*, you will have access to any of the files in that directory. A file you save now will automatically be saved in *C:\WP51\DOCS* with the filename appended. For example: *C:\WP51\DOCS\MYFILE*.

UNIT 17 Working with computer files

In your job as a computer user you will probably use application software. Each time you need to work with a particular application, that application program must be *loaded* into the computer's memory (RAM) from the disk where it has been **installed**. (When a program is installed, it is tailored to your system and your needs.) Application programs, such as those for spreadsheets, word processors and databases, are supplied on diskettes. Where a hard disk system is in use, all the application software needed will no doubt have been copied on to the hard disk from the program diskettes.

To load an application program from a hard disk system

1 Switch on the computer and wait until the **C:\>** appears
2 Change to the required program directory, for example *WP51*
Type **CD WP51** and press **Enter**
3 Type **WP** and press **Enter** (to load the *WordPerfect* program)

To load an application program using a dual floppy disk system

1 Insert the **DOS/System Disk** in **Drive A**
2 Switch on the computer. Wait for the prompt to appear **A:\>**
3 Remove the **DOS Disk** and insert the **Program Disk** in **Drive A**
4 Insert a formatted diskette in **Drive B** for your work
5 Type **WP** and press **Enter** (to load the *WordPerfect* program)

Using application software

During a work session, no matter which application program you are using, you will generally be called upon to do one of the following:

1 Enter new data or text
Store it as a file on disk
Print out a **hardcopy** (paper copy)
2 Retrieve an existing file from disk
Change its contents or layout
Resave it on disk
Print out a hardcopy of the new version

Any data or text you enter will appear on the screen and will be temporarily stored in the computer **memory**. While it is in the memory, you can view your data/text, revise it, erase it and reorganise it with the help of the special functions and features of the application program you are using. For example, when word processing, you can use the **move** function to reverse the order of two paragraphs. When using a spreadsheet, you could delete a section of the worksheet with the **range erase** function. When you have finished your text/data entry, you issue an instruction to **save** your work. The system saves your work as a **file** on either the hard disk or a diskette. You may also issue an instruction to **print** the file.

Opening a file/saving a file

Some application programs allow you to start entering your data/text right away and only when you have completed your input do you open a file for it and save it on the disk. Other programs require you to provide a filename before you start keying in. The input, however, is *not stored on disk* until you wish to save it and give the necessary command to the system to do so. **Opening a file** means more or less what it does in the manual sense — reserving space for the file. Instead of allocating a file folder and space in the filing cabinet for the file, space is allocated on the disk.

Filenames

Each file that you store on a disk must have a distinctive **filename**, so that it can be identified easily. A filename can be made up of a combination of letters and/or figures up to a stipulated number of characters. This depends on the computer's operating system. DOS filenames can be up to eight characters long followed by an **extension** made up of a period (.) and up to three characters. It helps to use filenames that describe the contents of the files. For example, BUDGET1 for the first month's budget, and FEBRUARY.RPT and MARCH.RPT for monthly reports. The filename extension given in the second example makes it easy to identify similar types of files. Grouping files by their extension enables you to erase or copy the entire group with one system command. For example, you could extract and copy all the report files from the disk in Drive A to the disk in Drive B simply by entering the command **copy A:*.RPT B:** (the * is known as a **wildcard character**, used to match any filename).

Retrieving a file

The reason for giving a file a distinctive name is, of course, mainly to identify it for retrieval later. When the filename is entered, the system knows what to look for and will go directly to the place on the disk where the file has been stored (this is **direct access**). The contents of the retrieved file will be displayed on the screen immediately. It is important when retrieving a file to enter the exact name under which it was stored. If there is the slightest difference in the letters or figures entered, the system will not find the file. To help you select the correct file, most application programs display the disk directory as soon as the command is given to retrieve a file. The directory is sometimes referred to as the **index** or **list**.

Re-saving a retrieved file

When you have finished making the required changes to the file, you save it once more on the disk. You can save it under the same filename, in which case the updated version will overwrite the original, ie it will replace the original. If you wish to keep both the old and the new versions, you must give the updated file a new filename.

Ending a session on the computer

Follow a simple but set procedure each time you terminate a session on the computer:

1 **Save** (store) the file on which you have been working on your work disk if you wish to keep it. You must give the system appropriate instructions to save the file. These will vary according to the application program you are using.
2 **Exit** from the application program.
3 Remove the floppy disks from the disk drives and return them to their envelopes.
4 Switch off the monitor, the printer and the computer.

UNIT 18 Terminology

Terminology

A number of words and terms have been used so far which you have perhaps found somewhat strange. Nevertheless, I hope that you have made a point of learning these terms and that you are now familiar with their use in connection with information processing. Some of these terms have been particularly selected and listed as 'keywords'. Many specialist occupations, such as banking, insurance, legal and computing, have their own special words and terms (**terminology**). Obviously, to be successful in your chosen field of work it is essential to become familiar with any terminology used in that field. Each term has a specific meaning which should be clearly understood by all in that particular business or profession so that when it is used there is no risk of misunderstanding. Terminology also eliminates the need for long and tedious explanations. Without it the risk of misunderstanding increases and time is wasted. Terminology is an aid to effective communication, which is essential to the efficiency of a business.

Knowing the terminology of information processing will benefit and speed up your initial practical training in business computing. Later it will help you, when training on a new system or application program, to understand the instructions given in the operator's manual and/or by the trainer, as both will use terminology. Additionally, when you attend a job interview an employer might well attempt to test your knowledge of information processing by questioning you on the subject, making a point of using terminology associated with it. Even if you are good at operating your school/college word processor or computer, you could still fail to impress the interviewer if you do not understand the terminology used.

Adapting to change

There are many different makes/models of computers on the market and, when you first go out to work, you will almost certainly encounter a different system to the one on which you were trained. You can also expect that when you change jobs the hardware and software you will be required to use will again be different. Even if you remain in the same job for any length of time, it is possible that your company will at some stage change over to another system or add other application software. From all this you will see that you will have to be flexible. You will have to be prepared to accept changes and adapt to them as quickly as possible. This will not be difficult:

1 if you have a good background knowledge of information processing and know the terminology
2 if you are aware that, while basic functions of software for a particular application (eg word processing or accounting) are the same, the labels or words used for the function keys might be different.

For example, to rearrange text on one system, the key marked MOVE would be used, but on another system to perform the same function a key marked CUT might be used, or perhaps COPY.

An overview of different application programs presented in Section 6 will give you an indication of the type of information processing you will probably be involved with in the work situation.

SUMMARY — Key Points

1 Everyone who uses a computer in business needs to know: **a** how to get the system started; **b** how to use frequently needed operating system commands; **c** how to load and use application software; **d** how to end a session on the computer.

2 Software can be divided into three types: **a** programming languages; **b** system software; **c** application software.
3 A programming language is a particular way of coding instructions so that the computer will accept them.
4 System software includes *operating systems, compilers and interpreters, communication software* and *diagnostic programs*.
5 The *operating system* is the core of computer software.
6 The operating system most popular for personal computers is **DOS** (Disk Operating System).
7 Other operating systems growing in popularity are **windows** and **OS/2**.
8 Startup procedures differ slightly depending on the type of system you have: you logon to a network; boot-up from Drive C when using a hard disk; and use a systems disk in Drive A on a two diskette computer.
9 The default drive is the drive presently in use.
10 Frequently used **DOS** commands are: DIRECTORY, FORMAT, COPY, TYPE, RENAME, ERASE.
11 The storage space on a hard disk (the root directory) is usually divided into subdirectories, and different groups of files are stored in different subdirectories.
12 Each time you need to work with a particular application, that application program must be loaded into the computer's memory from the disk where it has been installed.
13 Each file on the disk must be given a unique filename. DOS allows filenames to be up to eight characters long, followed by an extension of up to three characters.
14 At the end of a work session, save your work before you exit from the application program and switch off the computer.
15 It is necessary for those working with computers to understand computer terminology.

Knowledge Check on Section 5

Keywords (try to explain the meaning of these terms in your own words).

Application software	DOS command	Programming language
Backslash	DOS prompt	Root directory
Bootup	Format	Source disk
Change directory	Hardcopy	System disk
Default drive	Installed	Target disk
Direct access	Logon	Wildcard character

Complete each of the following items and then check your responses either with your tutor or with the answers on page 79.

1 Match each term in the first column with its meaning from the second column:

a

____	*1* Communication programs	*a*	Enable the system to run a series of self-tests.
____	2 Diagnostic programs	*b*	Carry out specific business tasks.
____	3 Application programs	*c*	Transfer data from one computer to another.

b

____	*1* A programming language	*a*	Is specially coded instructions to the computer.
____	2 The default drive	*b*	Is the startup procedure of loading DOS.
____	3 Booting up	*c*	Is the current drive or drive presently in use.

c

____	*1* The Format command	*a*	Displays the disk directory.
____	2 The Dir command	*b*	Examines the contents of a file.
____	3 The Type command	*c*	Prepares a new disk for use.

2 Label the following statements true or false:

a ____ The source disk is the disk you are copying from.
b ____ A wildcard character is a character over which you have no control.
c ____ The root directory is represented by a backslash (\).
d ____ A programmer writes computer programs.

3 Fill in the blanks:

a After booting up, DOS looks for the ____ file and then carries out the commands in it.
b The application program is on the ____ disk.
c DOS stands for ____ ____ ____.

Answers

1 **a** *1c 2a 3b*
b *1a 2c 3b*
c *1c 2a 3b*

2 **a** T **b** F **c** T **d** T

3 **a** Autoexec.bat **b** program **c** Disk Operating System

Additional questions on Section 5

1. What do you think are the advantages of packaged software to a business? State your reasons.
2. Discuss the sort of problems that you think you would encounter if you had to operate a stand-alone personal computer at work but had no knowledge or experience of any of the system commands needed for managing disks or files.
3. Discuss the statement 'Computer jargon is used by someone who works with computers just to impress others and encourage them to think that the job is more complicated than it actually is'.

Assignment 5

a Format a new diskette.
b If you have a double disk drive system:
Put the formatted diskette in drive **B**
Then make drive **B** the default drive.
c Check the directory of your system disk in drive **A**.
If there are too many files to see them all, display the files in a wide format across the screen.
d Make a note of the number of files and number of bytes free on the disk.
e Take a printout of the directory
Press **Shift** and **Print screen** keys.

6 Application software

Broadly speaking, the paperwork in an office can be divided into five different areas:

1 order processing, stock control, invoicing, accounts receivable/payable, payroll, etc
2 financial budgeting, forecasting and analysis
3 maintaining records of customers, suppliers, personnel, etc
4 dealing with external and internal correspondence
5 filing and retrieving the information generated from the above

When we talk about application software, we are referring to programs which have been written to handle tasks such as these on the computer, ie accounting, spreadsheet, database and word processing programs. In this section, we will examine and explore programs for each of these applications in turn — what they are and what they do, what they are used for and by whom, what features they have and their uses. You are already familiar with filing and retrieving information which was dealt with in Unit 17

UNIT 19 Word processing software

Many different word processing packages have been developed to run on computers of various types and configurations. Developers are also keen to constantly upgrade their products to incorporate new and better features. This is not surprising, as word processing usually plays a substantial role in any business operation. In most offices you can expect to use one of the following popular word processing programs and the features described in this unit are common to all these programs:

WordPerfect	DisplayWrite	WordStar
MultiMate	Word	Wang

What is a word processing program (or word processor) and what does it do?

A word processing program allows you to use a computer to produce virtually anything that you can type and then reproduce it without further effort on your part. Taking advantage of the computer hardware, you can enter, store, display and print one or more copies of your document. Furthermore, the program puts at your disposal a host of features which can be used to quickly and easily control the contents and look of each printed page.

Who uses a word processing program and what are its applications?

A need for word processing can be found in practically any office in both the public and private sectors, from large organisations to people working on their own, such as writers or consultants. Word processing is generally used by word processor operators (whose main job is word processing) and by secretaries and typists who combine it with other office tasks.

It is used by word processor operators (*a*) for repetitive typing tasks, such as mail shots, standard letters, standard paragraphs and anything that needs regular updating, eg mailing lists, price lists and directories; and (*b*) for servicing the general correspondence needs of several departments.

It is used by secretaries and typists as (*a*) above, but to a lesser degree, and also for reports, specifications, contracts, minutes, etc and general correspondence.

It is sometimes used by business executives and others for memos, notes, general correspondence and drafting reports and any complicated document.

What features do word processing programs have and what are their uses?

After the word processing program has been loaded in the computer's memory, all the program's features will be available for you to use as you wish. You should follow the prompts on the screen to open a file or create a new document — each program has its own procedures. When the status line shows a blank page 1 on the screen, you may start keying in your letter, memo, etc immediately. The words will appear simultaneously on the screen.

Creating a document

When text is being entered, the cursor, when it reaches the right margin will automatically return to the left margin of the next line, taking with it the word which does not fit on the typed line above. This feature is known as **word wraparound**. The clear space between words (required space) indicates to the system the start of each new word. The operator does not have to press the **Enter** or **Return** key unless a blank line is required, such as between paragraphs or at the end of a short line.

Editing features

Editing features cover all correcting and rearranging of text. Each system has a set procedure for the operator to follow when any of these functions is being carried out.

1 The text to be edited has to be identified to the system. This is generally done by placing the cursor on the first letter to be corrected or rearranged.
2 The appropriate edit function key is then touched; for example, if the text is to be deleted the DELETE key is touched.
3 The system must be told whether it is a character, word, sentence, paragraph, etc that is affected. Some systems have keys labelled for this purpose. On other systems, touching the spacebar will indicate a word, while touching the full stop will indicate a sentence and touching the RETURN key will indicate a paragraph.
4 The majority of systems acknowledge the instruction by highlighting either the text indicated or the screen behind the text. This gives the operator the opportunity to check that the correct portion of text has been identified.
5 The final step in the sequence is to give the system the go ahead to carry out the transaction by touching the **Enter** or some other specified key.

Errors made during the keying in stage can be corrected simply by overtyping or a combination of overtyping, deleting or inserting. The purpose of **delete** is to remove the text specified (eg character, word, sentence, etc) and automatically readjust the rest of the text so that there is no gap to show where the text was removed. The purpose of **insert** is to add any amount of new text within an existing document. New text is simply keyed in where it is required and the existing text from that point on moves along as the new text is entered. The automatic readjustment of text to accommodate inserted or deleted characters is an extension of the **word wraparound** feature mentioned earlier.

Move and copy

The purpose of **move** is to highlight specified and consecutive text in one part of a document and move it to another part of that document (*see* Fig 6.1). Some programs allow columns of text or figures to be moved and positioned vertically somewhere else in the document. This feature is very useful if, for example, the order of two columns needs to be reversed. The purpose of **copy** is to highlight and copy a portion of text in one part of a document to another position in that document. This means that the text indicated (highlighted) will appear both in the original position *and* in the new position. A useful feature if, for example, the same paragraph of text has to be repeated in, say, a contract or report (*see* Fig 6.1).

Locate features

All features which enable you to **retrieve a file** or a document, or **locate**

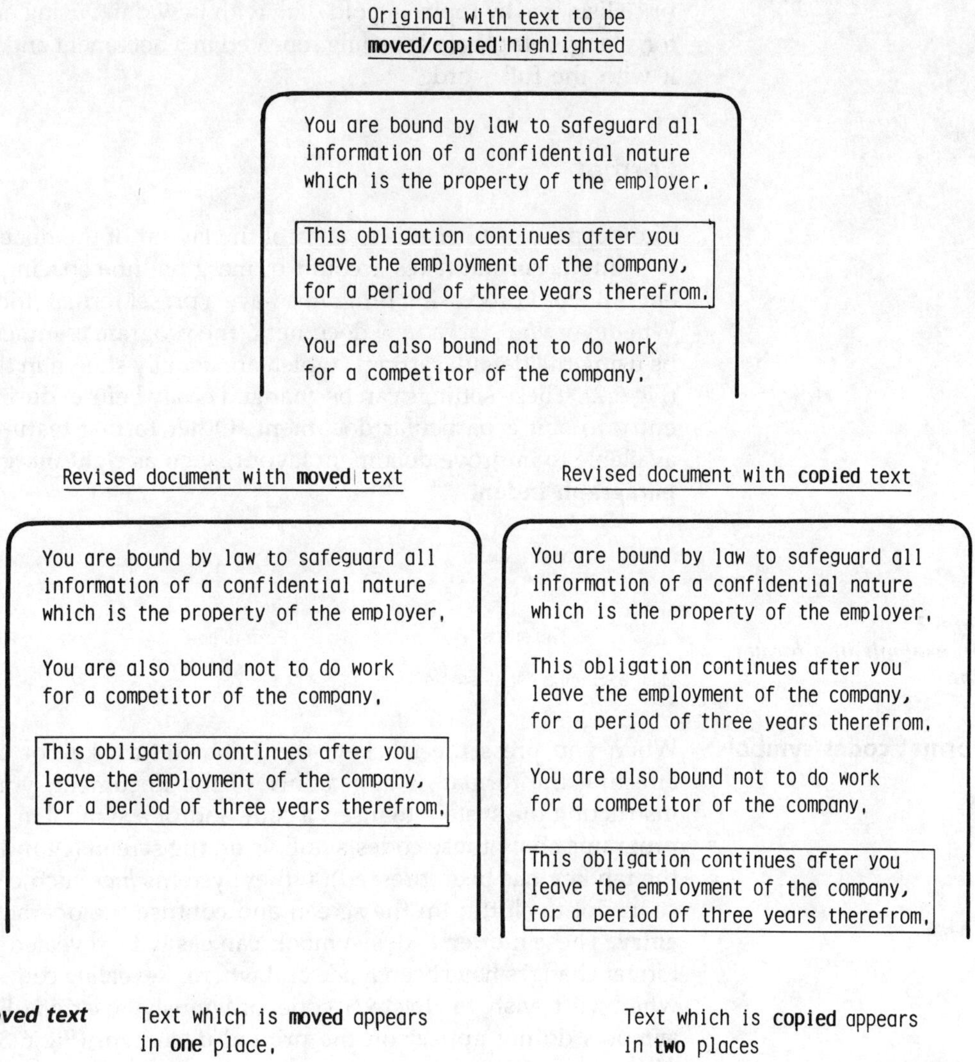

Fig 6.1 Examples of moved text and copied text

a page of a document, or **find a word**, **character** or **string of characters** within a document are locate features.

Search and replace

The purpose of **search** is to find and stop at a specified string of characters in a document. This feature can be combined with an instruction, if you wish, to **replace** these characters with other characters/words. The system can also be commanded to work its way right through the document and automatically make all the changes required. This is called **global search and replace**. This feature has many useful applications, eg replacing a wrongly spelt word(s) with the correct version; substituting a more appropriate word or phrase for an inappropriate one; updating notices, price lists, etc by replacing old data with new data; using an abbreviation for a long, complicated spelling repeated in a document and later replacing it with the full word.

Format

The purpose of **format** is to control the layout of the document when it is printed. **Format** takes account of margins, line spacing, tab settings, etc. All word processing programs have a preset format (format **defaults**). Whenever you start a new document, the program assumes that you will be using the default settings, which are usually shown in the **format line** (Fig 6.2). These settings can be changed easily before, during or after text entry to suit a particular document. Other format features are readily available to improve document layout, such as **right margin justify** and **paragraph indent**.

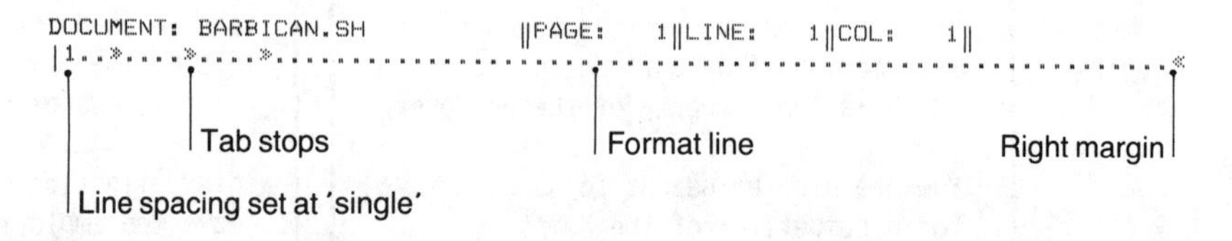

Fig 6.2 An example of a format line

Format codes/symbols

When you press the tab key, the **Enter/Return** key or any other key affecting the format or appearance of the document, you are actually instructing the system to insert a code and/or a symbol in the text. Some programs show these codes/symbols on the screen (eg indicating where the tab key has been pressed). Other systems *hide* such codes/symbols, so as not to clutter up the screen and confuse the operator **during text entry**. These hidden codes/symbols can easily be revealed to show what format changes have been made and where. Revealing codes is also useful when you wish to delete a code previously inserted. Format codes/symbols do not appear on the printed document (Fig 6.3).

Centre and justify

The purpose of the **centre** feature is to centre text automatically on a line, while the purpose of the **justify** feature is to provide an even right margin. This means that each line of type ends at exactly the same character position.

Decimal tab and indent

The purpose of the **decimal tab** feature is automatically to align columns of figures on the decimal points. This feature can also be used to right justify a column of text or a column of figures without decimal points. The **indent** feature allows for two or more consecutive lines to start a set number of places in from the left margin (at a tab stop) without the operator having to use the tab key at the start of each line.

Page and repagination

The purpose of the **page** feature is to define when one page of text should end and another should start. Most programs do this automatically according to the **page length** specified when setting up the original format

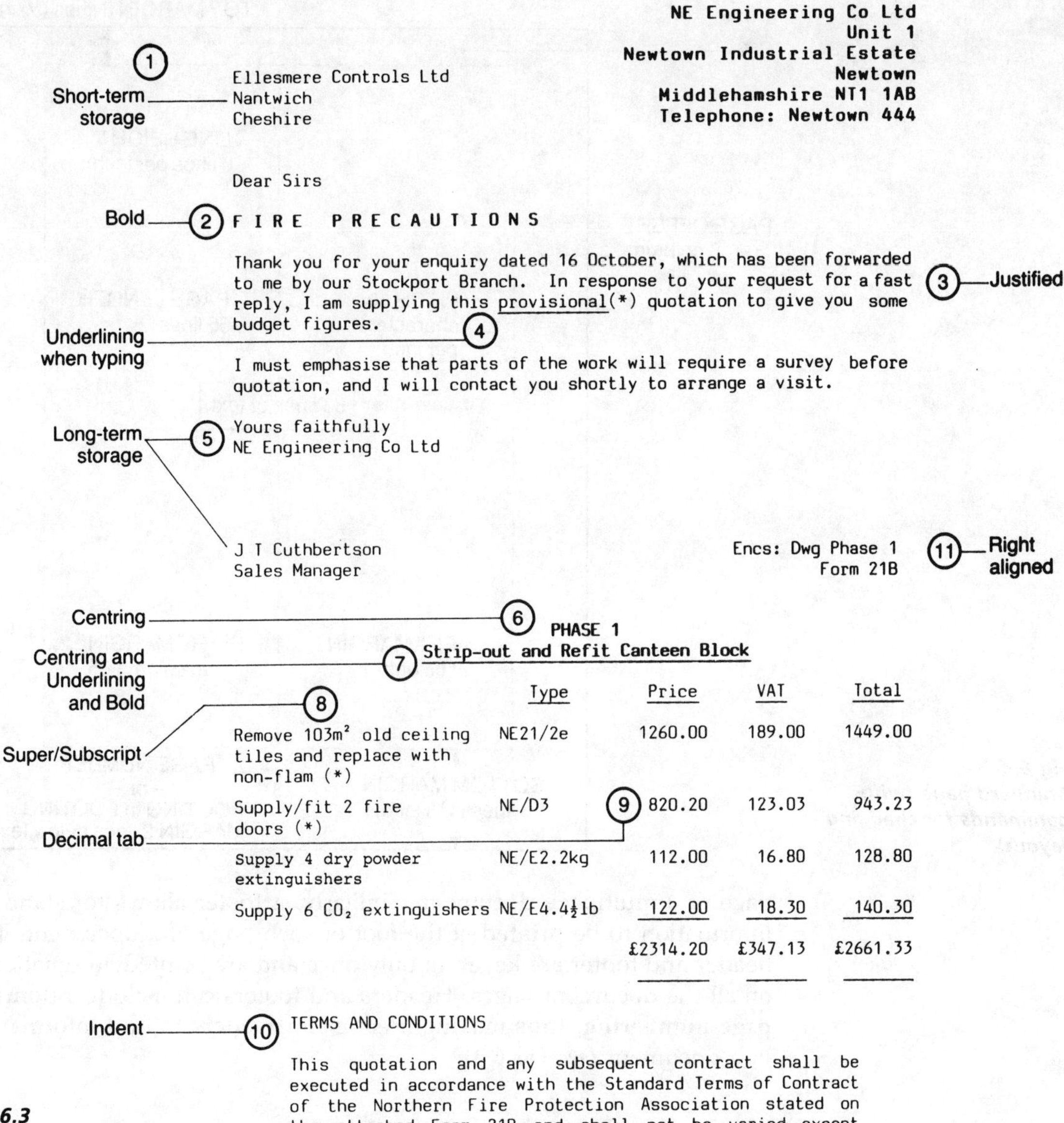

NE Engineering Co Ltd
Unit 1
Newtown Industrial Estate
Newtown
Middlehamshire NT1 1AB
Telephone: Newtown 444

Ellesmere Controls Ltd
Nantwich
Cheshire

Dear Sirs

F I R E   P R E C A U T I O N S

Thank you for your enquiry dated 16 October, which has been forwarded to me by our Stockport Branch. In response to your request for a fast reply, I am supplying this provisional(*) quotation to give you some budget figures.

I must emphasise that parts of the work will require a survey before quotation, and I will contact you shortly to arrange a visit.

Yours faithfully
NE Engineering Co Ltd

J T Cuthbertson
Sales Manager

Encs: Dwg Phase 1
Form 21B

PHASE 1
Strip-out and Refit Canteen Block

	Type	Price	VAT	Total
Remove 103m² old ceiling tiles and replace with non-flam (*)	NE21/2e	1260.00	189.00	1449.00
Supply/fit 2 fire doors (*)	NE/D3	820.20	123.03	943.23
Supply 4 dry powder extinguishers	NE/E2.2kg	112.00	16.80	128.80
Supply 6 CO_2 extinguishers	NE/E4.4½lb	122.00	18.30	140.30
		£2314.20	£347.13	£2661.33

TERMS AND CONDITIONS

This quotation and any subsequent contract shall be executed in accordance with the Standard Terms of Contract of the Northern Fire Protection Association stated on the attached Form 21B and shall not be varied except in writing by a Director.

Fig 6.3
Page design

for the document (*see* Fig 6.4). Even so, there will be many occasions when entering text that you will prefer to define your *own* page breaks as you proceed through the document. For example, you will not wish to have a page break occur in the middle of a piece of tabulation or some other type of display. The purpose of **repagination** is to allow existing page breaks to be changed. The system searches through the entire document and deletes all the old page breaks. The document can then be repaginated as required.

Headers and footers

The purpose of a **header** is mainly to identify or classify a document (eg as 'confidential'). It is a standard heading to be printed at the top of each

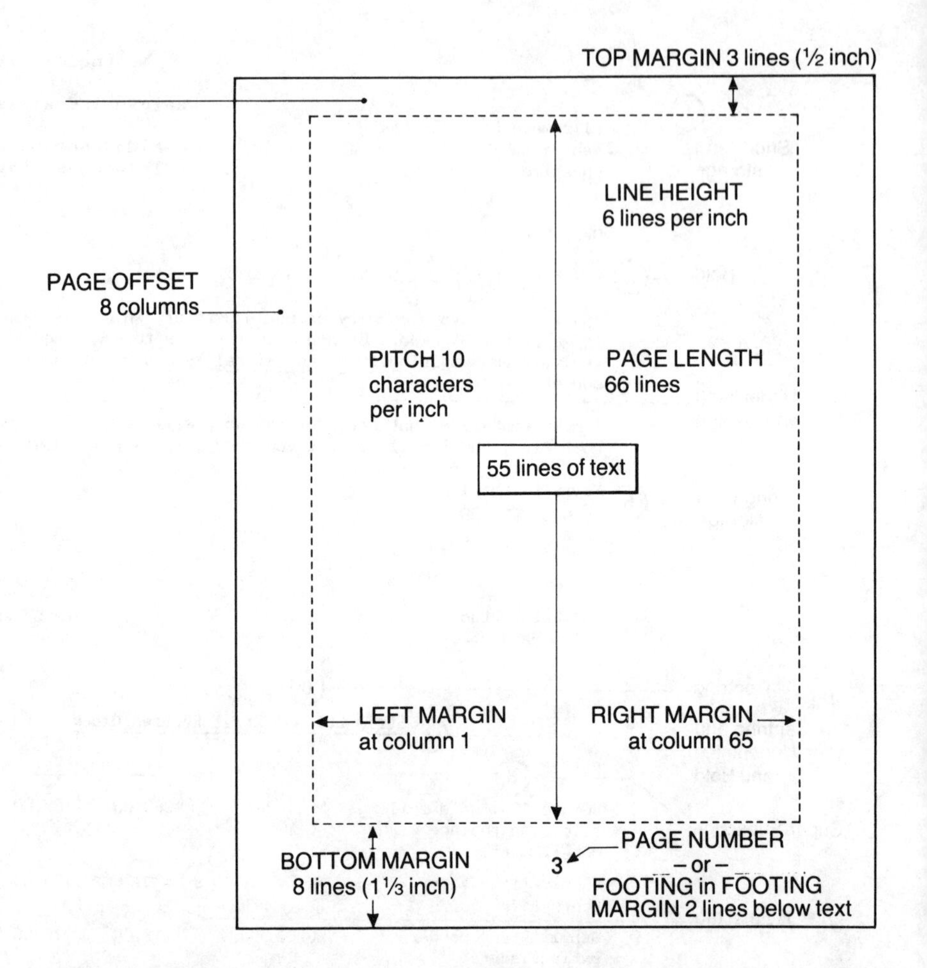

Fig 6.4 Standard page (with commands for changing layout)

page of a multipage document. Similarly, a **footer** allows for standard information to be printed at the foot of each page of a document. The header and footer are keyed in only once and are printed automatically on all the document pages. Headers and footers can include **automatic page numbering**, thus making it easier for readers to find information in a document (*see* Fig 6.4).

Saving a document

Saving your work is very important and should be done regularly throughout the work session. Some word processing programs automatically save each page when the specified page length is reached. In any event, save the file immediately you have completed work on it and before printing. Follow the instructions to **save** either through the menu and prompts on the screen or as given in the user manual. Most word processing programs require you to name the file before entering text; a few ask for the filename when you give the **save** command (filenames are dealt with in Unit 17). If you retrieve a file for editing, you may save it again after the corrections have been made; you will have the option of saving the old version as well. If you want a copy of both the old and new versions on disk, you will have to give your updated copy a new filename, otherwise the new version will replace the old.

Printing a document

Instructions for print enhancements, such as **bold face**, **underline**, **superscript/subscript** can be given while text is being keyed in. There are a number of other print enhancements, although not all of them may be available on your printer. Certain print instructions can also be issued when you are ready to print the document. These could include the page number on which printing is to start and finish, the number of original copies and page numbering. An opportunity may also be given to change the line spacing, set the left margin and select print density and typestyle. Before commanding the system to print your work, you should always ensure that the printer is properly loaded with the right type of paper and that it is **on line** (ie plugged in, switched on and ready to print).

Bold face and underline

The purpose of the **bold face** feature is to highlight certain words within the text. **This is an example of BOLD FACE print**. The **automatic underline** feature is also used to emphasise words.

Subscript/superscript

The purpose of the **subscript/superscript** feature is to enable formulas, equations and footnote reference numbers to be positioned slightly below or above the line as appropriate.

Special features

Most word processing programs offer nearly all the following special features.

Macros

A **macro** is a special command you create to *remember* a set of key strokes. You can then repeat the key strokes *automatically* with one simple command. The key strokes you create and save as a **macro** can contain text, commands or a combination of both. For example, you could create a macro for the address of a client/associate to whom you write regularly, or a paragraph that is often used. A macro could be created to change the margins and line spacing for a document that has to be typed in draft form. Creating a macro is a simple procedure, no matter which word processing software you use. Usually, you will be required to press the **macro key**, name the macro, enter the key strokes for your text or the command, and press the macro key again to save the macro. When using your word processing program any text or any instructions that you can enter at the keyboard can be saved as a **macro** to be entered automatically by the system each time you run the macro.

Foreground and background

This feature allows the operator to edit on the screen (**foreground**) while printing another document on the printer (in **background**).

Maths feature

The purpose of the **maths feature** is to enable the operator to perform calculations on the system while word processing and insert the result in the text. Generally, figures appearing anywhere on the work area of the screen can be calculated (using the standard operators: +, −, ×, ÷ and %).

Spelling checker

A **spelling checker** is an 'add-on' to the word processing program with which it interacts. The purpose of the spelling checker is to locate any misspelled word and give you the option of replacing it, adding the word to the spelling checker dictionary or to a supplementary dictionary, or ignoring it. For example, the checker might mark the addressee's name in a letter as a misspelled word because the spelling does not exist in its dictionary, in which case you would ignore it. For each misspelled word, the program gives you a list of possible correct spellings from which to choose. A supplementary dictionary is useful for creating lists of words that are difficult to spell and which are frequently used in your business. One of the main advantages of spelling checkers is the speed and thoroughness with which they handle **proofreading**. However carefully an operator reads a document, it is very easy for the human eye to overlook an error on the screen. If the operator is in a hurry and proofreading is carried out manually, several mistakes might slip through. One thing a spelling checker does not do and that is identify an incorrectly used word within the text. So long as the word has been correctly spelt, the checker will pass over it, eg if the word 'affect' were used instead of 'effect'.

Graphics

The purpose of **graphics** in word processing is mainly to construct forms, diagrams and charts, such as order or personnel forms, block or flow diagrams, organisational or bar charts. Using horizontal and vertical lines, such graphics can be easily constructed on the screen. The graphic elements can be changed or moved around just like blocks of text. Forms can be programmed with codes for the completion of standard information. As each item is filled out on the form later, the system 'tabs' on to the next one. All graphic structures can be saved to disk for future use and can of course be easily updated. Text sections can be added at any time (Fig 6.5). (*See also* Unit 26, *Developments to aid information presentation*.)

Multiple text columns

There are two types: **parallel** or **related** columns and **newspaper-style** columns. (The latter is dealt with in the next Section, Unit 26, *Developments to aid information presentation*).

Parallel or **related columns** run parallel across the page, with each column, from left to right, containing related information. The columns

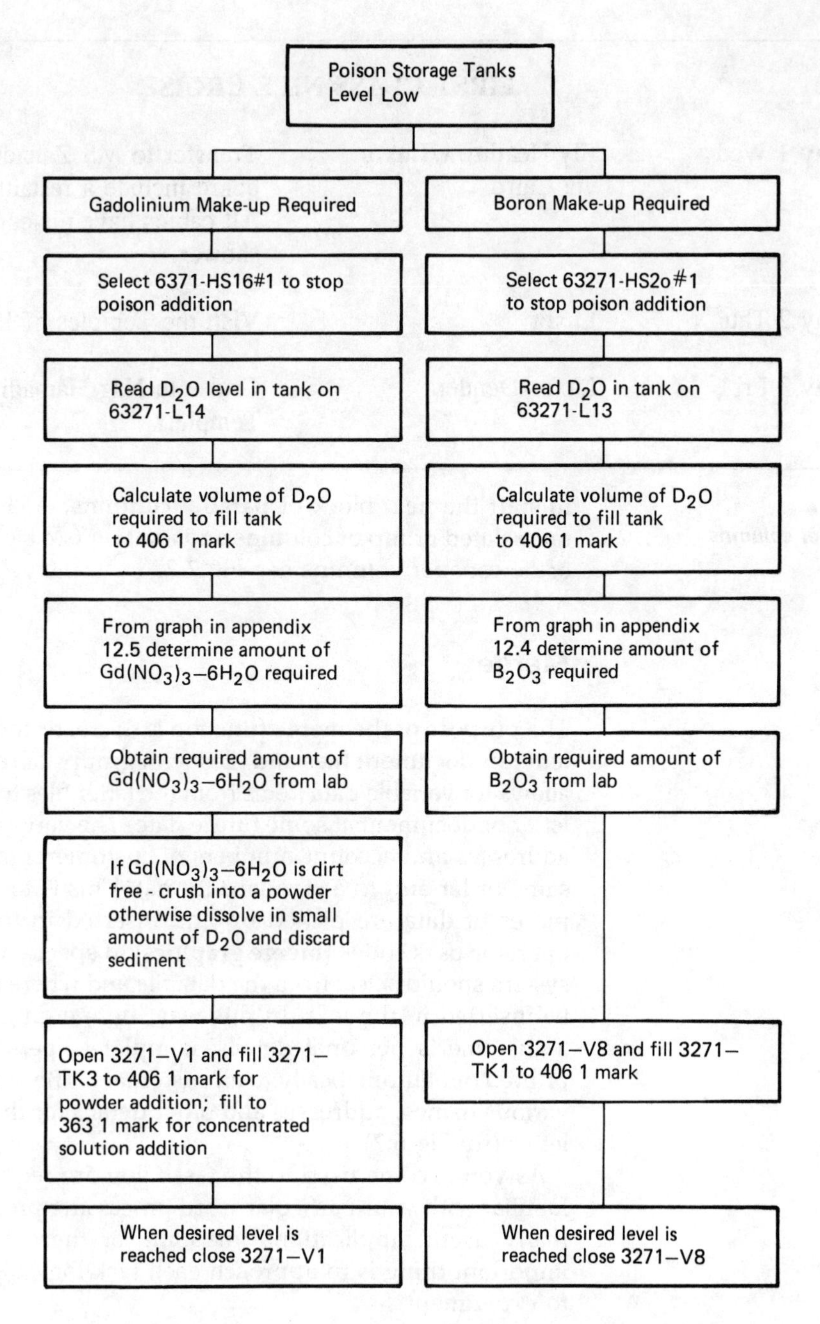

Fig 6.5
Example of a flow chart

line up horizontally on the first line of text in each column but columns do not have to be the same length. Therefore, this type of column is ideally suited to applications such as *itineraries, minutes,* etc. Columns must be defined before you start typing, which means that you have to tell the system how many columns you need and how wide each column should be. During text entry, the cursor wraps around at the column width. After keying in the text in one column, a code is entered to move the cursor to the first line of the next column. When the last column has been entered, the same code positions the cursor at the left margin once again

FIRST-CLASS NILE CRUISE		
Day 1 Wed	Fly Heathrow/Luxor via Cairo	Transfer to MS Zanadu. Facilities on board include a restaurant, bar, shops. All cabins have air conditioning and shower.
Day 2 Thu	Luxor	Visit the Temples of Karnak and Luxor.
Day 3 Fri	Luxor/Dendera	Cruise to Nag Hamadi and visit Abydos Temple.

Fig 6.6
Parallel columns

to start the next block of **parallel columns**. A clear line is left between one related group of columns and another (*see* Fig 6.6). For an illustration of newspaper columns see Fig 7.2.

Merge

The purpose of the **merge** function is to create and save on disk standard letter or document files and files with groups of relevant data items. This allows for variable data items from the latter files to be added to a standard letter or document at some future date. The various data items (eg names, addresses and account numbers of customers) must be recorded in the same order and to a standard format. This is to ensure that the correct pieces of data are picked up and inserted in the standard letter. The operator uses codes (**merge graphics**) to specify which items of data the system should select from the data file and where these data items should be inserted in the text. In this way, by merging a standard letter with a customer's personal details, completely personalised letters can be printed out automatically to all customers. The system will substitute the various names, addresses and other details for the codes in the standard letter (*see* Fig 6.7).

As you become used to the tasks you are required to do at work and familiar with your particular word processing program, you will discover many useful applications for some of these features/functions. The important thing is to approach each task logically and yet not be afraid to experiment.

Example of a customer record file with various data items

(1) Mr Peter Aims	12 Rose Gardens	Eltham	London SE9	(5) Mr Aims	(6) 23451
(1) Mr David Alders	29 High Street	Eltham	London SE9	(5) Mr Alders	(6) 23249
(1) Mrs Una Evans	6 Yule Crescent	Blackheath	London SE3	(5) Mrs Evans	(6) 23455
(1) Mr John Jones	35 Castle Road	Catford	London SE6	(5) Mr Jones	(6) 23344
(1) Ms Myra Loft	125 The Heights	Beckenham	Kent	(5) Ms Loft	(6) 23454
(1) Mr Don Meeds	3 Pratt Street	Eltham	London SE9	(5) Mr Meeds	(6) 23250
(1) Miss Ida Vidler	48 Oak Avenue	Bromley	Kent	(5) Miss Vidler	(6) 23349

Fig 6.7
Example of a standard letter with merge graphics

↕1

Dear ↕5

I am writing to you personally as I feel that
there must be a very good reason why your
account, number ↕6, remains unpaid.

Up until 3 months ago your cheque was always
received by us within a few days of our statement being sent to you.

I would be happy, ↕5, to discuss the matter
with you as my company values your custom.

Yours sincerely

G Finch
General Manager

Example of a personalized letter using the standard letter and variable data

Mrs Una Evans
6 Yule Crescent
Blackheath
London SE3

Dear Mrs Evans

I am writing to you personally as I feel that
there must be a very good reason why your
account, number 23455, remains unpaid.

Up until 3 months ago your cheque was always
received by us within a few days of our statement being sent to you.

I would be happy, Mrs Evans, to discuss the matter
with you as my company values your custom.

Yours sincerely

G Finch
General Manager

UNIT 20 Spreadsheet software

Along with word processors, spreadsheets are the most widely used software. They have become an important calculating and financial planning tool for people in business who have to produce figures and for managers who have to make decisions based on those figures. The secret of the electronic spreadsheet's success is that you do not have to be a computer expert, financial wizard or mathematician to use one.

What is a spreadsheet program and what does it do?

If you wanted to work out how much you would be able to save over the next six months, you would probably rule up a sheet of paper as a worksheet with columns and rows. You would then fill in the appropriate titles (headings) and figures for income and expenses for each week or month in the period and calculate your savings. The major drawback of this is the time it takes to recalculate and alter your worksheet if you change just one item of information. A spreadsheet is an electronic version of your worksheet which overcomes this disadvantage. A **spreadsheet program** puts at your disposal, for use on a computer, a worksheet of virtually whatever size you need, to be displayed on the screen. This worksheet has columns going down, which are identified by letters, eg A, B, C, D, and rows going across, which are identified by numbers, eg 1, 2, 3, 4. The spreadsheet, therefore, consists of **cells** (like little boxes), with each cell having a column/row **cell address** (*see* Fig 6.8). For example, take column B, row 8. The address of this particular cell is **B8**. A single piece of information can be placed in each cell: this could be a number, a formula or a **label** (title).

Basically, a spreadsheet program will calculate your data entries, allow you to change the contents of a cell as often as you like, and each time immediately recalculate the entire spreadsheet for you. This feature enables you to ask '**What if?**' questions. For example, 'What if I spend

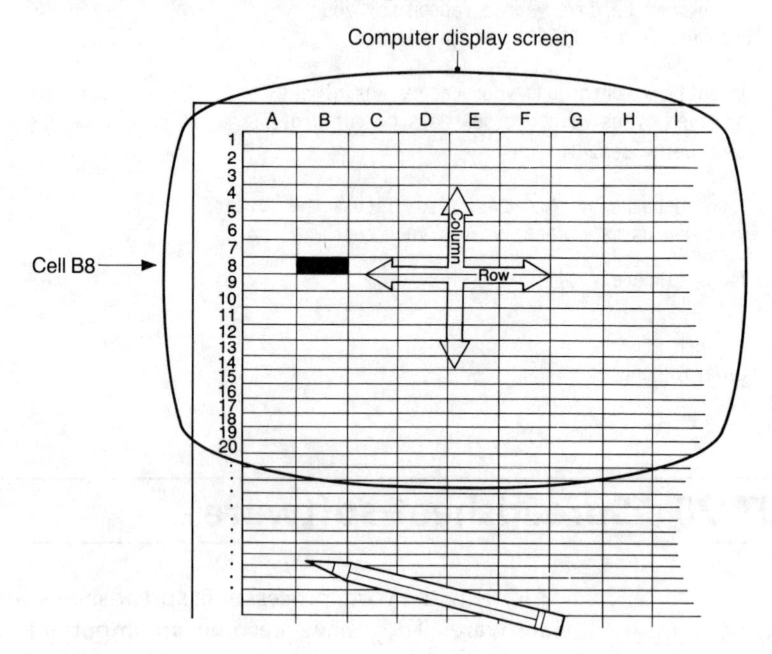

Fig 6.8
Screen worksheet

10 per cent more on advertising? What effect will this have on sales?' When you enter the new figure or formula, the spreadsheet will immediately show you the effect.

Who uses a spreadsheet program and what are its applications?

A spreadsheet is a multipurpose tool, capable of handling a wide variety of jobs, even technical and scientific applications. In business, the majority of people, from directors to clerks, have to work with figures some of the time and a spreadsheet can be tailored to various uses.

It is used by managers and accountants for financial planning, 'what if?' forecasting, business analysis, such as profitability, pricing and cash flow analysis, budget planning and sales figures.

It is used by clerks, office administrators/secretaries for general ledger, stock control, payroll, time sheets, petty cash, expense accounts and other statistical applications depending on the company's business.

What features do spreadsheet programs have and what are their uses?

A spreadsheet program allows you to tailor the worksheet for the use you have for it. It is a good idea first to design the worksheet on paper or in your head and then construct it on the computer. When the program has been loaded into the computer's memory, you should follow the prompts until the screen shows a worksheet ready for you to make your entries with the **cursor** or **cell pointer** positioned on cell **A1** (*see* Fig 6.9). All the spreadsheet's features will now be available to you.

Creating a spreadsheet

The position of the **cell pointer** indicates where the entry you make (label,

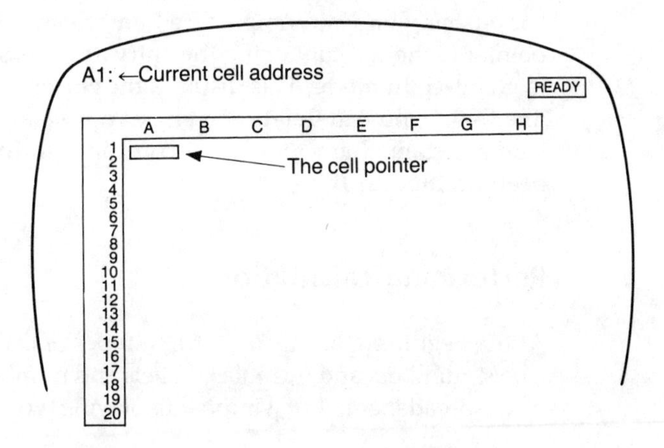

Fig 6.9
The current cell and cell pointer

number or formula) will be placed. For example, if you were to enter the word TOTAL with the pointer on cell A1, immediately you pressed the **Enter** key, TOTAL would appear in cell A1. Therefore, when making entries into a spreadsheet, the sequence is always

1 position the pointer on the cell in which you wish the entry to be placed;
2 key in the label, number or formula;
3 press **Enter** or **Return**.

The purpose of the **navigation keys** on the right of the keyboard (explained in Unit 12, *How the operator communicates with the system*) is to move the pointer around the worksheet.

Labels and numbers

The purpose of a **label** is to act as a title or heading for each column or row of numbers you enter. Spreadsheet programs treat labels and numbers differently. As a title, a label can be more than one word and can span across several cells. Numbers, on the other hand, are confined to individual cells. Some spreadsheets require you to identify every label entry with a prefix, eg single or double quotes (' or ") before you begin to key it in. Others only require you to use a prefix if the label you are entering starts with a number but should be treated as text (such as a date). If the first character you enter is a number, spreadsheet programs assume that you are entering a value. Therefore, when entering a number in a spreadsheet cell, it is important to determine whether you want the number to be treated as a value to be calculated or text, which is not calculated.

Editing features

When you key in an entry, it remains in the **status line** (sometimes called the **command line** or **control panel**) until the ↵ is pressed. Errors which occur while the entry is still in the status line can be easily corrected by backspacing and retyping. A cell entry can be replaced by moving the pointer to the cell containing the entry and pressing the appropriate key(s) to go into **Edit mode**. This displays the current cell's contents in the status line. Now you can **delete** the entry completely and retype it or you can delete certain characters only. You can also **insert** characters that have been omitted.

Performing calculations

At the beginning of this unit, three types of cell entries were mentioned: labels, numbers and formulas. Labels and numbers are the building blocks of a spreadsheet, but simply displaying your labels and numbers in columns and rows is of little use. The power of the spreadsheet lies in the third type of entry — **formulas**.

Formulas

The purpose of **formulas** is to instruct the program to perform calculations automatically. Formulas also allow you to establish relationships among cells. Cell addresses play an important role in formulas. Generally you enter cell addresses in a formula, rather than actual numbers. The spreadsheet program automatically uses the numbers stored at these addresses whenever it calculates the formula. Then if you change the number in any of the cells referred to in the formula, the program automatically re-calculates all the entries in the worksheet affected by the change (*see* Fig 6.10).

D13: (C2) [W12] +D6+D7+D8+D9+D10 READY

	A	B	C	D	E	F
1						
2						
3						
4			1992	1993	Change £	Change %
5		------------	------------	------------	------------	------------
6		Rent	£4,800.00	£4,800.00	£0.00	0.00%
7		Heat	£675.72	£634.00	(£41.72)	-6.58%
8		Entertainment	£1,874.62	£1,782.90	(£91.72)	
9		Electricity	£145.50	£163.39	£17.89	10.95%
10		Phone	£710.15	£756.23	£46.08	6.09%
11						
12		------------	------------	------------	------------	------------
13		Total	£8,205.99	£8,136.52	(£69.47)	-0.85%
14						
15						
16						
17						

Fig 6.10
Formula in cell D13

Functions

most spreadsheet programs offer several built-in **functions**. The purpose of a **function** is to shorten and simplify the writing of a formula. For example, the formula in Fig 6.10 would be easier to enter and need not be edited if additional rows were added to it. Figure 6.11 illustrates how one spreadsheet program's **Sum** function works.

Cell ranges

When you execute commands such as **copy**, **move** and **erase** or enter formulas, you often need to refer to a group of cells. The purpose of using a **cell range** (as in the formula entered in Fig 6.12) eliminates the need to enter each cell address individually.

D13: (C2) [W12] @SUM(D6..D10) READY

	A	B	C	D	E	F
1						
2						
3						
4			1992	1993	Change £	Change %
5		----------	----------	----------	----------	----------
6		Rent	£4,800.00	£4,800.00	£0.00	0.00%
7		Heat	£675.72	£634.00	(£41.72)	-6.58%
8		Entertainment	£1,874.62	£1,782.90	(£91.72)	
9		Electricity	£145.50	£163.39	£17.89	10.95%
10		Phone	£710.15	£756.23	£46.08	6.09%
11						
12		----------	----------	----------	----------	----------
13		Total	£8,205.99	£8,136.52	(£69.47)	-0.85%
14						
15						
16					Avg Cost Increase	
						0.026155
17						

Fig 6.11
Use of the sum function to express the formula in cell D13

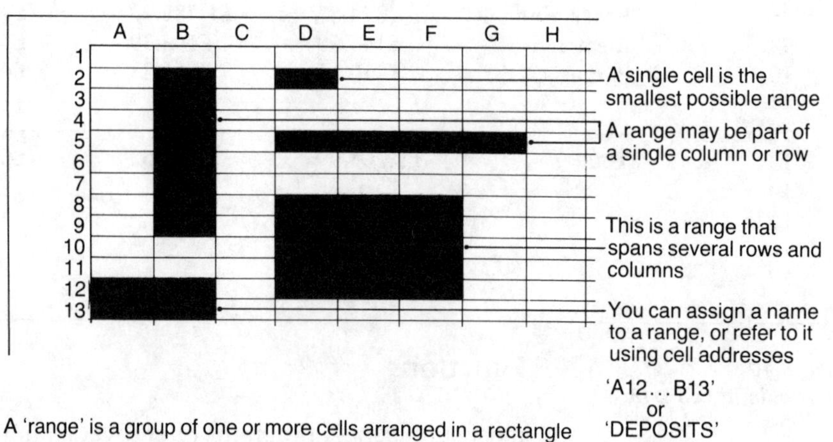

Fig 6.12
Cell range

Copy, move and erase commands

Each spreadsheet program has several commands. We refer to three useful and common commands here. The purpose of the **copy** command is to reduce the amount of work and time required to construct a worksheet. With the **copy** command you can quickly copy a range of cells to another location on the spreadsheet (Fig 6.12). The command works with formulas as well. The **erase** command is used to erase the contents of cells, either one at a time or a range of cells. Similarly, the **move** command will move one cell or a range of cells as specified.

Formatting a spreadsheet

The display of a worksheet affects how easy it is to read and to use. Although each program provides initial entry format settings, there are several commands which allow the user to alter these settings.

Number format

Number entries can be displayed in various ways, eg as general (25), as currency (£25.00), as per cent (25%) or as a date (25-04-87). Formatting only affects the display of the cell, not the actual contents.

Label prefixes

While labels are automatically aligned to the left of a cell (and numbers to the right), a one-character **label prefix** can centre a label or right align it.

Column widths

The purpose of this command is to alter the **column width** to accommodate the cell entry. Columns can all be the same width or each column width can be set individually. Column width is an important factor in the cell's appearance on the screen.

Inserting and deleting rows and columns

The purpose of the **insert** command is to allow rows and columns to be added as future additions to the worksheet are required. Similarly, the **delete** command allows for columns and rows to be deleted from the worksheet if no longer required. Spreadsheets automatically make corrections in any formulas that are affected.

Saving a spreadsheet

The purpose of **saving** your work on disk is that you will be able to retrieve it later for re-use. It is advisable to save each page and essential to save each worksheet before starting another or switching off the system. If you do not, **all** information in the worksheet will be lost. Give the worksheet a meaningful file name and use the same one to retrieve it later. When you save the worksheet a second time, you will be given the opportunity to replace the old version with the new by using the same file name. Should you wish to save *both* versions of the worksheet, you will be required to provide a new file name for the amended one. This file name should show the connection between the two worksheets.

Printing a spreadsheet

Printing provides a **hardcopy** of your work, ie a printed copy. Ensure that the printer is loaded with appropriate paper and is **on line** (plugged in, connected, switched on and in a 'ready' state). Your spreadsheet program should be loaded. As each program has its own print procedures, you should follow these from the user manual or the screen prompts. Some programs allow you to do additional formatting after issuing the **print** command.

Wide spreadsheets

Large spreadsheets are often wider than 80 characters. Spreadsheet programs print such worksheets in two or more strips if the printer is not able to accommodate the extra width (*see* Fig 6.13). This is not always convenient for the reader. Alternatives are to compress the type (if your printer has this facility) so that you can squeeze 132 characters on one line. There are also programs available which allow spreadsheets to be printed **sideways**. Any width can then be accommodated.

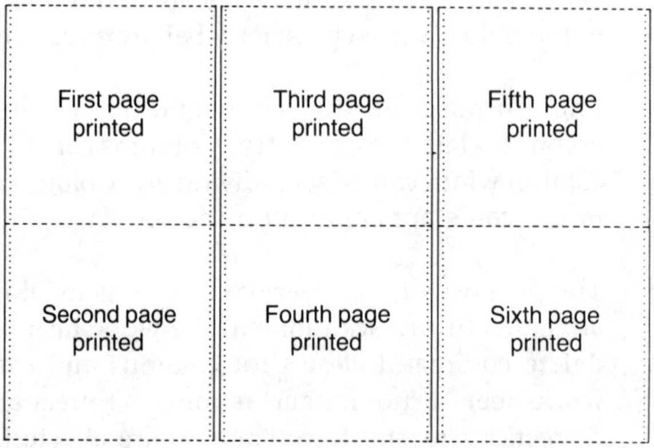

First page printed
Third page printed
Fifth page printed
Second page printed
Fourth page printed
Sixth page printed

Fig 6.13
Printing a report in strips

UNIT 21 Database software

Every business needs to have relevant information readily available. Therefore, one of the most popular uses for microcomputers in business is to store needed information in a **database**. This could be anything from a simple list of customers to multiple files which can be cross-referenced.

What is a database program and what does it do?

A **database** is an organised collection of information or data. Your address book, for example, is a database holding the names and addresses of people you know, probably organised in alphabetical order. A computer database is like a card index system, with each card holding the name and details of a particular customer. To examine a customer's record in a card index system you would go through the cards, searching through the names until you found the one needed. Using a computer and a database program, you could look up customers not only by name, but by account number, location, etc. This is not the only advantage that a computerised database has over a manual system. Information can be retrieved very much faster, according to the criteria you establish, and the retrieved information can be presented in an orderly fashion. One of the greatest benefits is the ease with which a computer database can be updated.

Who uses a database program and what are its applications?

Everyone in business deals with information of some kind and in some way. Organising and storing information in such a way that what is needed can be accessed when it is needed and in the form that it is needed is essential to carrying out a job efficiently. Databases are used by top management through to filing clerks.

They are used by managers and executives to store, access, examine and manipulate information on which day-to-day business decisions can be based, eg customer/client and stock records, personnel and sales staff records, reports, etc.

They are used by accountants/ledger clerks to maintain customer and supplier files, order and stock files, and generate invoices, statements and account summaries; to maintain staff records, payroll, etc.

They are used by secretaries to maintain mailing lists, parts lists, price lists, expenses, etc.

What features do database programs have and what are their uses?

Database programs vary widely in the features they offer. Some of the simpler ones are known as **flat-file** databases. These store, organise and output data sequentially and may suit the needs of a small business or an occasional user. A popular type of database program is the **relational** database, which is able to 'relate' (link) two or more files together through at least one common field (*see* Fig 6.14). The third type of database has programming facilities, which can be used to tailor a database to a company's particular needs. Whichever database program you use, once the program has been loaded in the computer's memory, all its features and functions will be at your disposal. You select and use what you need for the job you have in hand.

Creating a database

Information which is stored on index cards and alphabetical lists, etc is known as **structured information**, ie the information is organised in a certain way. Examples would be mailing lists, stock cards, personnel records. When such information is entered into a computer, the computer requires it to be organised in **file format**. (Text, on the other hand, is unstructured and therefore, when word processing, can simply be keyed in.) A **file** is a group of similar **records** kept together. In a personnel file,

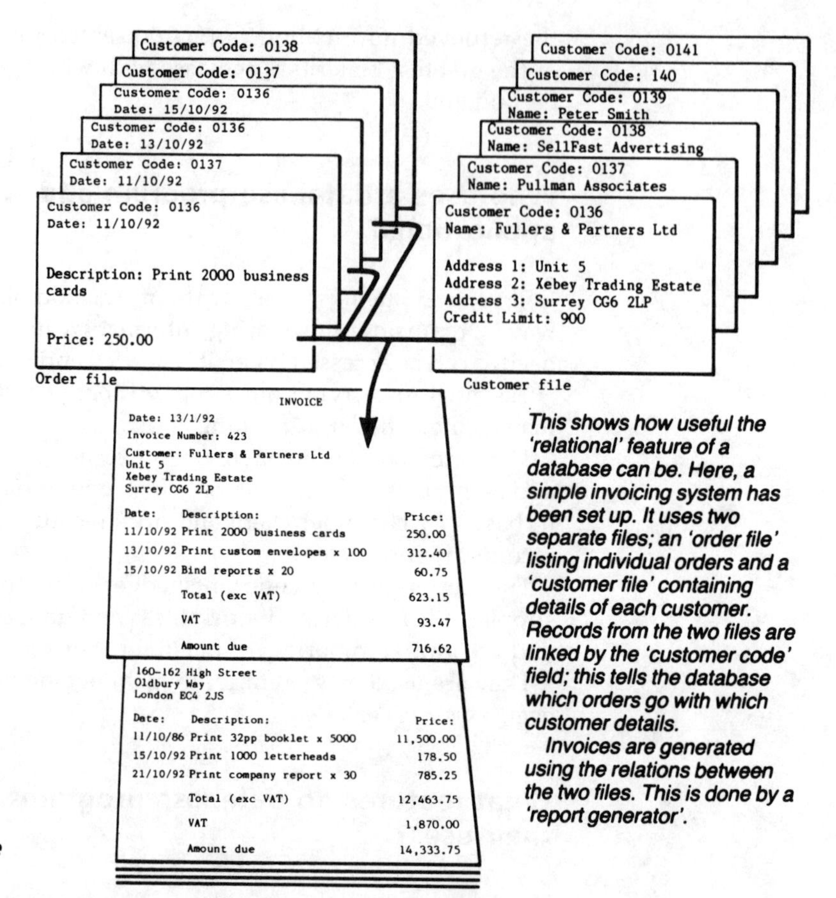

This shows how useful the 'relational' feature of a database can be. Here, a simple invoicing system has been set up. It uses two separate files; an 'order file' listing individual orders and a 'customer file' containing details of each customer. Records from the two files are linked by the 'customer code' field; this tells the database which orders go with which customer details.

Invoices are generated using the relations between the two files. This is done by a 'report generator'.

Fig 6.14
How a relational database works

```
. display structure
Structure for database      :   B:NAMES.dbf
Number of data records      :   10
Date of last update         :   01/03/92
Field  Field name      Type        Width
   1   LASTNAME        Character      10
   2   FIRSTNATE       Character      10
   3   ADDRESS         Character      20
   4   CITY            Character      14
   5   STATE           Character       2
   6   ZIP             Character       5
** Total **                           61
```

Fig 6.15
Example of a database file structure

these would be the records of all the company's employees. Each employee record would be made up of separate items of information called **fields**, such as employee's last name, first name, works number, grade number, department, etc. When structuring a database file, you are normally required to specify the maximum width of each field (ie maximum number of character spaces). You also need to identify each field as 'character' of 'numeric' (ie made up of numbers which can be calculated). The employee works number for example, would be identified as a character field because the number is not a calculable number. Fields in a record must be organised consistently. For example, each record in the employee file must have exactly the same number of fields in exactly the same order. You cannot enter a first name in the last name field, or a works number in the grade number field. It is a good idea to plan the structure of your database before you set it up, considering the type of information you want to have in it. Figure 6.15 is an example of a database file structure.

Entering data

Data is entered in a **data-entry form**, based on the structure designed by the user (*see* Fig 6.16). Data-entry forms allow you to set up a database quickly and easily and can help to avoid certain errors. Whoever is entering the data simply fills in each blank. When the last blank has been filled in, the record is added to the end of the database file and a blank data-entry form for the next record appears on the screen. The navigation keys on the right side of the keyboard are used to move between fields and records.

```
LASTNAME     Cooke
FIRSTNAME    Jonathan
ADDRESS      568 East Westbourne
CITY         Misson Ridge
STATE        SD
ZIP
```

Fig 6.16 Example of a data-entry form

Editing features

Records can be edited during entry or later by first displaying the incorrect record on the screen.

Deleting and inserting

Typing errors can be corrected by overtyping. Unwanted characters can be deleted and those omitted can be inserted.

Viewing the database

Figure 6.17 shows how the database filed the information entered, ie in a table with rows and columns. The field names are displayed as column headings and each row is one complete record. Each database program has several commands to view a database. Records may be DISPLAYED one at a time, in a group or all records may be DISPLAYED a screenful at a time, or LISTED by scrolling. A particular record can also be displayed when required.

```
. display all
Record#  LASTNAME    FIRSTNAME   ADDRESS                CITY            STATE  ZIP
      1  Neuhoff     Luann       8653 Rita Drive        Bloomington     IN     47401
      2  Lakeland    Lionel      4902 Bluffisde Road    Muskegon        MI     49450
      3  Butler      Sarah       45 Macedonia Road      Raleigh         NC     27606
      4  assist      John        87899 Gallatin SW      Roanoke         VA     24018
      5  Randolph    Charles     894 Grigsby Road       Knoxville       TN     37922
      6  Greystoke   Arthur      8897 Plaines Lane      Cheyenne        WY     82005
      7  Lock        Joseph      5788 Certified Way     Carson City     NV     89701
      8  Campbell    Chester     2716 Etoile Way        LaFayette       KY     42254
      9  Cooke       Jonathan    568 East Westbourne    Misson Ridge    SD     57557
     10  LYMAN       WILLIAM     78 Rye Street          Topeka          KS     66699
.
```

Fig 6.17
Example of a database file

Saving a database file

The object of creating a database is to have the information it contains available for use as and when required. Therefore you must save your database on disk, preferably at regular intervals, while you are entering the information or immediately after you have made all the entries. You should not move on to processing other work or switch off the computer until you have saved your database. Saving a file only takes a moment. Each database program has its own procedures for doing so. Follow the screen prompts or the instructions in the user manual. You will be asked to provide a filename for the database. This should indicate the type of information that the database contains. See Unit 17 for more details on files and filenames.

Maintaining a database

A database is only useful if the information in it is accurate and up to date. It is essential therefore to **maintain** a database. This means making any changes that are necessary, such as deleting unwanted records, updating existing ones (eg people change their addresses) and adding new records.

Deleting a record

To **delete a record**, it is necessary first to retrieve the file which holds the record. Some systems require that the actual record is first displayed on the screen. Others allow you to give the command to delete immediately. The record number must then be included in the command.

Updating a record

Updating a record means changing the record's existing information. This is done by first displaying the record and then making the alteration by using the editing features. Some programs provide the facility to BROWSE through the file, selecting those records that need updating.

Adding a new record

The new record is entered in the data-entry form for that particular database so that the same data fields can be entered in exactly the same order as the previous records. Some database programs require the user to move first to the end of the file before entering new records, while others have an APPEND command which automatically stores the new record at the end of the file.

After updating a database, the file must be saved again or the changes will not be recorded. This would generally be done under the same filename.

Using a database

The benefit of a computerised database is that once the information has been entered, there are many ways in which you can use it, which is just not possible with a manual system. Common functions are to **sort**, **find** and **extract** information from the database. You may want to sort the entries into a particular order, find specific information or extract data in a special format. By using field names, you can tell the database program exactly which records you want to sort, find and extract.

Sort command

The purpose of this function is to **sort** the database so that you can view the records in an organised fashion. A database can be sorted on any one of its fields. For example you might want to have the database sorted alphabetically by surname. You would therefore sort on the field **last name**. You could choose to have the sort performed alphabetically in ascending order (A–Z) or descending order (Z–A). Sorting can also be carried out numerically, for example on the area code (zip code). Database

Fig 6.18
Example of sorted data

Unsorted Data:

Order Received	Customer	Product Line
03/01/92	Armstrong & Sons	Invaders
27/01/92	Van Wyk's Hobby Shop	Chess
02/02/92	Erral Software Co.	Block Buster
10/05/92	Martin & Co. SA	Star Wars
17/07/92	Armstrong & Sons	Attack
25/10/92	Erral Software Co.	Block Buster

Sorted Data:

Order Received	Customer	Product Line
17/07/92	Armstrong & Sons	Attack
03/01/92	Armstrong & Sons	Invaders
02/02/92	Erral Software Co.	Block Buster
25/10/92	Erral Software Co.	Block Buster
10/05/92	Martin & Co. SA	Star Wars
27/01/92	Van Wyk's Hobby Shop	Chess

programs generally allow you to command a sort on more than one field at the same time. In a **multiple sort** the ordering details for each column and the priorities are specified. In Fig 6.18, column 2 was sorted alphabetically: this was the **primary sort** (first order of priority). Column 3 was arranged alphabetically – this was the second order of priority. Column 1 was the third order of priority and was sorted chronologically (in date order).

Find command

The purpose of this function is to **find** and view only those records in the database that meet a certain condition (criterion). For example, records that were created after a certain date; those customers with a bill outstanding for more than 60 days; or customers located in a particular area. Therefore, before invoking the **find** command, you should consider exactly what it is you are searching for. Once this is decided you can set up the criterion (this includes the field to be searched) by which the program can locate those records that pass this test. Most database programs allow you to use more than one criterion. There are two ways in which multiple criteria are used:

1 a record can be selected only if it fits ALL the criteria, ie both criterion A AND criterion B
2 a record can be selected if it fits ANY ONE of the criteria, ie, *either* criterion A OR criterion B.

Extract command

With the **find** command you will generally only be able to display records. The purpose of **extract** is to allow you to copy to another location or take a printout of records that meet certain criteria.

Printing a database

Save your work. Check that the printer is loaded with suitable paper and plugged in, switched on, connected and 'on line'. Follow the print instructions for your database program.

UNIT 22 Graphics software

The graphics capabilities of a computer are determined by three separate items: the graphics adapter (commonly called a graphics card or graphics board) the monitor displaying the graphics and the software used to generate the graphics. Both microcomputer hardware and software are now capable of presenting high-quality graphics. As a result, the use of computer graphics in business is gaining in popularity. Graphics can communicate information much better than numbers and words, instantly highlighting comparisons, trends and patterns.

What is a graphics program and what does it do?

A graphics program allows you to use the computer to show data in different formats — such as charts and graphs on screen — and print it out on a printer or plotter. You can key in new data or use data previously stored on disk, or a combination of the two, and then select in which pictorial form you wish the data displayed on the screen. You have the flexibilty to switch to another pictorial form at any time. Text can, of course, be added to the graphic display in the form of titles or an explanation. Graphic images can be stored on disk in the same way that text and data can. (*See also* Graphics software under Unit 26, *Developments to aid information presentation*.)

Who uses a graphics program and what are its applications?

Sales and marketing executives use it to illustrate sales projections, profits, product lifecycles, comparative sales figures, market share, trends, relationships between sales figures, changes, etc.

Accountants and managers use it to illustrate 'what if?' situations, to compare periodic income and expenditure figures, departmental costs, profits and budgets.

What features do graphic programs have and what are their uses?

When the graphics program is loaded into the computer's memory, all the program's features are available for you to use as you wish. The features mentioned above are common to all graphic programs. There are a few powerful programs available which allow images to be retrieved in a group, sorted into the desired order and presented as a slide show. Other imaginative features have also been introduced, with which you can add colour and special effects to your graphs.

Creating a graph

Before you draw a graph, you will need to decide which data it is that you want to see in graph form. The data will then have to be entered on a worksheet or data sheet. Alternatively, you might want to construct a graphic image of data previously entered and saved. Make sure that your data is organised and filtered so that the graph does not include unwanted data.

Defining a graph

The purpose of this is to decide on how the data should be displayed. Most graphic programs offer a choice of at least five types of graph — **bar**, **multiple bar**, **stacked bar**, **XY**, **line** — and **pie charts** (*see* Fig 6.19). You should select the type of graph which will present the data most effectively and illustrate any important relationships. For example, a pie chart would illustrate each department's percentage share of a company's overall annual expenses. At the same time, it would allow for quick comparisons to be made of individual departmental expenses. You might, therefore, find it helpful to make a rough sketch of how you would like the graph to look before you actually create it.

1 *Bar graph*: this type of graph can be used if you are interested in comparing different quantities over time, among other things. For example, comparing the sales of four different makes of cars within the same price range over a certain period of time. Another example would be comparing the fuel consumed by the same four cars over a certain mileage (*see* Fig 6.19a).

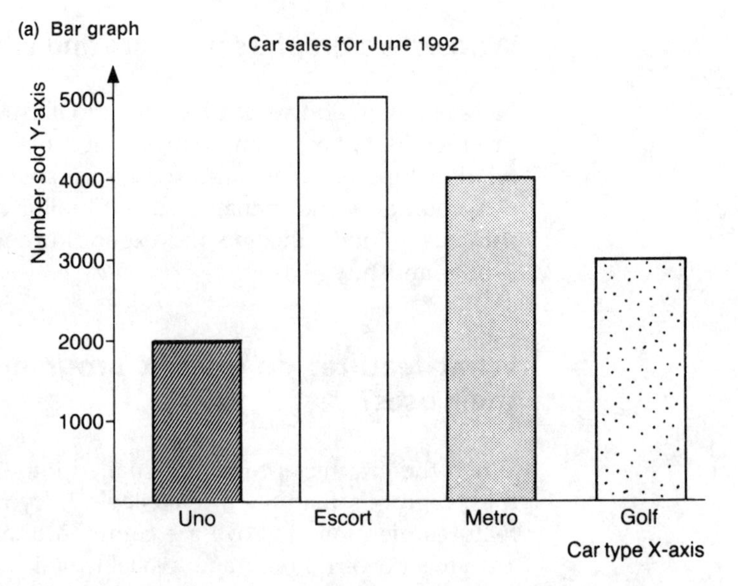

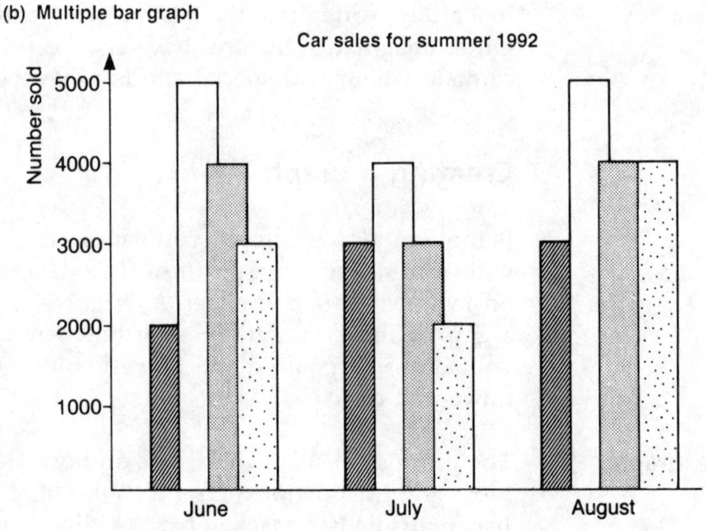

Fig 6.19 (a–d) Graphs

2 *Multiple bar graph:* bar graphs can also be used to advantage to depict additional ranges in the same graph. This will be shown as sets of bars (multiple bars) evenly spaced, instead of individual bars. For example, you could compare the monthly sales figures for the four cars over a few consecutive months (*see* Fig 6.19b).
3 *Stacked bar graph:* this is like a multiple bar graph, except that the bars in each group are arranged one on top of the other instead of side by side. This allows you to compare the total of each group of bars as well as the individual bars themselves. For example, you could compare the sales of the individual cars over the consecutive months *and* compare the total sales of the group month by month.
4 *XY graph:* an XY graph is useful for showing the relationship between two numeric values. For example, if you wanted to illustrate the miles

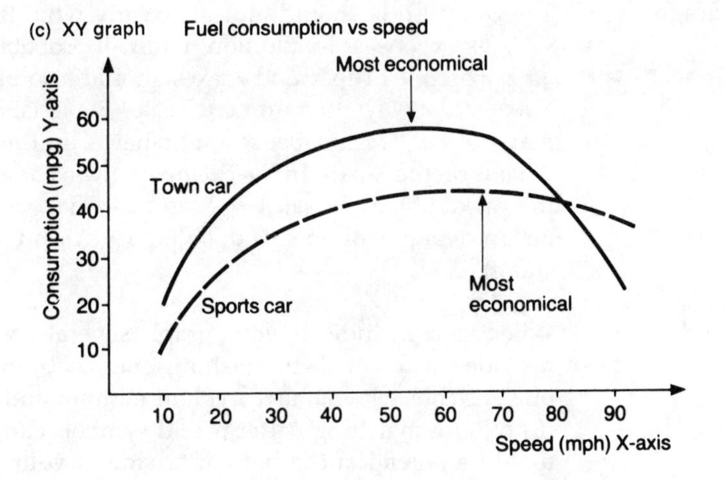

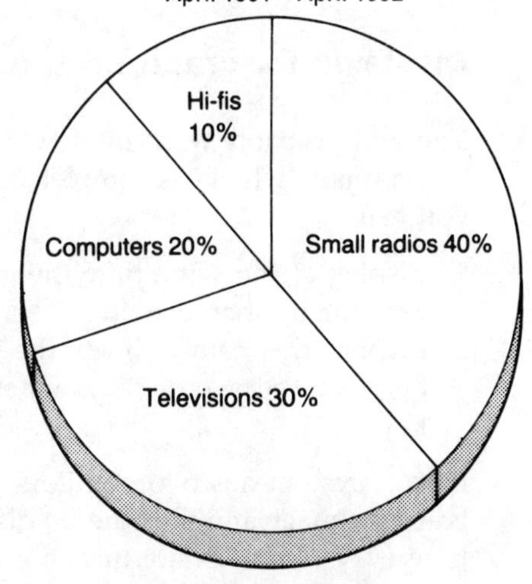

per gallon each car obtained travelling at certain speeds, ie miles per hour, this graph would indicate the speed at which to drive each car in order to obtain the best miles per gallon: one could also see instantly if and where any unexpected occurrence takes place, such as a sudden and drastic reduction in miles per gallon after reaching a speed of, say, 70 mph (*see* Fig 6.19c).

5 *Line graph*: line graphs depict how patterns in numeric values change over specific periods. For example, you could plot the profits of each department over the year and see the times of the year when the departments exceeded or did not meet the targeted profit figure.
6 *Pie chart*: this is useful for comparing fractions or percentages of a total quantity (a whole). For example, comparing the profit contribution of each department to the company's total profit (*see* Fig 6.19d).

Adding titles and labels to a graph

Titles and labels give meaning to a graph, increasing its effectiveness. The overall title should indicate clearly what the graph is showing, eg sales vs expenses. In addition, you will probably need a Y-axis title and an X-axis title. The Y and X axes should also be labelled. Labels on the Y-axis are always to a numeric scale, while labels on the X-axis may or may not be. Try to label so that what is on the Y-axis is *dependent upon* what is on the X-axis. In the examples given earlier, car sales depend upon the make of car, so sales = Y and car make = X. Similarly, miles per gallon depends upon speed, so mpg = Y and speed = X (see Fig 6.19a and c).

Adding legends

When you include in your graph several sets of data, the program provides ways of distinguishing one set from another. Colour is the obvious choice if you have a colour monitor and colour printer or plotter. If not, crosshatching patterns and symbols can be used. It is important to add a **legend** at the bottom or side of your graph to indicate which colour, crosshatching or symbol corresponds to which set of data. Each legend should show both the distinguishing mark and the explanation.

Displaying a graph on the screen

You will probably want to view your graph during the refining process and certainly when it is completed. If your system has a graphics adapter, you can

1 display at the same time the graph and the data from which it was generated (**shared mode**);
2 display the data only or the graph only, moving back and forth between the two displays whenever you wish, simply by pressing a key.

If your system has two monitors, you can use both, one to display the graphics image and the other to display the data, but not simultaneously. If your system does not have a graphics adapter, your monitor will not be able to display a graph at all.

Redrawing a graph

When your display screen is in **shared mode**, you will be able to make changes to the data and see how your graph instantly responds to the change. This gives you the opportunity to do 'what if?' graphing. For example, what if you increased the June advertising budget by 10 per cent? Changing that figure illustrates on the graph the rise in sales that you could expect as a result of more advertising in June.

If you decide that you wish the data to be depicted in a different style of graph, it can quickly be redrawn again based on the same data. Labels and legends can be changed, if you wish, by simple editing. The majority of graphics software is menu-driven, encouraging and assisting the user to create graphs by moving through a series of menus, step by step.

Saving a graph

Save your graph along with your worksheet or data sheet before changing over to another job or switching off the system. All titles, labels and legends can be saved with the graph. Provide appropriate filenames for the graph *and* datasheet.

Printing a graph

Daisywheel printers are not suitable for the printing of graphs. Printing a graph requires a plotter or a dot matrix, ink jet or laser printer. The printing process is usually much slower than printing data or text. For this reason, some programs do not print graphs directly, but store the specifications for the graph image in a **graph file**. Graph files can be printed out one by one as required or as a batch during off-peak periods when the printer is not required for data or text printing. To print graphs, make sure that the printer is loaded with appropriate paper and is on line when you issue the print command.

UNIT 23 Accounting software

Accounting, with its repetitive number crunching activities, is ideally suited to computerisation. In fact, accounting was one of the first business applications to be handled by mainframe computers but, because of the high cost of these systems, only large organisations were able to take advantage of it in those early days of computing. Now cheap, powerful microcomputers and packaged software have brought the benefits of computerised accounts within the reach of virtually all businesses. The result has been considerable interest and rapid growth in accounting software for micros. Today, users have many different account programs to choose from — a far greater choice than can be found in any other business application area.

What is an accounting program and what does it do?

Basically, an accounting program allows you to use a computer to do what a bookkeeper or an accounts clerk does manually; that is, to 'keep the books' or records of everything that a business owns, uses, buys and sells. All you have to do is enter details of sales and purchases, invoices and payments, and other relevant data. Behind the scenes, the accounting program keeps all your ledgers up to date and balanced. It also prints out invoices, statements and bad debt lists to speed up payment for goods and services provided. A major benefit of an accounting program is its ability to analyse the data stored and quickly produce comprehensive reports which keep managers informed and allow them to monitor the business operation.

Accounting programs vary widely in their capabilities. Some have limited features and are suitable only for small businesses with undemanding and routine accounting needs. The more powerful and sophisticated packages, suitable for medium to large businesses, are usually sold as accounting suites, made up of several modules. Each module deals with a specific accounting function. Figure 6.20 shows the **suite menu** of an integrated accounting package with modules for several functions. A company buys only those modules which are needed in its business. For example, a sales ledger is useful to companies with account customers, but it would not be needed by a chain of supermarkets supplying the general public on a cash basis.

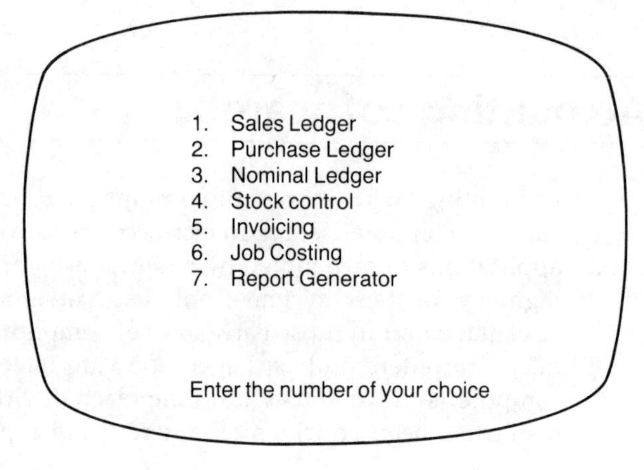

Fig 6.20
Example of an accounting suite menu

Who uses an accounting program and what are its applications?

Although order processing, stock control and ledgers are to some extent interdependent, in a business operating a manual accounting system only the ledgers will normally come under the umbrella of 'accounts'. A computerised accounting system makes it possible for office functions which are interdependent to be linked or **integrated**. The idea of having an integrated accounts package is that you only have to enter the data once. Where the same information has to be duplicated through several modules, the computer will update all of the modules automatically in an integrated accounts system. For example, order processing links with stock control, invoicing and the sales ledger. When an order is processed from stock, entries will be made automatically in the inventory (stock control), sales and nominal ledgers, and an invoice generated. Many accounting software packages, therefore, offer order processing, stock control and other interdependent functions as modules which can be integrated with general accounting modules. This means that the area of accounting is expanded to cover these other office functions. As a result, staff not normally connected with accounts also use accounting software. Fortunately, users do not need to be accountants, account clerks or bookkeepers in order to use the program, although an understanding of accounts is useful.

An accounting program is used by managers to obtain an overview of the business operations — to check on the financial status of the business, the cash flow, sales, purchases, expenses, outstanding debtors and to make budget comparisons.

It is used by accountants to set up reports and produce analysis of data, statutory accounts and returns and to run internal audits.

It is used by accounts staff for job costing, purchase tracking, audit trails, month end returns to file away completed transactions, trial balances, payroll and other specific accounting functions.

It is used by clerical staff for inputting and updating data; generating invoices, statements and payments.

It is used by accounting firms to audit clients' accounts and for tax work.

What features do accounting programs have and what are their uses?

The process of installing a computerised accounting system takes time. Staff have to be trained to use the system and all data from the company's current account books must be keyed into the computer in the format required by the accounting program. However, once the changeover has been made and the computerised system is running satisfactorily, the benefits are substantial, particularly if an integrated accounts package is in use. If you recall, information is entered once only, whereas in a manual accounting system each new entry must be duplicated in several different ledgers and record books.

Special features

Additionally, accounting programs include features for ease of use, flexibility and security, such as help screens, menus and error messages, choice of formats for invoices, reports, etc, passwords, self-checking and automatic audit trails.

If you are going to use an account program, you should know the purpose and function of each module and how it links with other modules, as well as its special features. The information given below is to provide you with this background knowledge.

Order processing

The purpose of this module is to keep track of all orders received up to the time of despatch/delivery. It links with stock control and later with invoicing and the sales ledger. The special features of this module are:

1 *Default values*, eg the current date is automatically entered on the order unless the operator inserts another date. Default values eliminate the need to enter standard information wherever possible. Each new order is also automatically numbered in sequence as it is entered.
2 *Free-format design forms* — the business can design its own forms to suit its order entry requirements. This makes it clear to clerical staff what data has to be entered and where.

Invoicing

This module produces sales invoices of products and services or stocks. Invoicing is not always a separate module: it can be part of the sales ledger or stock control modules. Depending on the business, invoicing can be either 'order entry' or 'point-of-sale'. In an order entry system, the invoice is only printed after the order has been entered, processed and the advice note produced. In a point-of-sale system, for example where goods are sold over the counter, the invoice is printed immediately. Invoicing links with the sales ledger, updating the customer's account by adding the new invoice figure, and with the stock control module by adjusting the stock records accordingly. Special features of this module are:

1 *Default values* — the current date is automatically entered on each invoice and invoices are numbered in sequence, for example. This is a useful feature when **batch processing**, ie when invoices or other documents are processed in a batch at the end of a day or other working period, rather than individually immediately the data are available.
2 *Checking of credit limit* — the customer's credit limit is displayed on the screen and the operator is warned if this is exceeded.

Sales ledger

The purpose of the sales ledger is to record the details of all sales made by the business and accordingly adjust the accounts of the individual customers to whom sales have been made. It has links with invoicing, stock control and the nominal ledger. Special features of this module are:

1 *Statements* — these are produced at the end of the month for each customer.

2 *Aged debtors list* — a list of everyone who owes money to the business and how old the debt is (reminder letters to these debtors can then be produced).
3 *Sales analysis reports* — sales can be broken down in many different ways, eg product, area, price, and these reports provide management with useful information.

Stock control

The purpose of this module is to keep an up-to-date record of all items held in stock. This record includes relevant information on each stock item, such as its description, stock number, price, supplier. The module links with order processing, the sales ledger, invoicing and the nominal ledger. The special features of this module are:

1 *Stock lists* — these can be printed out at any time, allowing a stock-take at a moment's notice.
2 *Price lists* — a price list can be generated with all product codes, descriptions, prices and quantities per pack and sent out to customers when needed.
3 *Stock level check* — the user is alerted when re-ordering of any stock item is necessary.
4 *Stock analysis reports* — these can be produced as required and will indicate stock movement, trends and provide an indication of future stock needs.

Purchase ledger

The purpose of this module is to keep an up-to-date and detailed record of all purchases made by the business. It links with the nominal ledger and stock control. Special features of this module are:

1 *Payment date calculation* — the system will calculate the most advantageous date on which to make payment to a supplier so that the purchasing company may gain the greatest benefit from its cash or the discounts allowed.
2 *Supplier lists* — these will show individual suppliers and their products. Lists can also be obtained showing the products and those who supply them.

Payroll

The purpose of this module is to record details of employees relating to their pay, and to calculate the payment due to them on the basis of these details. It also calculates and deducts tax and national contributions from the employee's pay, and any other authorised deductions. Payroll links with the nominal ledger, passing on information. The special features of this module are:

1 *Pay slips, cheques and bank giros* — these are produced by the system for each employee on regular payment days.
2 *Coin analysis* — this is a breakdown of the coins and notes required if employees are paid in cash.

Nominal ledger

The nominal ledger is the centre of the accounts system. Its purpose is to keep track of the company's funds. It records the balances on company sales, expenses, assets and liabilities and balances the books. The nominal ledger, therefore, is linked with the other modules, from which it draws its information. The special feature of this module is:

1 *Special accounts and returns* — profit and loss accounts, balance sheets and statutory returns can be produced and printed out instantly.

Report generator

The purpose of this module is to produce reports which will give management an overview of the business, its financial state and its operation. It links with all the other modules and collects information from them in order to produce analysis and reports on various aspects of the business. The special features of this module are:

1 *Predefined reports* — this ensures that reports contain the information required in a standard format, although they can be edited or re-drafted to cope with specific requirements.
2 *Passwords* — this module produces company information reserved for management. Security is, therefore, important, and any user must satisfy the password requirements before gaining access.

Computerised stock control

It is not possible here to go into the detail of using a full accounting package. However, we will look more closely at a computerised stock control system, as many of you already understand how a manual stock control system operates.

Stock control programs

Generally, stock control programs are easy to operate. Some of them are menu-driven, and you choose the function you want from the list presented to you on the screen. Many also display a straightforward message whenever the system requires input from the keyboard.

Entering data

When a stock control system is first set up, details of every stock item/product must be entered into the computer and the stock file(s) containing all the information must be saved on disk. The initial information about each stock item may be entered simply in rows with a maximum number of characters allocated to each field of data, eg Stock Code: up to 10 characters; Description: up to 40 characters. More sophisticated programs usually use a stock record form (see Fig 6.21), and the operator fills in the appropriate spaces; a fresh record form is used for each product. New stock items or products can be added to the stock file at any time by using the same format to enter the new details. Those products no longer stocked can be deleted easily from the file. Each time the file is updated

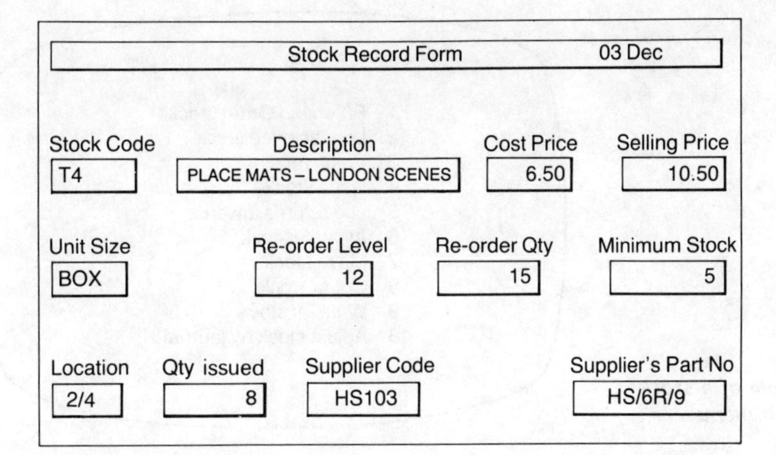

Stock Record Form			03 Dec
Stock Code	Description	Cost Price	Selling Price
T4	PLACE MATS – LONDON SCENES	6.50	10.50
Unit Size	Re-order Level	Re-order Qty	Minimum Stock
BOX	12	15	5
Location	Qty issued	Supplier Code	Supplier's Part No
2/4	8	HS103	HS/6R/9

Fig 6.21
An example of a stock record form

in any way, it must be saved again on disk under the same filename in order to record the amendments permanently.

Examine the information contained in the stock record form (Fig 6.21).

1 Stock Code: Each item/product is identified by a unique stock code.
2 Description: This provides a helpful description of the product.
3 Cost Price: This is useful in evaluating stock.
4 Selling Price: This is required for invoicing purposes.
5 Unit Size: This allows you to define the product's standard unit, such as 'each' or 'pack' or 'metre'.
6 Re-order Level, Re-order Quantity and Minimum Stock: Enable you to maintain adequate stocks of all products.
7 Location: Indicates where the stock items are stored.
8 Supplier Code: This is used as a fast and reliable method of identifying the product supplier. Each supplier has a unique code.
9 Supplier's Part No: Identifies the item instantly when re-ordering.

Stock transactions

Once the initial information about a product has been set up, the stock transaction facilities are used to record stock levels, movements and values. Figure 6.22 shows a stock transaction screen menu, allowing you to carry out 10 different types of transaction.

If a quantity of stock is delivered, you would select Function 2 from the menu and Function 5 if a customer returns a quantity of goods. You would then make the appropriate entries so that the stock records can be updated.

Additional features

Global price changes

Price changes can be made automatically throughout the file or to specific items only. Such increases or decreases can be made by percentage or by a fixed amount.

1 Purchase Order stock
2 Log received stock
3 Value receipts
4 Issue stock
5 Log returns inwards
6 Allocate stock
7 Move stock
8 Count stock
9 Write off stock
10 Adjust stock by journal

Fig 6.22
An example of a stock interaction menu

Search facilities

The file can be searched on all fields and parts thereof to match criteria established by you. For example, you might want to identify all products with a cost price above £50 and take a printout of a detailed list of these items.

Reports

The system can produce reports showing stock balance and value, stock on order, stock below minimum, sales analysis, cost variance, etc. These reports can be produced at any time on the screen or in hardcopy form. In a manual stock control system, the production of any one of these reports would involve many hours of tedious checking and recording.

UNIT 24 Integrated software

As mentioned at the beginning of this section, the needs of most users can be met by word processing, database, spreadsheet, graphics and accounting application software. However, it is often necessary to share and transfer information between these applications. This was made apparent in Unit 23 when integrated accounts were examined. This Unit looks at the integration of applications other than those under the umbrella of accounts, ie word processing, databases, spreadsheets and graphics.

What is an integrated software program and what does it do?

An integrated software program combines the functions that are found in several stand-alone application programs, such as word processing, database, spreadsheet and graphics programs. However, the functions of the combined applications are usually limited, lacking the power and sophistication of stand-alone programs. There are, of course, exceptions, where at least one application in an integrated package has all the capabilities and power of any similar stand-alone program. The reasons for the limitations are that:

1 the more functions there are, the more difficult a program is to use, so it would be impracticable to include all the functions for each application that would normally be found in powerful stand-alone programs.
2 the integration of several applications takes up a lot of memory (RAM) and more functions would mean even less working memory

None the less, an integrated software program provides the user with a variety of business tools with which to work – all in one package.

Who uses an integrated software program and what are its applications?

A secretary who only occasionally uses a database, but whose daily workload requires the help of advanced word processing functions, will find that stand-alone programs will better suit his/her needs. The main users of integrated software programs are those who work on projects requiring the use of multiple tools; people who are trying to put information together and present it effectively. Usually, they do not have the skill or the need for the specialist functions included in stand-alone programs.

Integrated software programs are used by managers and executives to handle their own data and information requirements; to prepare budgets, make financial projections, analyse data and trends, write reports, letters, memos and combine information from a variety of applications.

They will be used by business people new to computers who wish to learn to use one or more of the popular applications, taking advantage of the integrated program's user-friendly features.

What features do integrated software programs have and what are their uses?

Apart from the features which are basic to the applications in the integrated program, eg correcting and moving text in word processing and sorting a database, the special features of integrated software programs are explained below.

Using the same procedures

Each application in the package works in a similar way, so that the skills and procedures you learn using one application can be used as you expand into other applications. For example, files are opened, saved and retrieved using the same procedures for all the applications. In this way, you can learn to use several applications much more quickly than it would take you to learn them individually as stand-alone programs.

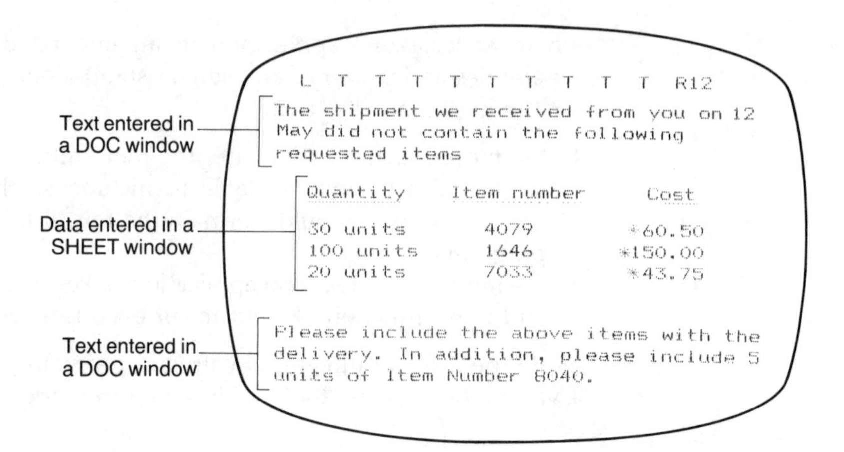

Fig 6.23
Sheet entries in a document

Move or copy information between applications

Information can be moved quickly between all the applications in the program. For example, Fig 6.23 shows data taken from a spreadsheet and incorporated in a word processing document.

Each integrated software program has its own specific procedures for copying and moving information between applications. The important thing to remember is that, before giving instructions to the system to copy or move information, you must make sure that there is sufficient room in the receiving document, spreadsheet or data file to accommodate it. Information will normally be transferred to the position specified by the cursor/pointer. If the space you create for the new data is too small, it will overwrite (**erase**) existing data.

Combining data from two stand-alone application programs

It is possible to transfer data between two different stand-alone application programs. Many individual programs now have this facility. However, transferring data between two separate programs necessitates a good understanding of both the application programs involved and the instructions must be followed through precisely. This is usually quite a complicated and lengthy procedure, hence the popularity of integrated software programs.

Summary — Key Points

1 The paperwork in an office can be divided into five areas:

a order processing, stock control and accounting
b financial budgeting and analysis
c maintaining records
d dealing with correspondence
e filing and retrieving information

2 Programs which have been specially written to handle these tasks on a computer are accounting, spreadsheet, database and word

processing programs respectively, generally referred to as business application software.

3 A word processing program allows you to use a computer to produce and automatically reproduce anything that can be typed, providing special features for editing and formatting of documents.

4 The main users of word processing programs are word processing operators and secretaries, whose job it is to produce printed copies of documents for internal and external distribution.

5 A spreadsheet program allows you to set up a variety of worksheets on a computer, automatically calculating and recalculating your data entries for you.

6 The main users of spreadsheet programs are managers and accountants, whose job it is to analyse previous and current company figures, and project and budget future income and expenditure.

7 A database program stores in an organised structure any information you enter into the computer and allows selected information to be rapidly retrieved from the database according to the criteria established by you.

8 The main users of database programs are managers whose job it is to examine information, such as customers', stock and personnel records, on which day-to-day business decisions can be based.

9 A graphics program allows you to display any data entered into the computer in pictorial form, eg as graphs and charts.

10 The main users of business graphics programs are managers, sales and marketing executives who wish to highlight trends, relationships and comparisons by displaying data input in graphic form.

11 An accounting program allows you to use a computer to 'keep the books' or records of everything that a business owns, uses, buys and sells.

12 Some accounting software may include modules for order processing, stock control, invoicing, sales ledger, purchase ledger, nominal ledger, payroll and a report generator.

13 The main users of accounting programs are clerical/accounts staff, whose job it is to input and update data, generate invoices, statements and payments, prepare the payroll and carry out specific accounting functions.

14 An integrated software program combines the functions that are found in several stand-alone application programs, such as word processing, database, spreadsheet and graphics programs.

15 The main users of integrated software programs are those who work on projects requiring the use of more than one application, where the output of one program often has to be combined with the output of another.

Knowledge Check on Section 6

Keywords (try to explain the meaning of these terms in your own words)

Accounting suite	Default values	Legend
Application program	Field	Macro
Batch processing	Global search	Merge
Boldface	Glossary	Shared mode
Cell address	Hardcopy	Word wraparound
Criterion	Integrated software	Worksheet
Database	Justified text	

Complete each of the following items and then check your responses either with your tutor or with the answers on page 122.

1 Match each term in the first column with its meaning from the second column:

a ____	*1*	The move feature	*a*	Copies information in one position and repeats it in another specified position
____	2	The copy feature	*b*	Places new information in a specified position.
____	3	The delete feature	*c*	Deletes specified information from its original position and transfers it to another specified position.
____	4	The insert feature	*d*	Deletes or erases specified information.
b ____	*1*	A primary sort	*a*	Sorts information according to numbers, either in ascending or descending order.
____	2	A multiple sort	*b*	Sorts information in more than one order of priority.
____	3	A numerical sort	*c*	Sorts information in date order.
____	4	A chronological sort	*d*	Sorts information according to the first order of priority.
c ____	*1*	A purchase ledger	*a*	Records the balances of sales, expenses, assets and liabilities.
____	2	A sales ledger	*b*	Records details of all sales made by the business.
____	3	A nominal ledger	*c*	Records details of purchases made by the business.

2 Label the following statements true or false.

a ____ When word processing, a spelling checker automatically corrects misspelt words in a document.

b ____ When you use a spreadsheet, you need only enter the cell addresses and not the actual numbers to be calculated.

c ____ Data is organised in file format.

d ____ If your computer system does not have a graphics adapter, you will not be able to display graphics at all.

e ____ When you retrieve a file for editing or updating, you can save both the old and the new version if you save the file again under the old filename.

f ____ Graphic images can be stored on disk in the same way that text and data can.

3 Multiple choice: select the letter that best answers the question.

1 Which of the following serves the same function as the cursor? ________.
- *a* symbol
- *b* cell pointer
- *c* tab stop
- *d* label

2 The function of a database is ________.
- *a* to check all input data
- *b* to check all spelling
- *c* to collect and organise input data
- *d* to output data

3 Which of the following is sometimes used instead of the term status line? ________.
- *a* format line
- *b* on line
- *c* headline
- *d* command line

4 Fill in the blanks:
- *a* Spreadsheet labels are aligned automatically to the ____ of a cell and numbers to the ____.
- *b* A ____ is an organised collection of data.
- *c* Before commanding the system to print your work, check that the printer is ____ ____.
- *d* A list showing who owes money to the business and the age of each debt is called an ____ ____ list.
- *e* ____ features allow you to make corrections and changes to your work.
- *f* A ____ is a group of similar records kept together and each record contains specified ____ or items of data.

Answers

1a *1c 2a 3d 4b*
b *1d 2b 3a 4c*
c *1c 2b 3a*
2 *a* F *b* T *c* T *d* T *e* F *f* T
3 *1b 2c 3d*
4 *a* left, right *b* database *c* on line *d* aged debtors *e* edit *f* file, fields

Additional questions on Section 6

1 Suggest some of the word processing features you would use in order to ensure that the final printout of a six-page report is attractively and effectively displayed. Give examples to illustrate where in the report you would use these features and why.
2 Discuss the benefits of using the following when working on a spreadsheet:
  a cell addresses
  b cell ranges
  c formulas
  d functions.
3 Which department in an organisation or which type of business do you think would benefit considerably from the use of business graphics? Give reasons for your answer with examples.
4 Compare the advantages and disadvantages of integrated software and stand-alone business application programs.

Assignment 6

a Enter two paragraphs of text with a left margin of 10 and a right margin of 60.
Proofread it.
Save it, using the filename "first.try". Take a printout.
Retrieve "first.try".
Change the margins to 15 and 65.
Indent the second paragraph a further five spaces to the right.
Save the file, using the filename "second.try".
Take a printout of the new format.

b Design a spreadsheet, whether or not you have the software to run it. Draw up the worksheet, using columns and rows so that each cell has an address. Your labels (headings) should be: SALARY, RENT, FOOD, FARES, ENTERTAINMENT and SAVINGS.
If you have the software, run the spreadsheet program, entering appropriate figures for four months from August to November inclusive. The program should total your salary and expenses over the period and calculate your monthly and total savings.
Save the spreadsheet under the filename: SAVINGS.NOV

Take a printout of the spreadsheet.
Retrieve the spreadsheet: SAVINGS.NOV
Add another monthly expense: CLOTHES, for the same period.
The spreadsheet program should recalculate your SAVINGS.
Save the spreadsheet, overwriting the original file.
Take a printout of the new spreadsheet.

7 Presentation of information

In this Section we discuss the **presentation of computer generated information**. There is now immense interest in this subject. What has stimulated and motivated this interest in and need for well-presented information? How has the computer industry (both hardware and software) responded? What skills do computer users need to develop in order to meet this new challenge?

UNIT 25 The need for well-presented information

The main objective of business computing is the **processing** of information. PC technology has played a major part in achieving this objective. However, the ever increasing speeds at which data is being processed create a new problem — that of assimilation. The more information that is processed, the more time is required to read and digest the information. Good presentation will help towards alleviating this problem. Information which is well presented can be more easily read and absorbed and salient points more quickly noted. It follows, therefore, that the next objective is **presentation**.

It is important that information is presented in such a way that:

1 It is easy to read and digest
2 It is brief, clear and concise
3 The main facts are highlighted
4 Trends and relationships are immediately apparent

1 *It is easy to read and digest* This means that the **format** (design and layout) of the page should guide the reader easily from one piece of information to another.

Areas that affect the format are:

Paper size and type (always select the appropriate paper for the job)

Margins (set adequate margins at the top, bottom, left and right of the page)

Tab stops (set appropriate tab stops to allow sufficient space between columns of figures or to number and indent text from the margins)

Justification (align text between the left and right margins to obtain the desired effect, eg centred for emphasis; right-justified for neatness)

Line spacing (select appropriate line spacing for the entire document or for sections of the document)

2 *It is brief, clear and concise* Keep information factual and to the point and adopt an easy-to-read business style.
3 *The main points are highlighted* Use different fonts and print attributes, such as bold or underline. A text box can be used for a main heading or text inserted between graphic lines to really make a point.
4 *Trends and relationships are immediately apparent* Use graphs and other graphic capabilities to illustrate trends and relationships.

UNIT 26 Developments to aid information presentation

It is now possible for an office to produce work which, until recently, would have required expensive professional expertise. The following developments in PC hardware and software have made a marked impact on the presentation of information, both on paper and on screen.

Computer developments

1 *Faster systems with greater processing power* (essential to run software with presentation capabilities).
2 *Extended and expanded memory* (graphics and sophisticated printing techniques need substantial working memory).
3 *Increased hard disk capacity* (software and files incorporating graphics and other presentation features occupy huge amounts of storage space).
4 *High resolution monitors — colour or monochrome* (state of the art **Video Graphics Array (VGA)** and **super VGA** monitors to provide the operator with sharp, clear text and graphics).

Printer developments

Desktop laser printers are considered necessary in offices where emphasis is placed on the **presentation** of information. New developments include:

1 *Increased memory,* required for better handling of graphics, fonts (different typefaces) and complex pages.
2 *Greater selection of internal and external fonts* to generate professional looking output from software such as word processing, spreadsheets, databases, graphics and desktop publishing.
3 *Duplex printing* to print automatically on both sides of the paper.

4 *Easy to use control panels*, so that functions can be selected with the touch of a button, including page orientation (ie portrait or landscape), font selection and number of copies.
5 *Improved paper handling facilities* to accept two or more input paper trays at the same time. The standard paper tray holds A4 size sheets and the optional tray(s) can hold legal, letter and envelope sizes.
6 *Compatibility with any PC* by the provision of both Centronics parallel and RS232 Serial ports.

Software developments

1 *Greater printer support* supplied by software houses, especially the leading word processing manufacturers, who provide printer drivers (software settings) for a wide range of printers. This allows the software to control those printers for which a driver is supplied.
2 *Soft fonts and bitstream fonts*, supplied on diskettes and generated by software. Many word processing programs now have their own bitstream fontware to generate **scalable** fonts (fonts which provide characters in varying sizes from very small to very large) (Fig 7.1). These fonts are then available when using the program to create typeset quality documents.
3 *Exporting/importing and converting files* to and from one software package to another. It is now possible not only to import a file from one word processing program to another but also to convert that file into the format of the program into which it has been imported. Files can also be exported and imported between different types of software, eg a file from a graphics or spreadsheet program can be imported into a word processing program. The picture or graph can improve the presentation of the document and clarify the message.
4 *Enhanced presentation features* have been added to application software recently, with a view to improving the appearance and presentation of output.

Word processing software

1 **Newspaper columns:** This feature allows for several columns to be *snaked* across the page, to be read as a newspaper from the top to the bottom of each column. This gives a professional look to any *newsletter, information leaflet*, etc created within the company. Since this type of work need no longer be given out to a printing firm, time and money can be saved. Additionally, because the documents are produced *in-house*, the information is likely to be right up to date (Fig 7.2 newsletter).
2 **Graphics:** This feature provides for the drawing of boxes and lines in varying thicknesses, so as to create professional type forms, etc. Text can be inserted in the boxes. The background of such boxes can be shaded, so that the text is more pronounced. Special fonts and font attributes (*italics*, **bold**, etc) can be used for the text (Fig 7.2).

Graphic files (pictures, charts, etc) can also be imported into a document and inserted into text displayed in columns and the text made to wrap around the picture (Fig 7.2).

CG Times 4
CG Times 6
CG Times 8
CG Times 10
CG Times 12
CG Times 14
CG Times 16
CG Times 18
CG Times 20
CG Times 24
CG Times 36
CG Times 48
CG Times 60
CG Times 72

Fig 7.1
Scalable fonts

3 **Preview:** This is a feature which enables the operator to view the document before it goes to print. This feature provides a **wysiwyg** (what you see is what you get) view of the document. If the layout or the presentation does not look good, the operator has an opportunity to change things before sending it to print. This feature is extremely helpful when striving for good presentation.

Graphics software

Quality of presentation does not end with words. In today's offices, graphics programs are used to take the facts and figures of business and create charts and presentations similar to those produced previously by professionals. Current business graphics packages offer a wide range of capabilities and features:

1 **Create and edit**. Charts and graphs can be created and edited from data entered at the keyboard or from data imported from another program.
2 **Draw and text tools**, to add to charts and to create and manipulate shapes by rotating, stretching, pushing, etc.
3 **3-Dimensional effects** are available in all formats of graphs and charts (Fig 7.3).

WORD PROCESSING OR WORD PUBLISHING?

What's the difference between word processing, word publishing and desktop publishing? Are these terms different or are they the same? With advanced word processing software that blends text, fonts and graphics, these terms are moving closer together and distinctions begin to fade.

Word processing is character-based writing. In that respect, word processors are direct descendants of Gutenberg's movable blocks of type.

Desktop publishing is pixel-based word processing. In desktop publishing, the computer doesn't just see characters. It sees a graphic image made up of fine dots, each one a pixel, or unit of information.

By viewing characters this way, the computer can change the type size and style of individual characters. Since the computer sees pixels, not just characters, other pixels can easily be integrated into documents.

These pixels can take the form of circles, such as a clock or squares, rectangles or photographs.

When the computer displays all the type size and style, and graphic changes onscreen, it has a true *WYSIWYG* (What You See Is What You Get, pronounced "whizzeewig") display.

Word publishing is a new term that has become the bridge between traditional character-based word processing and pixel-based desktop publishing. Word publishing combines the most popular features of desktop publishing with the ease of use of a traditional word processor.

INTEGRATING TEXT WITH GRAPHICS

The smooth integration of text and graphics in advanced word processing programs makes designing newsletters, reports and professional documents much easier. A graphic image can be scaled, moved, and rotated. Sizing and cropping are quick and easy. You can indicate the style and thickness for printing a border, and include a caption. The graphic image can be placed anywhere on the page, inserted in a line, tied to a paragraph or included in a header or footer.

Text meets Graphics

Fig 7.2
Newsletter produced with WordPerfect word processing software

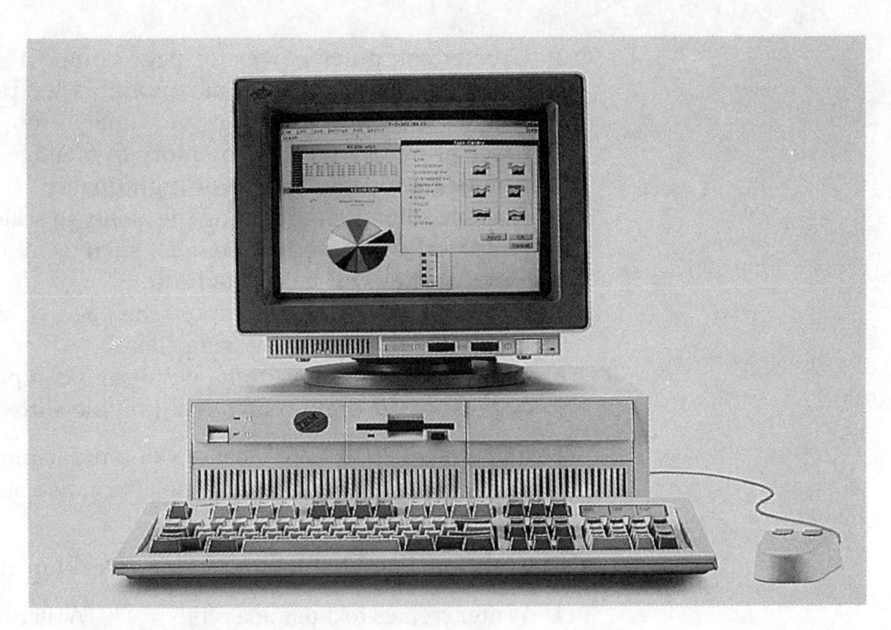

Fig 7.3
Three-dimensional effects

4 **Multiple charts** of different types can appear on the screen simultaneously.
5 **Clip-art material** can be supplied which includes business symbols and other images to improve presentation.
6 **Slide shows** — files created with graphic software can be turned into 35mm slides to produce a slide show with a slide projector.

Using a Personal Computer, a slide show can easily be created on a colour VDU by sequencing drawings, charts and/or pictures together. This will provide a number of benefits:

- The sequence in which the slides are displayed can be specified.
- Backgrounds of various designs can be used to fill in the area behind the chart on the screen.
- Special effects can be selected whereby, when one slide finishes, it fades out and the next slide scrolls in. These effects cannot be achieved with a slide projector.
- A PC can readily be set up at a client's office to run a slide show, whereas a slide projector is not usually available.
- Clients can be given a copy of the slide show to view at their leisure.

UNIT 27 Desktop publishing (DTP) software

These are programs that integrate text and graphics and create a publication. With the use of appropriate hardware, DTP software can replace all the stages of producing a published document that traditionally would be done by hand. Desktop publishing is the natural outcome of the following developments in hardware and software:

1 Greater computer power for page composition.
2 High resolution, large colour monitors for page design.
3 Image scanners to import graphic images into the computer memory.
4 Laser printers with extra memory to manage graphics and fonts and produce a finished article of high quality.
5 Scalable soft fonts, providing the ability to scale to a desired point size.
6 Graphical user interfaces (GUIs) such as **Windows** to see on screen exactly what will be printed out.
7 Publishing software to compose the page, deal with fonts, and import graphic and word processing files.
8 Word processing programs with page composing features.
9 Sophisticated draw, paint and graphic software.

To help you to appreciate what desktop publishing is all about, the stages of conventional publishing and the alternative stages offered by desktop publishing are listed here.

Conventional publishing

1 Writer creates text using a typewriter or word processor.
2 Typewritten copy is sent to the phototypesetter, who produces galley proofs (long columns of typeset text).
3 Galley proofs are sent to writer and editor for proofreading. Necessary changes are made to galleys.
4 A production artist makes a 'paste-up', arranging galleys into multiple columns on each page and leaving room for any photographs or drawings, etc that need to be included.
5 The paste-up is sent to the offset printer, who photographs the pages and artwork.
6 The printer makes a plate for the printing press from the negatives.
7 Final pages are produced.

Desktop publishing

1 Writer creates text using a word processor.
2 Publishing program takes over the text so that font sizes and page layout can be decided and text 'flowed' into the assigned number of columns.
3 Words and images are mixed if the graphic images are available. Images are positioned on the page to suit the required layout. Alternatively, space can be left on each page to accommodate photographs and drawings.
4 Completed pages are printed out by laser printer.

Required user skills for good presentation

Technology has provided the means with which to produce high-quality printed output and presentations. However, the final result depends on the skills of the computer user. Desktop publishing is a challenge to anyone — it requires the job skills of many individuals, all to be carried out by one person. One moment you will be using a word processor to prepare your text; the next you could be using graphics, draw or charting software. You will also have to don the various hats of typographer, editor and production artist! If desktop publishing is what you are interested in, then here are the skills you need to acquire.

Computer skills

As a DTP user, you should be familiar with the capabilities of system hardware: the processor, hard disk capacity and system memory. Desktop publishing software requires extended memory and a fast processor. You should also be well acquainted with laser printer facilities and operation. Some knowledge of scanners would also be useful.

Reasonably good word processing skills are needed, as text has to be prepared and edited with a word processing program. Those with experience, or even knowledge, of advanced word processing features, such as newspaper columns, style sheets, font selection, and graphics text and figure boxes, will already have acquired some basic DTP skills.

It is necessary to be familiar with **Windows**, as the main DTP packages operate in the **Windows** environment.

Working with a **mouse** is another skill that needs to be acquired.

Experience of using graphics/draw software would certainly be beneficial. Even if the graphic files are prepared for you, you will have to fine tune the images to fit your page design when they are imported into the DTP document.

Document design skills

Good document design is not something which happens when you throw everything together — some text here, a picture there, a few lines here and there and a variety of fonts to liven it all up! You need to *plan* your document and its layout, whether it is a simple newsletter or a publication of several pages. This is the way to achieve a truly professional looking document. Planning also involves defining your audience (the readers). After all, the object of the exercise is to communicate effectively with *them*.

It is worth spending time to learn about good document design:

1 **Key design principles** are simplicity, balance, proportion, contrast and consistency.
2 Learn about **kerning** (moving a character closer to the previous character) and **leading** (the vertical space between two lines of print, from the tops of the capital letters in one line to the tops of the capital letters in the next line).
3 Learn about **typefaces**, **typestyles** and **fonts**. Fonts can be defined according to the following criteria:

   Spacing This refers to the amount of space that each character occupies. There are **proportional spaced** fonts and **fixed spaced** (also called **monospaced**) fonts. Fixed spacing means that each character occupies the same amount of space. Proportional means that the space occupied by a character varies depending on the *shape* of the character. For example, a *w* or an *m* will take up more space than an *i* or an *l*, or even an *e*. **Courier** is an example of a monospace font, while **Times Roman** is an example of a proportional font. Proportional spacing gives a much more professional look to the printed article.

Pitch This refers to the number of characters per inch (cpi) and only relates to fixed spaced fonts, eg Courier 10 cpi or Courier 12 cpi.

Point size This refers to the *height* of the character, measured from the top of the character to the bottom of the character. There are 72 points to an inch. Therefore, a 36 point (36pt) font would be half inch in height and an 18pt character would be quarter inch in height (see Fig 7.1, *Scalable fonts*).

Style The style can be upright or slanting as in *italic*.

Stroke weight This relates to the stroke *thickness* of the character. Strokes can be light, medium or bold.

Typeface This relates to the *design* of the characters. Typefaces vary from the very plain to those that are quite elaborate.

Orientation This relates to the way in which the print is aligned on the paper. **Portrait** prints vertically on the page (on A4 paper 8.27 in × 11.69 in) and **landscape** prints horizontally (on A4 paper 11.69 in × 8.27 in).

Learn how to use *white space* and *colour* effectively.

Learn **desktop publishing terminology**. As you can see, it includes some strange words.

If you have acquired the skills and knowledge mentioned above *before* you attend a desktop publishing course, you will benefit so much more from the training. It helps tremendously if you feel comfortable working in the *Windows* environment and if you can manipulate a *mouse*. Desktop publishing courses are usually run over two days. Of necessity, these courses move at a fairly fast pace. The time is taken up with learning to use the particular desktop publishing program. There is little or no time to devote to teaching document design or other skills. This would only be possible on a longer course.

Summary — Key Points

1. The ever-increasing speeds at which data is being processed create a problem of assimilation.
2. The more information that is processed, the more time is required to read and digest the information. Good presentation helps to alleviate the problem.
3. When presenting information it is important that: *a* it is easy to read and digest; *b* it is brief, clear and concise; *c* the main points are highlighted; *d* trends and relationships are immediately apparent.
4. Developments in PC hardware and software have now made it possible to generate professional quality computer output. This has stimulated immense interest in presentation.

5 Computer development includes faster systems with greater processing power, extended and expanded memory, increased hard disk capacity and high resolution colour monitors.
6 Printer development includes increased memory, more internal and external fonts, improved paper handling, and control panels for immediate selection of functions.
7 Developments in software range from increased printer support, provision of soft fonts and bitstream fontware, exporting/importing files, and graphical user interfaces, to enhanced presentation features in application programs.
8 Word processing software includes presentation techniques such as newspaper column display and importing of graphic images.
9 Graphics software has developed capabilities to create 3-D effects and slide shows.
10 Developments in hardware and software have also revolutionised the publishing business by spawning desktop publishing.
11 Desktop publishing uses a computer to replace all the stages of producing a published document that, traditionally, would be done by hand.
12 Technology has provided the means with which to produce high-quality printed output and presentations, but the final results depend on the skills of computer users.
13 Computer skills useful to those entering the field of desktop publishing include word processing, use of graphics software, working in a windows environment and using a mouse.
14 A knowledge of document design principles, typefaces, typestyles and fonts would be helpful to anyone interested in presentation.
15 Good presentation involves planning your document, knowing your audience, and understanding and using the capabilities of the hardware and software.

Knowledge Check on Section 7

Keywords (try to explain the meaning of these terms in your own words).

Desktop publishing	Graphical user interfaces	Printer drivers
Duplex printing	Justification	Scalable fonts
Fonts	Kerning	Soft fonts
Format	Leading	VGA monitors
Galley proofs	Newspaper columns	Wysiwyg

Complete each of the following items and then check your responses either with your tutor or with the answers on page 135.

1 Match each term in the first column with its meaning from the second

column:

____	*1* Leading	*a*	Refer to printing in bold, italics, underline, etc.
____	*2* Kerning	*b*	Refers to the vertical space between two lines of text from the top of the capital letters.
____	*3* Scalable fonts	*c*	Provide characters in varying sizes from very small to very large.
____	*4* Font attributes	*d*	Means moving a character closer to the previous character on the same line.

2 List the four important considerations when presenting information:

____

____

____

____

3 Label the following statements true or false:

a ____ VGA monitors provide sharp clear text and graphics.
b ____ Software with presentation capabilities needs faster computers with greater processing power.
c ____ Soft fonts and bitstream fontware are part of computer hardware.
d ____ Newspaper columns refer to the way newspapers are stacked.

4 Fill in the blanks:

a To view a document in its printed form *before* it is printed, the operator would use the ____ function.
b ____ is 'what you see is what you get'.
c Desktop publishing requires ____ skills and ____ ____ skills.
d Printing on both sides of the paper is known as ____ ____.

Answers

1 *1b* *2d* *3c* *4a*
2 *a* It should be easy to read and digest; *b* it should be brief, clear and concise; *c* the main points should be highlighted; *d* trends and relationships should be immediately apparent.
3 aT bT cF dF
4 **a** preview **b** wysiwyg **c** computer, document design **d** duplex printing

Additional questions on Section 7

1 With good presentation in mind, which software features do you think you would make use of when working on (*a*) general correspondence, and (*b*) spreadsheets showing monthly sales figures of different products in the range. Give your reasons.
2 Computer technology will continue to develop systems capable of processing more information at even greater speeds. How will we deal with more and more information? Is an ever-increasing amount of information really necessary or even helpful? Discuss.
3 Assuming you were interested in obtaining a job in desktop publishing: (*a*) What interim goals would you set yourself to realise your ambition? (*b*) What do you think you could do in the meantime to develop a critical eye for layout?

Assignment 7

a Design a notice advertising a Disco at your college. Plan it first on paper and aim for a professional look. Key it in at the computer and take a printout.
b Design a newsletter for your sports club. Use newspaper columns, if your system has the facility. Take a printout.

8 Building good work habits

UNIT 28 Disk management

Files stored on computer disks (documents, worksheets, etc) should be given the same attention as traditional files in any organised office. Think of your disk as a filing cabinet. Files on disk should be appropriately named for easy identification and retrieval. No two files on a disk can have the same name. Each filename must be unique. (File naming was discussed in Unit 17, when it was suggested that a meaningful system of file naming/identification be used.) The same naming conventions apply to files stored on both hard disks and diskettes.

Files on diskettes

Work disks

When using a two-diskette system, all your files will be stored on diskettes. On no account save your work files on your **program disks**. These disks should only be used for loading the program. Have a supply of *formatted* disks ready to use as **work disks**. Save all your work on the **work disks**. During a work session on a two-diskette system, you would normally leave the **program disk** in drive **A** and place your **work disk** in drive **B**. If you make drive **B** the default drive, whenever you instruct the system to save a file, it will be saved on your work disk in drive B.

Diskette labelling

A set of loose labels can be found in each new box of diskettes. As each diskette is used, one of these gummed labels should be attached to the disk and the disk dated and numbered. Other information which would help to identify the contents of the disk should be added. File your disks in numerical, alphabetical or date order and store them in sturdy disk boxes (Fig 8.1). This will prevent your disks from being damaged, thus protecting the data on them.

As there is insufficient space on the label to list all the files stored on the diskette, an up-to-date printout could be taken of the directory of each work disk. This will show which files are on a particular diskette without having to insert the disk into the disk drive to examine the directory on screen. Each directory printout should be stored with the corresponding disk and should include the information on the label of that disk. This is to link the printout with the diskette should the two become separated at some time.

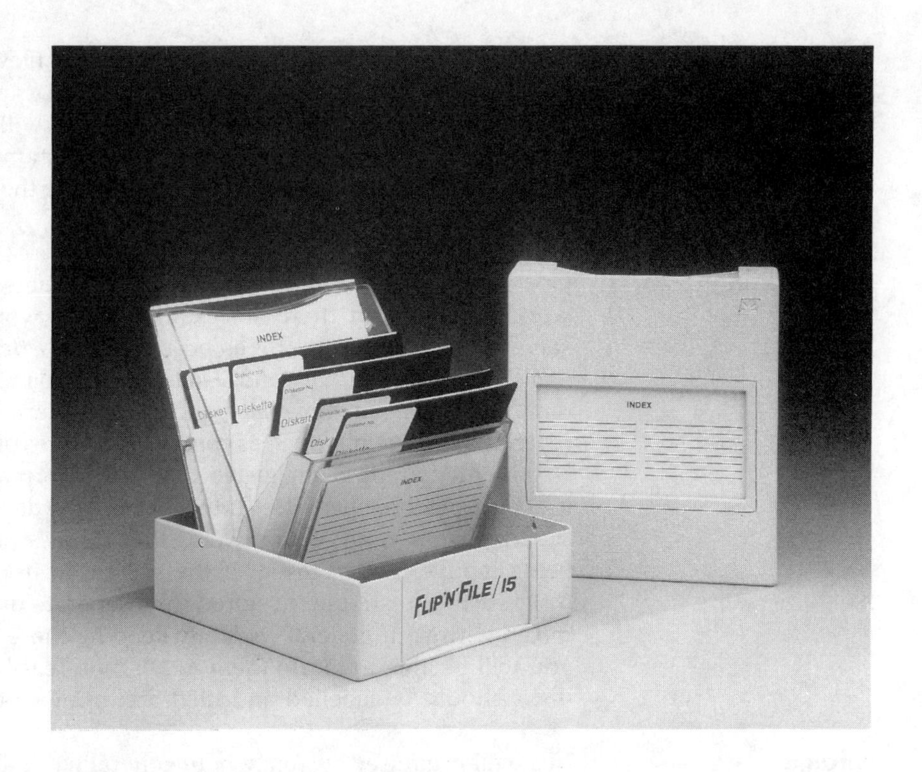

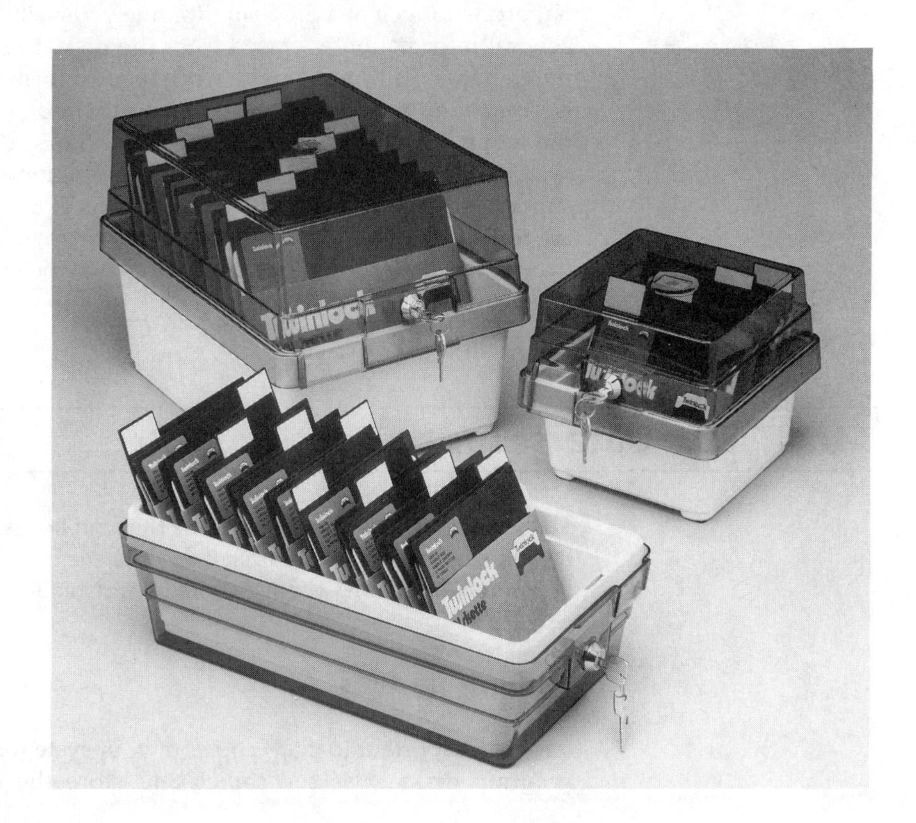

Fig 8.1
Disk storage boxes

When using a hard disk system, most of the files you save will be stored on the hard disk in a **subdirectory** created expressly for your work. However, there will be occasions when you will want to store a file or group of files on a diskette. The same suggestions given above for **work disks** and **diskette labelling** apply when using the diskette drive in a hard disk system.

Standardising tasks

One of the things computers are really good at is dealing with repetitive work. You should therefore examine your workload with a view to standardising as much of it as possible: *form letters* and *customer lists* for mailshots, *standard forms* and *standard letters* to merge with other variable data, and *standard paragraphs* and *blocks of text or data* for inserting in repetitive documents, such as contracts, minutes of meetings and financial statements, etc. It is suggested that you set up a separate subdirectory in which to store such files. If these standard documents/forms are kept separate from your general work, there is less risk of one of these files being inadvertently erased. If the system in use does not have a hard disk, such files should be stored on a separate diskette(s) and not intermixed with your general work. By keeping these files on separate disks, you will be able to locate them much more easily when needed. These disks should be labelled and filed according to their contents.

Purging

In a well-organised system where general work directories and diskettes contain no standard text, company data or special records, purging does not present much of a problem. Routinely, usually after a specified period, general information is erased from the disk. In some organisations the purge date is indicated on the work request form and, in others, a notice is sent round to originators informing them of a purge. It is then up to the originator to request that a particular file is retained. In a centralised system, purging might be left to the discretion of the centre manager/supervisor. Where a two-diskette system is in use, if only one or two files are to be retained on some disks, it is worthwhile copying these across to another disk, so that complete disks may be erased, ready for re-use.

UNIT 29 Data security

There are many simple precautions that can be taken to keep data secure. Backing up files is the first step in data security. The system must also be protected against theft, sabotage and malicious damage.

Backing up files

It is very important to make copies of your **system disk** and all **application program disks**. Use the copies and store the originals away safely.

Diskettes can be damaged by careless handling or by accident, resulting in the system being unable to read all or some of the information. There is also the possibility that a diskette can be inadvertently erased. The practice of making duplicates of diskettes, directories and files is called **back-up**. In many companies, back-up copies are made at the end of each day or work session of everything that has been processed. Others are more selective. It should be standard procedure in all companies to make at least one back-up copy of *system disks, application program disks*, directories and diskettes on which *standard letters, paragraphs, forms, customer files* and other *records* have been stored.

Back-up procedure using DOS copy or diskcopy commands

Diskettes have a **write-protect notch** (*see* Fig 8.2). When a diskette is **write-protected**, it is not possible for the computer to write new information on the disk. On the $5\frac{1}{4}$ in diskette, the disk is write-protected if this notch is covered with an adhesive tab (supplied with the disks). The adhesive tab can be removed at any time, when information can be written to the disk again. The write-protect window on a $3\frac{1}{2}$ in diskette is on the reverse side of the disk in the lower right corner (*see* Fig 8.2). To write-protect the diskette, slide the tab so that the window is *open*. Slide the tab back again to close the window, and the diskette is ready to accept new data. When using either the **DOS copy** or **DISKCOPY** command (the latter can only be used with a two-diskette system) to make a duplicate copy of a diskette, *write-protect the source disk*! This is particularly important when using **DISKCOPY** because, if you do not and a mix-up occurs when inserting the **source** and **target** disks into the disk drives, you will lose **all** the data on the source disk.

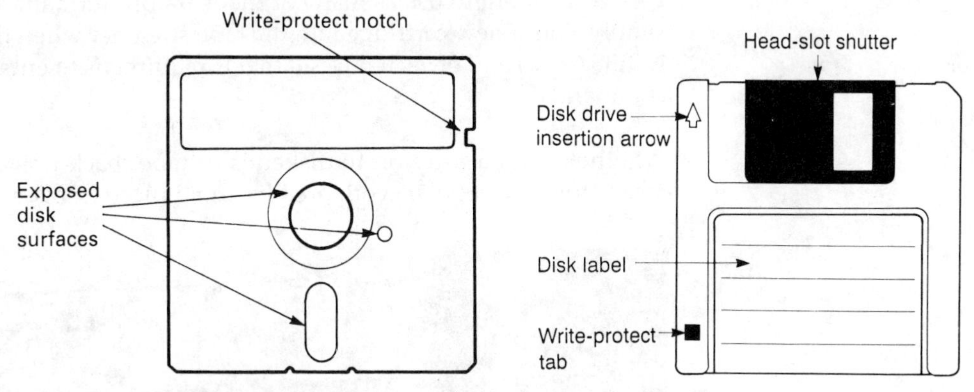

Fig 8.2
$5\frac{1}{4}$ in disk showing write-protect notch, and $3\frac{1}{2}$ in diskette showing write-protect window

Backing up a disk directory using the DOS BACKUP command

The **BACKUP** command is generally used to back-up files from the hard disk onto diskettes or tape at the end of each working day. Obviously, it is not necessary to back-up the entire hard disk every day, as this would take some time and use a number of diskettes, even though the **Backup command** compresses the files as it copies them. When the first diskette is full, you are instructed to insert diskette number 02, and so on. Since duplicates will already have been made of all application program disks, it is really only **work directories** that need to be backed up. For example, if your document files were stored in the directory *C:\WP51\DOCS* and you wanted to back-up all the files in that directory on to diskettes, you would simply enter:

C:\> **BACKUP C:\WP51\DOCS A:** and press **Enter**.

You would be instructed to place diskette 01 into drive A and, at the same time, receive a warning that any existing files in the **target drive** (drive A) would be erased. After the diskette has been inserted and the **Enter** key pressed, the back-up process would begin. The whole of the **DOCS directory** will be backed up onto diskettes. Even this is unnecessary and time-consuming on a daily basis. You really need only **append** (add) those files which were created or revised during that particular day. DOS has a way to do this. Key in the command as before, but add **/A** to the end of it. This instructs the system *not* to erase the existing back-up files on the disk (ie those from previous back-ups) but only to *add* any new or revised files. For example:

C:\> **BACKUP C:\WP51\DOCS A: /A** and press **Enter**.

Backing up a disk directory on to magnetic tape

In many offices, computer hard disks are backed up at the end of the day on to magnetic tape in the form of a **data cartridge**, which is inserted into a **tape streamer** (*see* Fig 8.3). This is a stand-alone drive unit, which can store enough data to fill 180 disks in 15 minutes. Data cartridges are very convenient to use as many of them are pre-formatted. The operator simply slots a new cartridge into the tape streamer when the existing one is full. At the end of each day, all that is required is to enter the BACKUP command.

Whether you back-up on to diskettes or tape, back-ups should be kept away from the regular work area in a safe place or even stored off-site.

Fig 8.3
A tape streamer

Storing off-line (archiving)

In legal offices, banks, building societies, insurance companies, hospitals, etc, the necessity to store files for many years has always presented problems, mainly of space. With computerisation, these organisations can use either cheap magnetic tape or a digital optical recording disk (DOR) to store these inactive files. The tapes and DOR disks on which such files are stored do not require to be under the direct control of the CPU. This is known as **off-line** storage. All discrete (separate) storage media such as disks (even floppy disks) and tape, which are removed from the system and stored somewhere else — on a shelf, in a storage cabinet or in a library perhaps — can be said to be stored 'off-line'. (Disks, tape, etc under the direct control of the central processor would be termed **on-line storage**). If well indexed, magnetic tape and disks stored off-line can be loaded on to the system with little trouble when required. DOR is seen as a viable alternative to magnetic tape for off-line storage. Unlike tape, DOR offers fast random access to stored information and vast storage capacity — one disk stores about 500 000 A4 pages. DOR is not limited to characters; images, too, can be scanned. Information of all types can therefore be stored, including pictorial information. Hospitals could, for example, store X-rays and patient data together.

Another term for off-line storage is **archive**. Archiving is carried out frequently in some organisations to make room for new input and to keep the system running efficiently. In such cases documents/files which are not in continuous use will be transferred to DOR, tape or other media and stored off-line. If the system is overloaded, the time required to retrieve and/or process data or text (**response time**) will be increased. Archiving is frequently necessary when using hard disks. As you will recall, these disks are fixed and not interchangeable. Even though the storage capacity of some of these disks can be greater than 200 Mbytes, purging and archiving will have to take place regularly in order to provide space for future input, if for no other reason.

Data protection

Data is the most valuable part of any computer system. That is why it is imperative to **back-up** your disks. Should, for any reason, some or all of your data on the hard disk be destroyed, you will be able to use the **DOS RESTORE command** and your back-up disks to replace the lost data. However, prevention is better than cure. Here are some suggestions to protect your computer system and prevent loss of data:

1 **Restrict access to hardware by:**
   - **a** locking the room(s) in which computer systems are kept whenever they are unattended
   - **b** locking the systems when not in use and storing the keys safely
   - **c** providing secure, fire-proof storage for diskettes and tapes

2 **Restrict access to software and data files by:**
 a using passwords to get into the system
 b using password protection on valuable data files
 c changing passwords from time to time
 d keeping passwords confidential

Computer systems also have to be protected against **virus infection**. A computer virus is a bug which spreads through the system and corrupts the data. It is usually 'injected' into the computer by the use of unauthorised software and diskettes. There are anti-virus programs now available to assist in *finding* and *removing* a virus (this is no easy task without such a program). These programs also have a facility to *check for viruses* and to *inoculate* against certain viruses. It is really only when a company experiences a virus attack that the extent of the damage that can be done is fully realised. Clearly, companies should ban unauthorised software from their premises.

Last but not least, on the subject of **data protection**, users should be encouraged to accept responsibility to protect, as much as is possible, their computers and data.

The Data Protection Act 1984

The Act is based on eight main principles. Data users (those who control the content and use of personal data) have to abide by all eight principles, but computer bureaux are only affected by the last principle.

1 Data shall be obtained fairly and lawfully.
2 Data shall only be held for specified purposes.
3 Data shall not be used in a manner incompatible with those purposes.
4 Data shall be adequate, relevant and not excessive to the purposes.
5 Personal data shall be accurate and kept up to date.
6 Data shall not be kept longer than necessary.
7 Individuals shall be entitled to have access to their data and, where appropriate, to have it corrected or erased.
8 Appropriate security measures shall be taken against unauthorised access to, or alteration, disclosure or destruction of, personal data.

It should be noted that the Act does not cover all information held on computers, but only **personal data**. This is data which relates to a living individual who can be identified from the data, eg name, phone number, National Insurance number.

UNIT 30 Care of materials and equipment

Computers are not fragile and have been designed for extensive use by experts and learners alike. Pressing the wrong key or inserting the wrong

Fig 8.4
Keep objects away from the system

disk will not damage the system. However, there are certain areas where special care is needed in order to provide trouble-free performance.

General care of the system

Nothing should be placed on the system at any time. It should be kept free of books, files, bags and other objects (*see* Fig 8.4). Food, drink and other liquids should be kept away from the system. This also applies to cigarettes, etc.

Disk drives

As with any high-precision electronic equipment, disk drives must be treated carefully. If the CPU, which houses the disk drives, has to be moved, it should be done with great care. It should not be moved if the system is switched on, neither should it be pushed or jolted, as the disk and/or the drive **read/write head** could be damaged. The head's function is to read information from the disk and write information to the disk. It normally floats a minute distance above the surface of the disk. If moved, it is possible for the head and disk to crash.

To avoid damaging the diskette drives, nothing must be inserted (apart from disks) into the diskette drive slots. Care must be taken not to force or jam disks into the slots.

Floppy disks

Although diskettes are made of durable material, they can be easily damaged if not properly cared for. Valuable information can be lost and hours of work wasted. To prevent loss or damage to disk contents, take the following precautions.

The magnetic material has a sealed protective jacket. This jacket must *not* be removed. It provides support for the disk and also protects it from dirt, dust and handling. In addition, the jacket has a special liner which continually cleans the disk surface and prevents static build-up, which makes particles stick to the disk.

Never touch the exposed recording surfaces or leave them unprotected. These are the areas of magnetic material which show through the jacket, ie the centre ring and the oblong cut-out beneath it on the $5\frac{1}{4}$ in diskette (*see* Fig 8.2). On good-quality disks, the centre ring is reinforced to protect it from warping or denting. If the centre ring is damaged, the disk will spin unevenly and the read/write head will not be able to keep track of it to read the data. The head reads and writes through the oblong slot. The small hole to the right of the centre ring is an index hole which generally indicates the start of the recording areas. Touching any of these exposed surfaces will transfer the natural oils from your fingers to the diskette. The $5\frac{1}{4}$ in diskettes should always remain in their storage envelopes (*see* Fig 8.2) whenever they are not actually in the drive.

It is not advisable to store disks in the cardboard boxes in which they are received from the supplier. If something heavy is placed on the box, the disks will not be protected. These boxes are also a tight fit and disks can be damaged when being removed from or returned to the box. Some manufacturers supply their disks in rigid plastic boxes which, when open, allow easy access to the disks. When closed, these boxes act as a strong 'library case' in which the disks can be stored in an upright position (*see* Fig 8.1). If data protection is needed, lockable storage boxes can be purchased for disks of different sizes (*see* Fig 8.1).

Although these are called floppy disks, they must *not* be bent. The name is somewhat misleading, but it refers to the thin, floppy plastic material from which the diskette is made. These disks are not intended to be bent, that is why they are supported in rigid jackets.

No magnetic object should come in contact with the disk, or even be placed in close proximity, such as a telephone. Examples of other magnetic objects would be paperclips, scissors, etc. Most metal objects can become magnetised, and magnets can erase the data/text stored on the disk.

Disks should also be kept away from radiators and other sources of heat or sunlight.

Disks should be properly labelled, but the labels should preferably be written out *before* being attached to the disk. If it is necessary to write on a label already on a disk, use a *felt-tip pen* not a pencil or a biro, which can damage the disk.

If you plan to keep a hard copy of the disk directory with the disk, do not attach it to the disk itself with a staple or paperclip, as this too will cause damage.

Insert disks gently and carefully into the disk drives (*see* Fig 5.2). Generally the system should be switched on before you insert a disk into a disk drive. On some systems, however, it is necessary to insert the disk first and *then* to switch on. Check the procedure to follow when using a new system. Remove disks from the disk drives before you switch the system off. There is a surge of power through the drives at such times that can cause damage.

Do not remove a disk from a drive when its in-use light is on.

Clean the heads of the floppy disk drives regularly with a proprietary head cleaning kit.

Visual display unit

Screens and keyboards collect dust and finger marks and need to be cleaned frequently by the operator. Special 'wipes' are available for the job.

Printers

Many of today's printers offer a variety of features and are capable of producing professional-quality output. As a result, the operating panel on some printers can appear to be quite daunting to a new user who does not know which touch-sensitive key to press or the meaning of the message, prompt or code which appears in the **display panel**. However, manufacturers do supply **operating manuals** and frequently include a detailed **operating panel display chart** (*see* Fig 8.5). A little time spent getting to know your printer will be well rewarded. Users who understand the various printer controls will be able to achieve the desired print results. An important point: users who know how to operate the equipment are also less likely to damage it. To ensure optimum performance from printers and users, the following should be displayed near the printer.

1 clear step-by-step **operating instructions**
2 a detailed **operating panel chart**
3 the printer **operating manual**
4 a list of **messages, prompts and codes and their meanings**

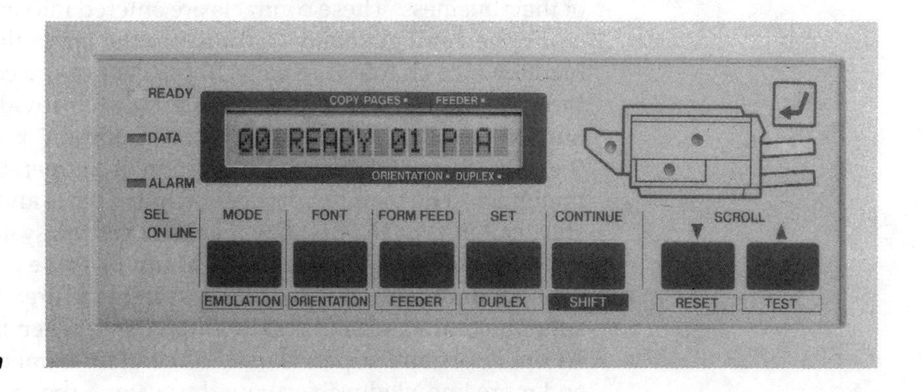

Fig 8.5
The operating panel of a laser printer

A **laser printer** will generally provide trouble-free operation. All you have to do is:

1 give it the correct print instructions
2 keep the paper tray(s) filled with paper of the correct weight and size
3 change the toner cartridge when indicated

Dot matrix forms tractor (paper feed)

If continuous paper is used, care must be taken to ensure that the paper is not under tension. The paper must be carefully fitted so that the holes at the side of the paper fit exactly over the pins and are accurately aligned. When printing stops, paper must not be ripped out of the printer. This is often the cause of problems. The majority of printers have an automatic paper feed (forward or backward) and this of course should be used to remove a printout. In its absence there is always the platen knob.

If fanfolded paper is used, the paper stack behind the printer must be straight, otherwise the paper will shift on the platen and eventually get churned up in the printer.

Print wheels

Print wheels have a limited life and will need to be changed periodically. Changing is a simple operation, but care is required.

New print wheels or those still required for use must be kept in their plastic cases for protection.

Ribbons

If one-time or single-strike carbon ribbons are always used, the cost of these alone per annum could be high. On average about 150 pages of print can be obtained from one carbon ribbon. Bulk purchase could reduce the cost, but proper storage and the risk of deterioration must be considered and offset against any saving. Carbon ribbon itself is very flimsy and likely to snap, so it must be handled carefully. It is, however, protected in a cartridge which snaps easily into place when changing ribbons.

Maintenance of equipment

Maintenance of computer systems is usually carried out by the suppliers of the equipment. Maintenance contracts are, in fact, a substantial part of their business. These contracts are entered into immediately the system is supplied and generally continue for the life of the system. The annual maintenance charge is usually 10 per cent of the cost of the system. For this the supplier will probably undertake to provide a fairly prompt call-out service. This is, of course, very important as it is essential to keep the period during which the system is inoperable (**down time**) to a minimum. The maintenance fee includes parts and labour. Understandably, call-outs in the first few months after the system has been installed will probably be quite frequent. Many of these calls, however, will be for help and support rather than system failure. Therefore, a technical support contract should also be entered into when the system is installed. As operators and supervisors become more familiar with the equipment and more knowledgeable about the system, they will be able to do a little simple 'troubleshooting' themselves, before calling for support or maintenance.

Problem solving or troubleshooting

The majority of operator manuals will have at the back a summary of error codes and error messages. It is useful to read through these a couple of times so that if any of the messages appear on the screen you will at least know where to look for further information or clarification of the fault. Some user manuals will go so far as to give details of recovery procedure. It is also useful when you get an error message to think about what you did just prior to the appearance of the message. Do not touch the keyboard in panic but think clearly and consult the summary of error messages. *If you enter blind commands you may not be able to recover your file.*

Failure checklist

The following is a general checklist should various parts of a computer system fail to operate:

Problem symptom	*Checklist*
Nothing works	Check power cord and plug for proper connection Check cables Check switches are 'on' Check fuses (technician) Check power source by plugging in another electrical device
Printer does not work	Check power connections Check fuse (technician) Check all settings and switches Check position of the paper support Try the printer in 'local'
Display does not appear	Check the VDU connector
Display freezes and the computer does not respond to commands	Check the keyboard connector Type Control C (Alt C) Press the reset button
Drive in use light does not light up	Check that there is a disk in the drive Remove the disk and insert it again Remove the disk and try another disk
System behaves strangely	Check back on operator commands Check system disk on another system and replace if necessary Press reset button Remove disks, switch off and start again

When confronted with a failure in the system, you should go through the appropriate checklist systematically before calling for external maintenance. Checking only takes a few minutes and the fault could be rectified. Sending for maintenance without a pre-check could mean that the system is unnecessarily inoperative for several hours at least. However, do not attempt to service the system yourself, and resist the temptation to 'tinker'. Keep a detailed maintenance record and also the phone numbers of the maintenance company and other assistance available, such as company technicians. During training, report the fault to your trainer. Make a point also of consulting equipment and operating manuals.

UNIT 31 Equipment environment

The environment of computer equipment is important to the efficiency of the system. There are many factors such as temperature, humidity and dust which affect not only people but also machines. In this unit we will discuss the environmental needs of computer equipment.

Location

The area or areas chosen for the siting of the equipment should be large enough to provide for the equipment to be adequately spaced out. There should be sufficient room on the desks for the components to be at least 6 in from the wall to allow for sufficient ventilation. Closer placement to the wall or a solid object can cause overheating. The desk space should also be large enough to accommodate work files, operator manuals, disks, etc required during operation of the equipment. Shortage of space will encourage operators to place objects on the equipment which, as noted earlier, they should not do.

Systems are known to grow and enough room should be allowed for expansion.

Space should be available in or adjacent to the location for supplies. Blank disks, print wheels, ribbons, printer paper, system and application program disks, all documentation and user manuals should be neatly stored close at hand. This will improve efficiency and encourage operators to return materials, disks and manuals no longer required to where they belong.

Temperature

Temperature and humidity should conform to the equipment manufacturer's recommendations. The equipment itself generates heat, and if there are several workstations in one room, the heat buildup from equipment will be considerable.

Seasonal changes need to be considered. Extreme cold or extreme heat will badly affect hard or fixed disks. These should not be subjected to rapid temperature changes.

Floppy disks, magnetic tapes and carbon ribbons can also be damaged if exposed to heat, cold or damp.

From the above it is clear that the equipment and supplies are sensitive to temperature and humidity. Therefore, to prevent the development of problems, an acceptable even temperature should be maintained at all times. This applies also at weekends and through holiday periods. Additionally, while avoiding draughts there should be a good circulation of clean air.

Power supply

Computers require an even power supply. Other equipment should not be plugged into the same outlets. It goes without saying that there should be a sufficient number of outlets, placed in such a way as to avoid trailing cables. A data/word processing centre should be designed so that the power is supplied unobtrusively where needed. In a local area network configuration, thought must be given to the arrangement of the equipment so that the shared components, while accessible to all workstations, are not sited in such a way as to be a nuisance or danger. Provision should be made for the cable linking the equipment to be neatly channelled from one to the other. If the equipment is placed against a wall, a sufficient gap can be left between the work surface and the wall for the cables to drop behind the equipment to plug into the wall sockets. A platform floor in the computer room is another way of coping with the proliferation of wires and cables required to run a computer system. Wiring can then be linked to each workstation from the appropriate point beneath the platform.

Furnishings

Furnishings and carpets should be of antistatic materials. Most office carpets are nylon or part nylon. This material cleans easily and wears well. It also causes static charges in equipment. It is possible to have such material treated, but the treatment must be carried out regularly, usually on a monthly basis. This is costly and also something of a nuisance. A wool carpet in the first place would be a better purchase. Cork tiles are also perfectly satisfactory for flooring, although a tiled floor might not look quite so comfortable. Consideration should be given, too, to furnishings such as seating and drapes or curtains.

Other considerations

No telephone should be close to the work area. A phone ringing on top of a disk or disk drive can erase the contents of the disk.

Disks must be stored in non-metallic cases.

Work surfaces must also be of non-metallic material.

Summary — Key Points

1 Files stored on disk should be given the same attention as files stored manually in an organised office.
2 Each file should be appropriately named for easy identification and retrieval.
3 When using a two-diskette system, store all the files you create on work diskettes; not on the program diskette.
4 Work diskettes should be labelled, dated and numbered, and then filed in sturdy disk boxes.
5 When using a hard disk system, save your work files in a subdirectory created expressly for your work.
6 Regular purging and archiving is necessary to ensure that the system is not overloaded and to keep it running efficiently.
7 Backing up files is the first step in data security. Some companies back up everything that has been processed.
8 Back-up copies must be made of system disks, application program disks and disks on which standard letters, paragraphs, forms, customer files and other records have been stored.
9 Data is the most valuable part of any computer system. Data can be protected by restricting access to hardware and software.
10 The Data Protection Act 1984 is based on eight main principles and data users have to abide by all eight principles.
11 Food, all liquids and smoking should not be allowed near a computer system.
12 Diskettes must be handled with care and monitors and keyboards cleaned regularly.
13 When confronted with a failure in the system, operators should systematically go through an appropriate checklist before calling maintenance.
14 Environmental considerations for the siting of a computer system include location, temperature and humidity, power supply, furnishings of antistatic materials and non-metallic furniture.
15 Computer supplies should be stored close to the system and instructions for operating the equipment should be clearly displayed on or near the appropriate hardware.

Knowledge Check on Section 8

Keywords (try to explain the meaning of these terms in your own words).

Append	DOR	Read-write head
Archive	Off-line storage	Response time
Back-up	On-line storage	Tape streamer
Computer virus	Personal data	Work disk
Data cartridge	Purge	Write-protect

Complete each of the following items and then check your responses either with your tutor or with the answers on page 152.

1 Match each term in the first column with its meaning from the second column:

____	*1* Write-protect your source disk	*a* So that the copies can be used and the originals can be stored away safely.
____	2 Back-up system and program disks	*b* So that the program disk is kept free of additional files.
____	3 Save your work on work disks	*c* So that all is not lost if you inadvertently place the diskettes in the wrong drive.

2 Label the following statements true or false:

a ____ Disks under the direct control of the central processor (ie those in use for the storage of documents being processed) are providing off-line storage.

b ____ The computer unit should not be moved, pushed or jolted when the system is switched on.

c ____ A popular means of backing up a hard disk is to use a data cartridge in a tape streamer.

3 Tick one or more of the following as appropriate:

a To protect data, restrict access to hardware by:

1 locking the computer room(s) when unattended

2 locking the systems when not in use

3 providing secure, fireproof storage for diskettes and tapes

b List the steps to be taken to restrict access to software and data files:

1 ______________________________

2 ______________________________

3 ______________________________

4 ______________________________

4 Fill in the blanks:

a A computer virus is usually injected into the system by the use of ____ ____ and diskettes.

b Computers require an ____ power supply.

c Computer equipment and supplies are sensitive to ____ and ____.

Answers

1 *1c* *2a* *3b*
2 **a**F **b**T **c**T
3 **a** *1*, *2* and *3* are appropriate.
b Use passwords to get into the system; use password protection on valuable data files; change passwords from time to time; keep passwords confidential (in any order).
4 **a** unauthorised software **b** even **c** temperature, humidity.

Additional questions on Section 8

1 What do you consider to be the essential elements of good file management when storing documents and files electronically? Answer fully.
2 Discuss the merits of backing up everything on disk as opposed to selective backing up.
3 The environment of computer equipment is important to the efficiency of the system. Discuss the factors to be considered.
4 What security measures should a data user or computer bureau take in order to comply with the eighth data protection principle?

Assignment 8

a Label your work disk with your name.
Take a printout of the directory of your work disk.
Add the date (if this is not already on the directory printout) and your name.
Write the same identity details on the diskette envelope.
Insert the labelled diskette and directory printout in the disk envelope.
b Delete all unwanted files from your work disk.
Take a printout of the disk directory (noting date and identity on it).
Discard the previous directory printout and keep the latest one for reference.

9 The people factor

We have considered the environmental needs of the equipment in order to keep the system functioning efficiently. It must be remembered, however, that people are needed to operate computer systems and therefore they too must be considered.

Frequently, people are expected to adapt their bodies, their work habits and their needs to fit in with the equipment they operate. While equipment has to be designed to carry out specific functions effectively, the comfort and ease with which operators can perform their part deserves some thought, if only in the interests of overall efficiency. An operator who is comfortable will work much better than one who is uncomfortable. Fortunately, in recent years there has been an increased awareness of this fact. Manufacturers are now keenly interested in designing electronic office equipment and furniture to suit the needs of the human body. The study of fitting the equipment to the operator, with emphasis on safety, comfort and efficiency, is known as **ergonomics**. In this section the environmental needs of those who operate computer systems will be highlighted and we will examine how ergonomics has affected the design of computer equipment and furniture. We will also consider the effects of information technology on office jobs.

UNIT 32 People environment

Temperature

Some of the factors which affect computers are also important to human comfort, such as temperature, humidity and draught-free ventilation. As VDU operators spend most of their time seated at the equipment, a temperature slightly higher than that in a normal working environment is required. On the other hand, the equipment itself generates heat and careful calculations will therefore have to be made in order to achieve the right balance. There are also other factors which affect personal comfort and which need to be considered in the general design of computer work areas.

Location

While there is a need for the location of the system to be readily accessible to users, it should not be in the middle of a traffic flow. This would be very distracting to operators. The site selected should be quiet and roomy.

Personal space should be large enough to provide comfort and privacy.

Acoustics

Nobody likes to work in a persistently noisy environment, and computer installations can be noisy — from the hum of the system to the clatter of impact printers. Acoustic hoods fitted to printers greatly reduce the noise level, and sound absorbent materials should be used for floors, walls and ceilings. For example, floors can be covered with cork tiles or wool carpet (both antistatic materials), and acoustic tiles can be used on ceilings.

Acoustic screens not only cut down the noise but also provide privacy.

Lighting

Proper lighting is essential when working with screen-based systems. Most offices are too brightly lit for the comfort of VDU operators, whose eyes are subjected to screen brightness and glare. 'Glare' is unwanted and unpleasant light. Soft, diffused and indirect lighting should be used in computer areas and all possible sources of flicker should be removed.

Windows should be fitted with blinds to eliminate bright sunlight.

General

Colour plays an important part in a computer environment. Natural shades of grey, brown, honey or beige are considered restful on the eyes, while white is a source of glare and should be avoided.

An arrangement of pictures, plants or flowers on which operators can focus from time to time provides relief from staring at the screen and is beneficial and restful for the eyes.

Furniture in the work area, such as desks, cabinets, etc, should have non-reflective surfaces to reduce glare.

Work surfaces or desks should be large enough to accommodate the workstation and allow sufficient space on the left and right of the terminal so that files, books or copy holders can be used on either side, according to personal preference.

Drawers, shelves or cupboards should be provided for user manuals, files, office supplies and personal belongings.

UNIT 33 Ergonomics

The majority of screen-based computer systems are now claimed to be ergonomically designed, with emphasis on the keyboard and screen as these are the components in constant use by operators.

Keyboard

Traditionally, typewriter keyboards were made with a fairly steep slope. Typists were taught to keep wrists raised and fingers bent in order to accommodate the slope of the keyboard and to produce the required amount of force with which to strike the keys. Ergonomically designed electronic keyboards now slope up very gently and only slightly at about 5° so that the operator's wrists can rest on the desk. Some computer keyboards even have an extended front piece on which to rest the wrists when inputting data. Not having to raise the wrists or kink them upwards enables the operator to relax the wrists and comfortably input at his/her optimum speed. Because of the very slight and gentle slope, key reaching presents no problem. Fingers too can be relaxed as very little striking force is required on an electronic keyboard. It is helpful to the operator if all keys have a built-in 'click' so that each key depression can be both felt and heard. Keys are generally sunken in the middle (**concaved**) to prevent fingers from slipping off.

Much thought has also been given to the layout of computer keyboards. **QWERTY** keys are positioned in the centre so that fingers can rest comfortably on and return naturally to the 'home keys'. Additional keys are grouped according to their function for the convenience of the operator. Many systems have an extra set of figure keys, grouped in rows like a calculator on the right of the keyboard, called a **numeric pad**. This is helpful if the workload includes a lot of figure entry, although it does not take account of anyone who is left-handed. The majority of keyboards are detached and connected to the system only by a coiled cable. This allows the operator to place the keyboard in the most comfortable and convenient position. It is recommended that the height of the keyboard should be such that the forearms are in a horizontal position (*see* Fig 9.1). This is lower than the normal writing level.

Screen

A screen size of between 12 in and 14 in is considered to be suitable for a 25-line 80-column display, where the distance between the screen and the operator is between $1\frac{1}{2}$ ft and 2 ft. The recommended character size is 6 mm ($\frac{1}{4}$ in). The characters on the screen are made up of dots and the number of dots in a given area, eg a centimetre, is called the **dot matrix**. The more dots in a dot matrix the clearer the character or picture.

Dark grey is usual as the screen background colour on **monochrome**

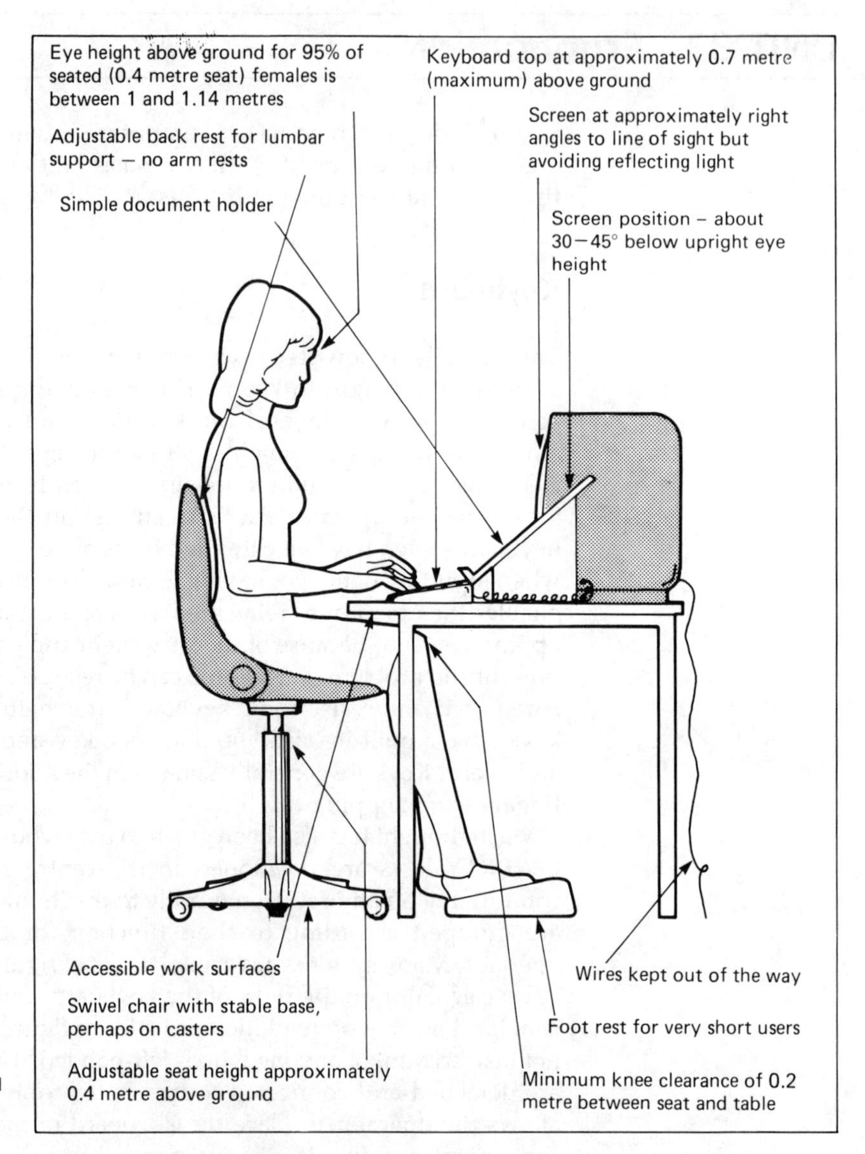

Fig 9.1
Good workstation principles
(taken from Association of Professional, Executive, Clerical and Computer Staff (APEX) Report of Office Technology Working Party)

(single-colour) monitors, with the foreground (character) colour often green or amber. Some manufacturers provide a white screen with black characters. This is believed to be easier on the operator's eyes when transferring the gaze from the source document to the screen and vice versa. However, **colour monitors** are becoming the norm. Colour is well-supported by application software, which permits users to change both background and foreground colour to suit their personal preference. This means that you can set the screen to display colours that you feel comfortable with. Selection can be made from a wide variety of both background and foreground colours.

VDUs are fitted with a brightness control, and brightness should be adjusted to take account of the level of lighting in the computer location.

One of the major causes of discomfort when working with a screen-based system is glare. Screens can be either reflective or non-reflective. Non-reflective (or antiglare) screens are now common and filters are available for screens that are reflective.

A good design feature is a swivel base. The screen can then be turned slightly to avoid glare. This facility is useful, too, if the operator changes position. Most VDUs can also be tilted up or down to avoid glare and provide for viewing at a comfortable angle to suit the operator. Ideally, the VDU should be on a level lower than the operator's eyes and should be tilted upwards. Looking up at the screen is tiring and can also result in aching shoulders and neck muscles.

Problems may arise from switching the eyes from the screen to the source material. Many types of document holders which improve source/ screen relationship are now available (*see* Fig 9.1).

Systems furniture

Most of the leading office furniture manufacturers have designed a range of furniture to accommodate computer equipment and users. Such ranges are referred to as **systems furniture** and are designed to be both functional and comfortable and also to facilitate new methods of working. Much thought has gone into the design of two items in particular, both of which are of great importance to the VDU operator — the desk unit and the chair.

Desk unit

Many desk units in the systems furniture range are free-standing and include built-in wiring for the full computer system (*see* Fig 9.2). This avoids trailing wires across work surfaces and around the operator's feet. Some ergonomically-designed desk units have extendable worktops with sections that slide out from the main body of the desk as required. Some units allow the keyboard to be positioned lower than the normal writing level. Other units are designed with split-level work surfaces for greater operating comfort (*see* Fig 9.3). As desk height is not generally adjustable, footrests should be provided for short users (*see* Fig 9.1).

Chairs

On the other hand, chairs for VDU operators have adjustable seat heights. The height of the chair seat can therefore be adjusted so that the user is in a comfortable position for operating the equipment. Some chairs are fitted with a footrest for short operators whose feet have to be raised above the floor level. Ergonomically designed chairs have a firm and fairly wide contoured seat, and a backrest that gives support to the lumbar region. A good backrest helps to relax the back, particularly when tasks require long periods of sitting down as is usual with computer operation. An excellent feature of many chairs is that both seat and back adjustments can be easily activated by the touch of a lever while the operator remains seated. Chairs are covered in materials of various textures and colours. Plastic should be avoided as it can be uncomfortable to sit on for any length of time.

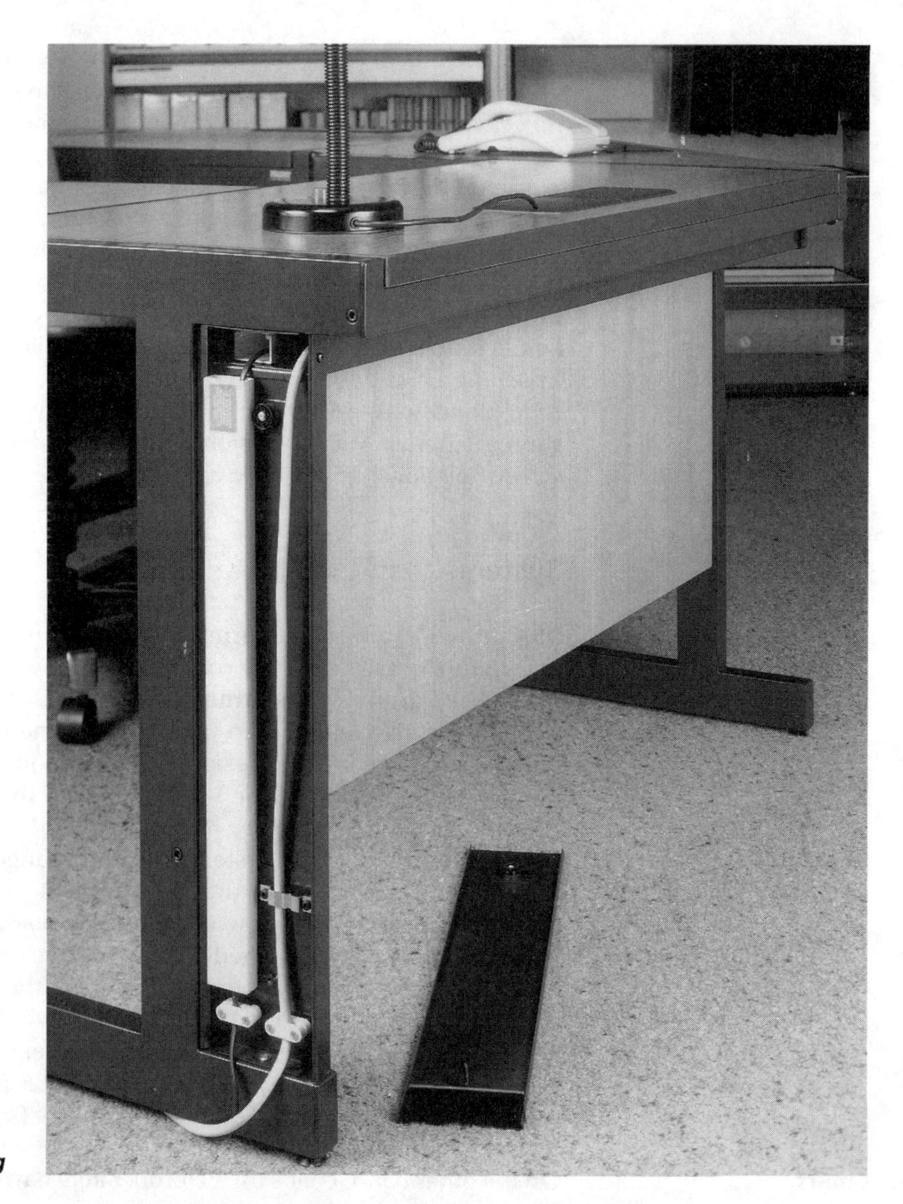

Fig 9.2
Example of built-in wiring

UNIT 34 Health and safety

Safety

Safety regulations established by the Health and Safety at Work Act 1974 apply to the work environment and use of all new office equipment, although this Act was not drafted with reference to computer technology.

Fig 9.3
Example of a split-level work surface

Common safety requirements relating to the handling of electrical and other equipment, maintenance, electrical wiring and power supply, etc, should of course be strictly adhered to. Any additional advice on safety given by the manufacturers with regard to the equipment should also be followed.

Health

VDU operators have so far complained mainly of fatigue, eye-strain and headaches. The causes of these complaints are not yet known for certain. However, it is thought that with proper training, well-planned work schedules and careful design of workstation furniture and the environment, such effects can be minimised. It is also suggested that, because of possible screen flicker and dot instability, those who suffer from epilepsy, migraine and nervous disorders should limit the time spent at the VDU.

Trade unions

Trade unions in several countries are researching the effects of computer technology on office workers. While it is their intention to continue to monitor the health, safety and environmental requirements of their members, various recommendations have already been made. The extract below is a checklist for health and safety considerations in regard to new technology. (What to look for when inspecting a screen-based system.) This is taken from the APEX publication *New Technology — Health & Safety Guidelines*.

Checklist for Health and Safety of New Technology. What to look for when inspecting a screen-based system. Tick Yes/No against this list.

	Yes	No
SCREEN		
Is the screen large enough?	□	□
Is the image stable and flicker free?	□	□
Is the image sharp and easy to read?	□	□
Is the contrast between the image and the background satisfactory?	□	□
Are there too many colours?	□	□
Are the words/numbers/graphs clearly set out?	□	□
WORKING ENVIRONMENT		
Are the chairs comfortable?	□	□
If NO — is the seat height easily adjustable?	□	□
Is the seat surface padded?	□	□
Is the height of the backrest adjustable?	□	□
Can the backrest be adjusted forwards and backwards?	□	□
Are the users clearly told how to adjust the chair?	□	□
Do you have sufficient leg room?	□	□
If NO — can the height of the terminal desk/table be adjusted?	□	□
Is there excessive glare in the work area?	□	□
If YES — are there reflections from windows?	□	□
Is the terminal facing a window?	□	□
Is the desk/table top too shiny?	□	□
Are the lights too strong?	□	□
Is the keyboard too shiny?	□	□
Is the noise level louder than you would wish?	□	□
If YES — is it persistent/continuous?	□	□
or is it intermittent and irritating?	□	□
Are printers fitted with hoods/covers?	□	□
Are printers in the same area as the terminals?	□	□

	Yes	No
Is the information on the screen too cluttered?	□	□
If YES — are the characters too small?	□	□
Are the characters too close together on the line?	□	□
Is it hard to distinguish between words?	□	□
Is there a clear space beween lines?	□	□
Is the central computer too noisy?	□	□
Do any users of the equipment complain of sore or tired eyes, headaches, backaches?	□	□
If YES — did they have an eyesight test before using the equipment?	□	□
Have they had an eye test since?	□	□
Do they wear contact lenses?	□	□
Do they wear bifocal spectacles?	□	□
Are source documents clear and legible?	□	□
Are these placed on a document holder?	□	□
Are any chemicals used in preparing output/printing?	□	□
If YES — which chemicals are used?	□	□
Are any recommendations given for their safe use?	□	□
Are they liable to give off unpleasant/harmful fumes?	□	□
Are they a fire hazard?	□	□
KEYBOARD		
Is the keyboard detachable from the terminal?	□	□
Can the keys be easily found?	□	□
Are they set out as on a typewriter?	□	□
Is there adequate space between keys?	□	□
Can you feel or hear feedback from the keys?	□	□
Do you have to use excessive pressure on them?	□	□
Are the keytop surfaces concave?	□	□

Legislation

It is difficult for health and safety legislation to keep pace with changing technology. It takes employers and employees some time to recognise possible health hazards in new equipment. This is particularly so as some health hazards may only become apparent after long-term exposure. It takes even longer for legislation and government regulations to catch up.

On 29 May 1990, the European Communities issued the following Council Directive to all Member States on the minimum safety and health requirements for work with display screen equipment. Member States must comply with this Directive by 31 December 1992.

The relevant provisions of the Health and Safety at Work Act 1974 are shown on page 166. The main provisions of the Offices, Shops and Railway Premises Act 1963 are shown on page 169.

EUROPEAN COMMUNITIES COUNCIL DIRECTIVE

of 29 May 1990

on the minimum health and safety requirements for work with display screen equipment (fifth individual Directive within the meaning of Article 16(1) of Directive 87/391/EEC)

SECTION I
GENERAL PROVISIONS

Article 1
Subject

1 This Directive, which is the fifth individual Directive within the meaning of Article 16(1) of Directive 89/391/EEC, lays down minimum safety and health requirements for work with display screen equipment as defined in Article 2.
2 The provisions of Directive 89/391/EEC are fully applicable to the whole field referred to in paragraph 1, without prejudice to more stringent and/or specific provisions contained in the present Directive.
3 This Directive shall not apply to:

(a) drivers' cabs or control cabs for vehicles or machinery;
(b) computer systems on board a means of transport;
(c) computer systems mainly intended for public use;
(d) 'portable' systems not in prolonged use at a workstation;
(e) calculators, cash registers and any equipment having a small data or measurement display required for direct use of the equipment;
(f) typewriters of traditional design, of the type known as 'typewriter with window'.

Article 2

Definitions

For the purpose of this Directive, the following terms shall have the following meanings:

(a) *display screen equipment:* an alphanumeric or graphic display screen, regardless of the display process employed;

(b) *workstation:* an assembly comprising display screen equipment, which may be provided with a keyboard or input device and/or software determining the operator/machine interface, optional accessories, peripherals including the diskette drive, telephone, modem, printer, document holder, work chair and work desk or work surface, and the immediate work environment;
(c) *worker:* any worker as defined in Article 3(a) of Directive 89/391/EEC who habitually uses display screen equipment as a significant part of his normal work.

SECTION II
EMPLOYERS' OBLIGATIONS

Article 3
Analysis of workstations

1 Employers shall be obliged to perform an analysis of workstations in order to evaluate the safety and health conditions to which they give rise for their workers, particularly as regards possible risks to eyesight, physical problems and problems of mental stress.
2 Employers shall take appropriate measures to remedy the risks found, on the basis of the evaluation referred to in paragraph 1, taking account of the additional and/or combined effects of the risks so found.

Article 4
Workstations put into service for the first time

Employers must take the appropriate steps to ensure that workstations first put into service after 31 December 1992 meet the minimum requirements laid down in the Annex.

Article 5
Workstations already put into service

Employers must take the appropriate steps to ensure that workstations already put into service on or before 31 December 1992 are adapted to comply with the minimum requirements laid down in the Annex not later than four years after that date.

Article 6
Information for, and training of, workers

1 Without prejudice to Article 10 of Directive 89/391/EEC, workers shall receive information on all aspects of safety and health relating to their workstation, in particular information on such measures applicable to workstations as are implemented under Articles 3, 7 and 9.

In all cases, workers or their representatives shall be informed of any health and safety measure taken in compliance with this Directive.
2 Without prejudice to Article 12 of Directive 89/391/EEC, every worker shall also receive training in use of the workstation before commencing this type of work and whenever the organization of the workstation is substantially modified.

Article 7
Daily work routine

The employer must plan the worker's activities in such a way that daily work on a display screen is periodically interrupted by breaks or changes of activity reducing the workload at the display screen.

Article 8
Worker consultation and participation

Consultation and participation of workers and/or their representatives shall take place in accordance with Article 11 of Directive 89/391/EEC on the matters covered by this Directive, including its Annex.

Article 9
Protection of workers' eyes and eyesight

1 Workers shall be entitled to an appropriate eye and eyesight test carried out by a person with the necessary capabilities:

— before commencing display screen work,
— at regular intervals thereafter, and
— if they experience visual difficulties which may be due to display screen work.

2 Workers shall be entitled to an ophthalmological examination if the results of the test referred to in paragraph 1 show that this is necessary.
3 If the results of the test referred to in paragraph 1 or of the examination referred to in paragraph 2 show that it is necessary and if normal corrective appliances cannot be used, workers must be provided with special corrective appliances appropriate for the work concerned.
4 Measures taken pursuant to this Article may in no circumstances involve workers in additional financial cost.
5 Protection of workers' eyes and eyesight may be provided as part of a national health system.

SECTION III
MISCELLANEOUS PROVISIONS

Article 10
Adaptations to the Annex

The strictly technical adaptations to the Annex to take account of technical progress, developments in international regulations and specifications and knowledge in the field of display screen equipment shall be adopted in accordance with the procedure laid down in Article 17 of Directive 89/391/EEC.

Article 11
Final provisions

1 Member States shall bring into force the laws, regulations and administrative provisions necessary to comply with this Directive by 31 December 1992.
They shall forthwith inform the Commission thereof.

2 Member States shall communicate to the Commission the texts of the provisions of national law which they adopt, or have already adopted, in the field covered by this Directive.
3 Member States shall report to the Commission every four years on the practical implementation of the provisions of this Directive, indicating the points of view of employers and workers.

The Commission shall inform the European Parliament, the Council, the Economic and Social Committee and the Advisory Committee on Safety, Hygiene and Health Protection at Work.
4 The Commission shall submit a report on the implementation of this Directive at regular intervals to the European Parliament, the Council and the Economic and Social Committee, taking into account paragraphs 1, 2 and 3.

Article 12

This Directive is addressed to the Member States.

Done at Brussels, 29 May 1990.

For the Council
The President
B. AHERN

Annex

MINIMUM REQUIREMENTS
(Articles 4 and 5)

Preliminary remark
The obligations laid down in this Annex shall apply in order to achieve the objectives of this Directive and to the extent that, firstly, the components concerned are present at the workstation and secondly, the inherent requirements or characteristics of the task do not preclude it.

1 EQUIPMENT

(a) *General comment*
The use as such of the equipment must not be a source of risk for workers.

(b) *Display screen*
The characters on the screen shall be well-defined and clearly formed, of adequate size and with adequate spacing between the characters and lines.
The image on the screen should be stable, with no flickering or other forms of instability.
The brightness and/or the contrast between the characters and the background shall be easily adjustable by the operator, and also be easily adjustable to ambient conditions.
The screen must swivel and tilt easily and freely to suit the needs of the operator.
It shall be possible to use a separate base for the screen or an adjustable table.
The screen shall be free of reflective glare and reflections liable to cause discomfort to the user.

(c) *Keyboard*
The keyboard shall be tiltable and separate from the screen so as to allow the worker to find a comfortable working position avoiding fatigue in the arms or hands.
The space in front of the keyboard shall be sufficient to provide support for the hands and arms of the operator.
The keyboard shall have a matt surface to avoid reflective glare.
The arrangement of the keyboard and the characteristics of the keys shall be such as to facilitate the use of the keyboard.
The symbols on the keys shall be adequately contrasted and legible from the design working position.

(d) *Work desk or work surface*
The work desk or work surface shall have a sufficiently large, low-reflectance surface and allow a flexible arrangement of the screen, keyboard, documents and related equipment.
The document holder shall be stable and adjustable and shall be positioned so as to minimize the need for uncomfortable head and eye movements.
There shall be adequate space for workers to find a comfortable position.

(e) *Work chair*
The work chair shall be stable and allow the operator easy freedom of movement and a comfortable position.
The seat shall be adjustable in height.
The seat back shall be adjustable in both height and tilt.
A footrest shall be made available to anyone who wishes for one.

2 ENVIRONMENT

(a) *Space requirements*
The workstation shall be dimensioned and designed so as to provide sufficient space for the user to change position and vary movements.

(b) *Lighting*
Room lighting and/or spot lighting (work lamps) shall ensure satisfactory lighting conditions and an appropriate contrast between the screen and the background environment, taking into account the type of work and the user's vision requirements.
Possible disturbing glare and reflections on the screen or other equipment shall be prevented by coordinating workplace and workstation layout with the positioning and technical characteristics of the artificial light sources.

(c) *Reflections and glare*
Workstations shall be so designed that sources of light, such as windows and other openings, transparent or translucid walls, and brightly coloured fixtures or walls cause no direct glare and, as far as possible, no reflections on the screen.
Windows shall be fitted with a suitable system of adjustable covering to attenuate the daylight that falls on the workstation.

(d) *Noise*
Noise emitted by equipment belonging to workstation(s) shall be taken into account when a workstation is being equipped, in particular so as not to distract attention or disturb speech.

(e) *Heat*
Equipment belonging to workstation(s) shall not produce excess heat which could cause discomfort to workers.

(*f*) *Radiation*
All radiation with the exception of the visible part of the electromagnetic spectrum shall be reduced to negligible levels from the point of view of the protection of workers' safety and health.

(*g*) *Humidity*
An adequate level of humidity shall be established and maintained.

3 OPERATOR/COMPUTER INTERFACE
In designing, selecting, commissioning and modifying software, and in designing tasks using display screen equipment, the employer shall take into account the following principles:

(*a*) software must be suitable for the task;
(*b*) software must be easy to use and, where appropriate, adaptable to the operator's level of knowledge or experience; no quantitative or qualitative checking facility may be used without the knowledge of the workers;
(*c*) systems must provide feedback to workers on their performance;
(*d*) systems must display information in a format and at a pace which are adapted to operators;
(*e*) the principles of software ergonomics must be applied, in particular to human data processing.

Health and Safety at Work Act 1974 (Relevant Provisions)

The purpose of the Health and Safety at Work Act is *to provide the legislative framework* to promote, stimulate and encourage high standards of health and safety at work.

The aim must be to promote safety awareness and effective safety organisation and performance, by schemes designed to suit the particular industry or organisation; and by the accumulation of influences and pressures, operating at many levels, in a variety of ways, and from a number of directions.

Contents of the Act

The Act is an enabling measure superimposed over existing health and safety legislation. The existing duties under, for example, the Offices, Shops and Railway Premises Act remain in force, the main provisions of which, for the time being, continue.

In addition to placing duties of a general character on employers, manufacturers, employees and the self-employed and others, the Act provides a wide regulation-making power.

Scope

All 'persons at work', whether employers, employees or self-employed, will be covered with the exception of domestic servants in a private household. About five million people, such as those employed in education, medicine, leisure industries and in some parts of the transport industry who have not been covered by previous health and safety legislation, are now protected for the first time.

The Act provides for the gradual replacement of existing health and safety requirements by revised and updated provisions, in the form of a system of regulations and approved codes of practice prepared in consultation with industry, so as to create an integrated body of requirements enforced on a common basis. New provisions made in regulations and approved codes of practice must be designed to maintain or improve the health and safety standards established by existing legislation, the objective being not only to rationalise and update the law, but also to improve the standards of protection which it affords to people at work and the public.

Regulations

These will be made by the appropriate minister (usually the Secretary of State for Employment), normally on the basis of proposals submitted by the Health and Safety Commission after consultation with appropriate organisations.

Codes of practice

Where appropriate, regulations will be supplemented by approved codes of practice, which will have a special legal status. They will not be statutory requirements, but they may be used in criminal proceedings, as evidence that statutory requirements have been contravened.

Existing codes of practice and other forms of practical guidance will be discussed with interested bodies before the Commission approves them for use under the Act.

General duties

Most employers and others with duties under this Act will have had responsibilities under previous legislation dealing with the health, safety and welfare of people at work, but some will have been subject to such legislation for the first time.

Much of the earlier legislation is retained, but the method of enforcement is changed and the powers of inspectors are increased. Where new responsibilities are imposed by the Act, these are now in force and they apply universally.

Duties of employers

Employers must safeguard, as far as is reasonably practicable, the health, safety and welfare of the people who work for them. This applies in particular to the provision and maintenance of safe plant and systems of work, and covers all machinery, equipment and appliances used.

Safety policies, organisation and arrangements

There is a statutory requirement for the employer of five or more people to prepare a written statement of his/her general policy, organisation and arrangements for health and safety at work, to keep it up to date by revision and to bring it to the notice of his/her employees.

Safety information and training

It is the duty of employers to provide any necessary information and training in safe practices, including information on legal requirements. Employers will need to consider the specific training needs of their organisations with particular reference to processes with special hazards.

Duties of manufacturers and suppliers

Designers, manufacturers, importers or suppliers of articles or substances for use at work must ensure that, so far as reasonably practicable, they are safe when properly used. They must test articles for safety in use, or arrange for this to be done by a competent authority. They must also supply information about the use for which an article was designed and include any conditions of use regarding its safety.

Anyone who installs or erects any article for use at work must ensure that, so far as reasonably practicable, it does not constitute a risk to health and is safe to use.

Duties of employees

Employees have a duty under the Act to take reasonable care to avoid injury to themselves or to others by their activities, and to co-operate with employers and others in meeting statutory requirements. The Act also requires employees not to interfere with or misuse anything provided to protect their health, safety or welfare in compliance with the Act.

Safety representatives and committees

In order that employers and employees can co-operate in promoting health and safety at work, regulations allow for the appointment of safety representatives and committees. Safety representatives with prescribed functions may be appointed by a trade union from among the employees in a workplace. Any two safety representatives may submit a written request to the employer for a safety committee to be formed.

Enforcement

If an inspector discovers a contravention of one of the provisions of the previous Acts or regulations, or a contravention of a provision of this Act s/he can:

Issue a prohibition notice if there is a risk of serious personal injury, to stop the activity giving rise to this risk, until the remedial action specified in the notice has been taken.

Issue an improvement notice if there is a legal contravention of any of the relevant statutory provisions, to remedy the fault within a specified time.

Prosecute any person contravening a relevant statutory provision — instead of, or in addition to, serving a notice.

Seize, render harmless or destroy any substance or article that s/he considers to be the cause of imminent danger or serious personal injury.

The Health and Safety Commission

The Health and Safety Commission consists of representatives of employers, employees and the local authorities. It takes over the responsibility for developing policies in the health and safety field from government departments.

The Health and Safety Executive

This is a separate statutory body appointed by the Commission which will work in accordance with directions and guidance given by the Commission. The Executive will also enforce legal requirements, as well as provide an advisory service to both sides of industry (employers and employees).

Employment Medical Advisory Service

EMAS will act as the medical arm of the Commission and will be the main channel of medical advice to the Commission and to the Inspectorates within the Executive. It will also be involved in work for which there has been no previous statutory responsibility but which will come within the scope of the Commission and Inspectorates, for example, laboratories and research establishments.

The Offices, Shops and Railway Premises Act 1963 (main provisions)

1. The premises, furniture and fittings must be kept in a reasonably clean condition. Floors, stairs and passages must be safe and kept free from slippery substances and obstructions.
2. The temperature in rooms that are not open to the public should reach at least 16°C (60.8°F) no more than one hour after work starts. Where an outside door is continually open, special means must be provided so that employees can warm themselves.
3. Rooms must be properly ventilated.
4. Lighting must be adequate for safety and to avoid strain.
5. The total space available must be sufficient to allow an average of at least 3.7 m^2 (40 ft^2) for each employee or 11 m^3 (400 ft^3) for each employee where the ceiling is below 3 m (10 ft).
6. Lavatories must be suitable, properly maintained and accessible. Separate facilities must be provided for men and women.
7. Suitable washing facilities must be provided, including hot running water, soap and towels.
8. Fresh drinking water must be available.
9. Where food is eaten on the premises, a suitable room must be provided.
10. Suitable facilities must be provided for keeping clothing not worn by employees during working hours (eg coats).
11. Employees who work sitting down must be provided with suitably designed and constructed seating, including footrests if their feet are off the ground. Where employees normally work standing up, at least one chair must be provided for every three employees and they should be allowed to sit down whenever possible.
12. No employee should be expected to lift or carry loads which are so heavy as to be likely to cause injury.
13. Dangerous parts of machinery must be protected or the machinery must be positioned so that there is no risk of causing injury to employees.
14. First-aid boxes must be provided and a record must be kept of all cases treated. Where more than 150 people are employed, there must be a person qualified to give first-aid available on the premises.
15. If an employee is disabled for more than three days (or dies) as a result of an accident on the premises, a written report must be submitted to the relevant government inspectorate.

UNIT 35 The effects of information technology on office jobs

To assess the effects of information technology in offices, we need to look at the changing role of offices. Offices are no longer just complementary to industry. Many of them are businesses in their own right. They are information industries such as civil service, banking, education, insurance, advertising, radio and television. In nearly all cases these are industries employing large numbers of staff. Because handling information is their actual business, information industries are already large-scale users of information technology. Additionally, the five basic functions of the office — to collect, transfer, verify, convert and distribute information — lend themselves to computerisation. Therefore, the effects of information technology in these offices often mean changes in office structure, working methods and conditions and job content. Consequently, what everyone does in such organisations and how they do it is affected. However, the effects on jobs are not uniform. It depends on the status of the job, the functions performed, the existing procedures and conditions and also the way in which the new technology is introduced. In offices of other industries, computerisation may be limited to data processing or text processing and the jobs of only some people in the organisation are then affected. Jobs most affected by and susceptible to new technology are routine jobs such as clerical work, typing, filing, printing/reprography and mailing.

Clerical

As you know, business computers can be programmed to handle a variety of functions, including the five basic office functions. Since all clerical work involves some or all of these basic functions, the routine work of bank clerks, insurance clerks, stock clerks, ledger clerks, order clerks, etc can be processed by computer. Traditionally, clerical jobs can vary greatly. What a bank clerk does is very different from what a stock clerk does. When computerised, however, there is not that much difference between clerical jobs. Many of the associated tasks originally done with each individual type of clerical job become part of the computer process. The data, be they banking data or stock data, have to be entered, read, filed, retrieved, updated or output by the clerk. This is all carried out at the computer terminal and the job title 'VDU operator' becomes appropriate. Consequently, jobs which would formerly have been advertised as 'order clerk' or 'ledger clerk' in a particular type of industry are now simply advertised as 'VDU operator'. This implies that knowledge of a particular type of clerical work is not so important when the job is computerised. This can be considered an advantage to both employers and employees as it provides greater employment flexibility within a variety of clerical capacities and industries.

Advantages

For employees the advantages are:

1 more job opportunities
2 the chance to gain experience of different industries
3 the acquisition of a new skill
4 the opportunity to progress to other areas of computing
5 possibly higher status
6 job satisfaction arising from being part of a workforce trained in the use of new technology

It has been suggested that VDU operators are merely machine minders, that skills are lost and job satisfaction diminished. While this might be true in some cases, more often than not the job of VDU operator is still a 'thinking' job, requiring skill and knowledge. Operators have to accept responsibility for the data they prepare and enter. Many operators found their former clerical jobs repetitive and, when compared with their present work, less stimulating.

Disadvantages

However, while some clerical staff welcome changes and any advantages they might bring, others will consider the disadvantages to be significant:

1 working with machines all day — many people would not be happy doing so
2 the 'personal' aspect of the job is lost
3 as the computer does the processing, less personal effort is required, which affects job satisfaction
4 the change in job status
5 experience and knowledge of a particular industry is no longer considered so important or so great an asset

Typing

In Section 3, when discussing the implementation of computerisation, some of the changes in the work routine of secretarial staff were brought out. Other typing jobs affected by new technology are those of audio and copy typists.

Audiotyping

Organisations which already use audio (rather than shorthand dictation or handwritten drafts) as the method of text origination, generally opt to continue to do so, using audio in conjunction with word processing. This has two advantages:

1 Little or no change is required in the work methods of the authors, who are often managers (adapting to changes in work methods or routine is time-consuming and management time is expensive).
2 Audio is the most productive method of text origination and word processing is the most productive method of text processing. If used together, the combined effect of audio and word processing produces even greater productivity gains and cost savings than is possible if these two technologies are used separately within an organisation. This is

known as a **synergistic effect**, meaning simply that the joint effect is greater than the sum of the individual effects.

While the kind of documents prepared by audiotypists in a centre might not change much when word processing is introduced, the effect of computerisation on work methods and the actual jobs of audiotypists is quite considerable. Audiotyping has always required a high degree of concentration to cope with both unseen material and the poor dictation techniques of some authors. Combining audio with another quite complex skill such as word processing makes the job of an audiotypist even more demanding. There are two separate sets of equipment to contend with and the operation of each requires a special knowledge and skill. Not all audiotypists are able to combine these skills, nor do they all wish to do so. However, the demand for those able and willing to combine audio with word processing skills continues to grow.

Copy typing

Computer technology has created a new demand for keyboarding skills. Copy typists who suffered a loss of job opportunities with the advent of cheap photocopying equipment are now able to train as word processor or VDU operators.

Telex

Facsimile telegraphy, usually known simply as **fax** (see under Unit 36, *Electronic mail*) has replaced **telex** in many offices, thus reducing the need for **telex operators**. Those organisations where telex is still a much used means of communication have switched to computer-based telex systems, on which text can be entered, edited and formatted swiftly and with ease. Telex operators today need word processing skills. Clearly, new office technology has severely affected the jobs of telex operators.

Advantages

The advantages to operators working with the new equipment are:

1 the acquisition of a new skill
2 wider job opportunities as a result of the new skill
3 increased job satisfaction working with new technology
4 ergonomically designed equipment provides not only greater operator comfort but also facilities such as a VDU to improve the presentation of work and increase efficiency
5 telex operators frequently worked in isolation because of the high noise level of traditional telex machines — this is not necessary when using computer-based equipment

Disadvantage

The disadvantage of computerised telex to existing operators is reduction in the number of telex operator jobs, as telex can become an integrated part of a data/word processing system — in such cases, telex would be handled by word processor or VDU operators with no special telex training.

Filing

Computerisation, with the storage of data on disks, has made the job of paper filing redundant in some offices. Where the job is carried out by secretarial or other clerical staff as part of their daily duties, such a step is welcomed. Obviously, disk and file management procedures have to be followed. In organisations where full-time filing clerks are employed to cope with heavy filing loads and/or the long-term storage of documents, a decision to make full use of electronic storage could have a significant effect on filing jobs. Initially, the paper system would run parallel with the electronic filing system, until the latter is fully implemented. This provides an opportunity for filing clerks to acquire the necessary knowledge of computer off-line storage and retrieval methods. They also have to be trained in the maintenance of tape or disk libraries. New work methods and new knowledge could provide greater job interest and satisfaction, improved status and better career prospects than that of filing clerk.

Reprography/printing/DTP

Combining conventional copier technology with advances in microelectronics and communications has resulted in new printing equipment such as intelligent copiers and desktop publishing systems. Reprography departments in organisations equipped with this new technology are capable of meeting all company printing needs in addition to the usual photocopying requirements. Staff need special training to operate the sophisticated equipment and also to cope with other aspects of printing, such as layout and type sizes. This is a far cry from using an ink duplicating machine and staff trained in these new methods with the accompanying new knowledge and skills will certainly gain improved job status. They will no doubt also have greater career opportunities open to them.

Mailing

Computer-based technology is already in use in many company mailrooms in the form of electronic weighing machines, computer addressing systems, etc. However, the mailroom is one area of the electronic office that faces a very much diminished workload in the future. The growth in communicating terminals through both intersite and local area networks is reducing the need for paper communication. This will naturally have a serious effect on mailroom jobs, including those of office messengers.

Summary — Key Points

1. Ergonomics is the study of fitting the equipment to the equipment operator, with emphasis on safety, comfort and efficiency.
2. Environmental factors important to the operator's comfort and well-being are temperature, location, privacy, noise level, lighting, colour, furniture and furnishings.
3. Ergonomics plays an important part in the design of today's systems. Features to improve operator comfort and efficiency are now standard on most keyboards and VDUs.
4. Systems furniture is office furniture designed to accommodate computer equipment and users.
5. Although not drafted with reference to computer technology, the Health and Safety at Work Act 1974 applies to the work environment and use of all new office equipment.
6. Trade unions are concerned about the effects of computer technology on the health, safety and jobs of their members. They are monitoring the situation and have already made many recommendations.
7. To assess the effects of information technology in offices we need to look at the changing role of offices.
8. Offices are no longer only complementary to industry — many of them are businesses in their own right, such as service industries or information industries.
9. The five basic functions of an office to collect, transfer, verify, convert and distribute information lend themselves to computerisation.
10. Jobs most affected by and susceptible to new technology are routine jobs such as clerical work, typing, filing, printing/reprography and mailing.
11. When computerised, the differences between various clerical jobs are reduced.
12. Audio is the most productive method of text origination and word processing is the most productive method of text processing, but combining the two makes the job of an audio/word processor operator very demanding.
13. Computerisation with electronic filing of data could make the job of paper filing redundant.
14. The mailroom is one area of the electronic office that faces a very much reduced workload in the future because of communicating terminals on site and intersite.
15. General advantages of computerisation to staff appear to be the acquisition of new skills, increased job satisfaction and more job opportunities.

Knowledge Check on Section 9

Keywords (try to explain the meaning of these terms in your own words).

Concaved	Glare	QWERTY keys
Dot matrix	Information industries	Synergistic effect
Ergonomics	Numeric keypad	Systems furniture

Complete each of the following items and then check your responses either with your tutor or with the answers on page 177.

1 List four environmental factors likely to affect the personal comfort of a VDU/word processor operator.

____

____

____

____

2 List three design features which could be incorporated in a VDU to help to avoid glare.

____

____

____

3 List four design features which would help to make an operator's chair more comfortable.

____

____

____

____

4 Label the following statements true or false:

a ____ The more dots in a dot matrix, the clearer the character or picture.

b ____ Systems furniture is just another name for traditional office furniture.

c ____ Screen brightness should be adjusted to the level of lighting in the computer location.

d ____ Document holders improve source/screen relationship.

5 Fill in the blanks:
 a It is difficult for health and safety ____ to keep pace with changing technology.
 b The five basic functions of the office are to ____, transfer, ____, convert and ____ information.
 c Jobs most affected by new technology are ____ jobs.
 d Audiotyping requires a high degree of concentration to cope with ____ material.

6 Examine Fig 9.1 for 30 seconds then return to this page and try to recall six good workstation principles.

____

____

____

____

____

____

Answers

1 Location; temperature; humidity; ventilation; noise level; lighting; privacy; colour; furnishings; furniture (any four).
2 Non-reflective screen; screen filter; a swivel base; tilting facility (any three).
3 Adjustable seat height; a backrest; a wide, contoured seat; seating material other than plastic; a footrest; easily activated levers for seat and back adjustments (any four).
4 *a* T *b* F *c* T *d* T
5 *a* legislation *b* collect, verify, distribute *c* routine *d* unseen
6 Eye-height above ground for seated female normally between 1 and 1.14 m; adjustable backrest for lumbar support — no arm rests; simple document holder; keyboard top approximately 0.7 m above ground; screen at approximately right angles to line of sight but avoiding reflecting light; screen position — about 30–40° below upright eye height; accessible work surfaces; swivel chair with stable base, perhaps on castors; adjustable seat height approximately 0.4 m above ground; wires kept out of the way; footrest for very short users; minimum knee clearance of 0.2 m between seat and table (any six).

Additional questions on Section 9

1 Discuss the environmental and other factors which affect the comfort of operators and which therefore need to be considered in the design of a computer work area.
2 Describe how the study of ergonomics has affected the design of computer equipment and furniture.
3 Health and safety are obviously important, yet the long-term effects on users of the new technology are not known. How do you consider this situation should be approached by employees, employers, unions and governments?
4 Discuss the effects of information technology on two different categories of office jobs.

Assignment 9

a Fill out the checklist for health and safety of new technology in this Section of the book, relating it to your computer system.
b Compile a list of safety rules to be followed by all those using the computer centre.

10 The electronic office

In earlier sections we examined the use of various application programs on business microcomputers. As the functional capabilities of systems and software have improved, so too have other aspects, such as speed, power and user-friendliness.

In this final section, we look at the diverse functions available on today's computers — functions that make these systems suitable for use throughout an organisation by general office staff, specialist staff and management. These systems are capable of supporting all the administrative and general management functions of the office, in addition to the standard word/data processing. They combine communications with computing. It is the co-ordination of these technologies that provides the variety of functions required in the office, where the average day's work evolves around a combination of communication and processing.

Computer systems offer particular help to senior management in providing access to and analysis of information, and rapid internal and external communications. There is also the facility of time management, which will assist with scheduling of meetings and appointments. Many of these jobs cannot be delegated to subordinates, yet the lack of information and delays in communication can erode the effectiveness of executives.

The area of communication is no longer restricted to conventional mail, the telephone and telegraph systems. The merging of computer technology with telecommunications has opened up many different means of communication and we will now take a look at some of these.

UNIT 36 Electronic mail

Sending information by conventional mail or messenger services is slow and unpredictable and subject to weather, traffic and other conditions. This is particularly frustrating in business today when we have all the computer power at our disposal and are able to process documents almost instantly. Transmitting such documents to other machines electronically has been an objective for some time. Now the technology has been developed and electronic mail is available in more than one form to anyone using a computer.

Electronic mail is not new. Telex is a form of electronic mail and has been used in business for many years. What is new and so exciting about today's electronic mail is the wide range of facilities and benefits that it brings.

Electronic mail over a local area network

Where a local area network is already installed, electronic mail can be added to the system to:

1 automatically collect, distribute and store mail within the network
2 allow users to specify different levels of priority and security for each item sent (eg personal or confidential items can be viewed only by the recipient)
3 allow users to sort messages by sender or topic, using keywords, and examine all mail not yet answered
4 allow users to send documents to more than one terminal at the same time, such as specified user group
5 automatically send such items as monthly reports to all those whose names are on previously set up distribution lists
6 include an editor with which the user can compose and edit messages

Electronic mail in a local area network environment is internal (*see* Fig 10.1).

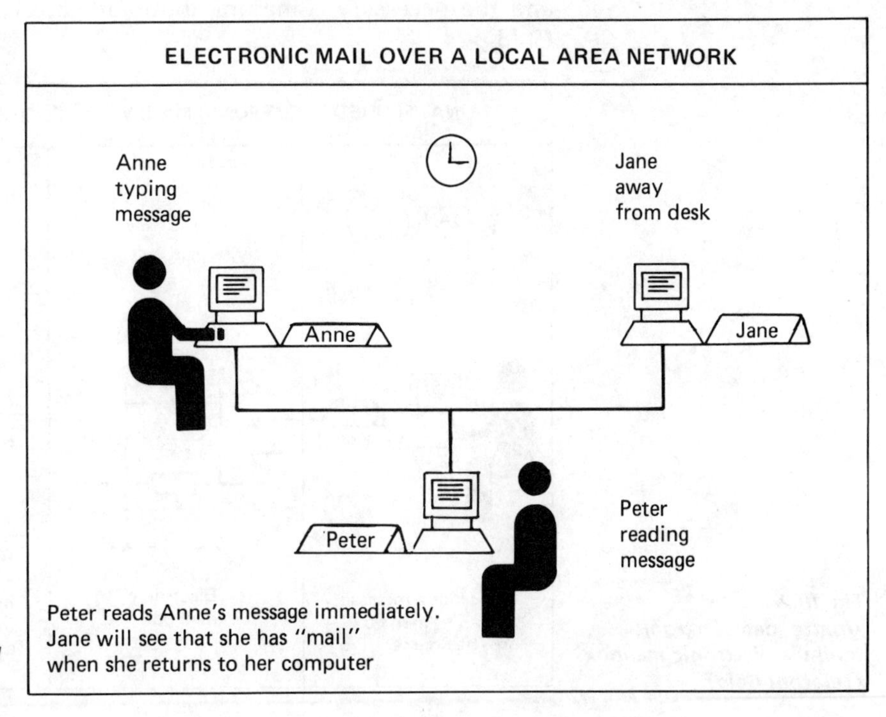

Fig 10.1 Electronic mail over a local area network

Telecom Gold

Naturally, greater benefits will accrue with inter-office electronic mail. One system that enables computer users to communicate with others externally, including internationally, is Telecom Gold. This is British Telecom's electronic mail service, which provides each subscriber with a unique mailbox number. The sender addresses the message using this number and other details of the recipient. The sender also supplies a subject heading. When the mail arrives at its destination, the subject heading is displayed on the screen. Urgent or other important messages which may have arrived while the terminal was unattended can be quickly spotted and dealt with first. The system stores all mail for later retrieval by keywords such as sender or subject. Confirmation of despatch and acknowledgement of receipt of a message can be provided. Replies can be appended to a message received, to save time. Confidential messages are protected by passwords (*see* Fig 10.2).

Telecom Gold provides users with additional services such as telemessages and telexes. Telexes can be sent and received by subscribers to Telecom Gold even if they do not have their own telex service. It is also possible for subscribers to use Telecom Gold's computers to store and process information which they might wish other users, such as branch personnel, to access.

As well as a substitute for a network service, Telecom Gold is used by companies to connect with branches, subsidiaries, suppliers and customers/clients. It is an *open* electronic mail system, which means that it is not restricted to a particular manufacturer's equipment. A company or an individual with a computer, word processor or electronic typewriter and the necessary communication software can subscribe to Telecom Gold.

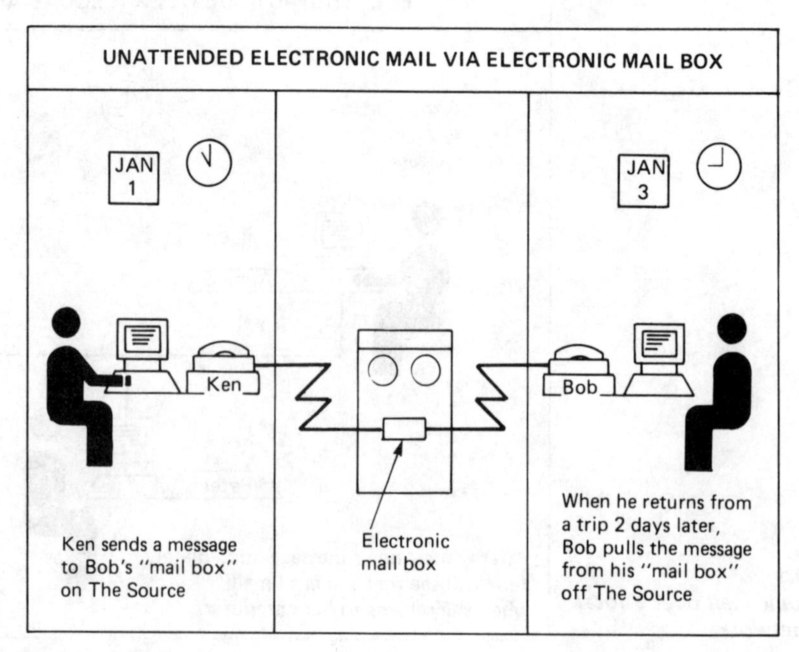

Fig 10.2
Unattended electronic mail via electronic mailbox (Telecom Gold)

The advantages of Telecom Gold are:

1 It is more reliable and faster than conventional mail delivery.
2 Messages can be transmitted at times convenient to the recipient and the sender.
3 It is cheaper to use Telecom Gold than the telephone. Therefore, telephone bills can be reduced.
4 It can reduce the time spent on the telephone trying to 'get through'.
5 Messages delivered on a VDU are not generally so formal as those received in an envelope through the regular mail. This encourages a quick response which can be similarly informal.
6 Telecom Gold is fast becoming a popular electronic mail service with links to other countries, in much the same way as the telephone system, providing access to a vast number of subscribers.

Direct electronic mail via modems

Another form of direct electronic mail is the sending of files and documents from one computer to another using a telephone line and a **modem**. The word *modem* is an abbreviation of *mo*dulator/*dem*odulator. A modem converts signals from the sending terminal into a suitable form for transmission over the telephone line (it **modulates**). At the receiving end, another modem reconverts the signals for the recipient terminal (it **demodulates**). In short, a modem allows data to be transmitted across ordinary telephone lines so that one computer can 'talk' to another computer over any distance (*see* Fig 10.3). To send and receive data, the modem must be connected to the computer and plugged into the telephone socket.

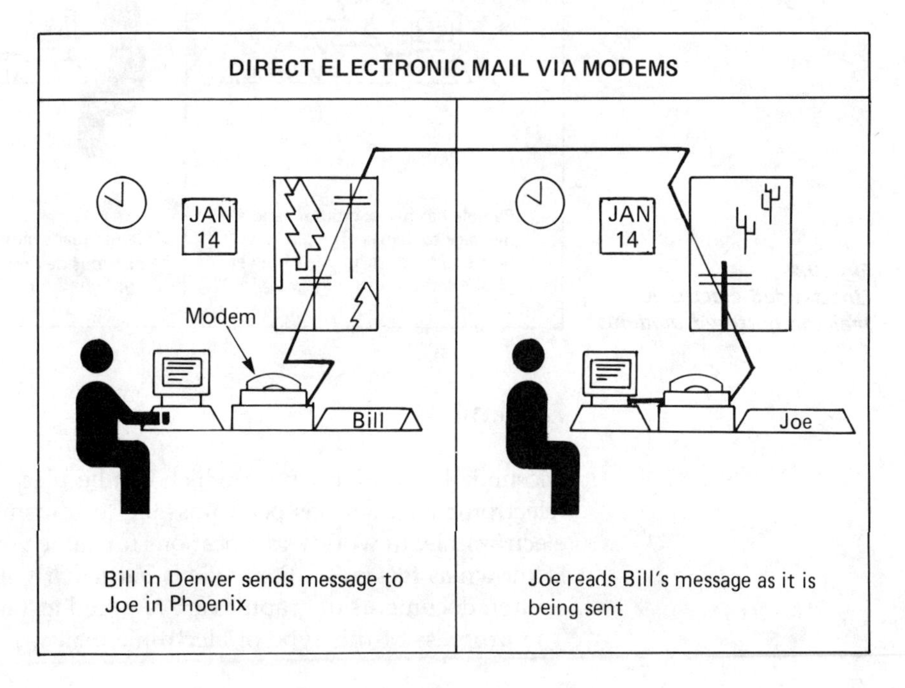

***Fig 10.3* Electronic mail via modems**

Baud rate

The 'baud rate' is the speed at which a modem can send/receive data. Some modems transmit and receive at much slower speeds than others. A baud rate of 2400/2400 is recommended for business use. This provides fast transfer of data in both directions, saving time and money. As with any telephone call, charges commence immediately upon connection. Therefore, your computer must be ready loaded with the data you wish to transmit before you dial the telephone number of the receiving computer.

Buffered modems

Mail can also be sent electronically from an unattended terminal to an unattended terminal, if necessary, using a buffered modem. The messages are stored in the modem buffer (a temporary store) of the sending machine awaiting a signal, and/or they can be stored in the buffered modem of the receiving machine until required (*see* Fig 10.4).

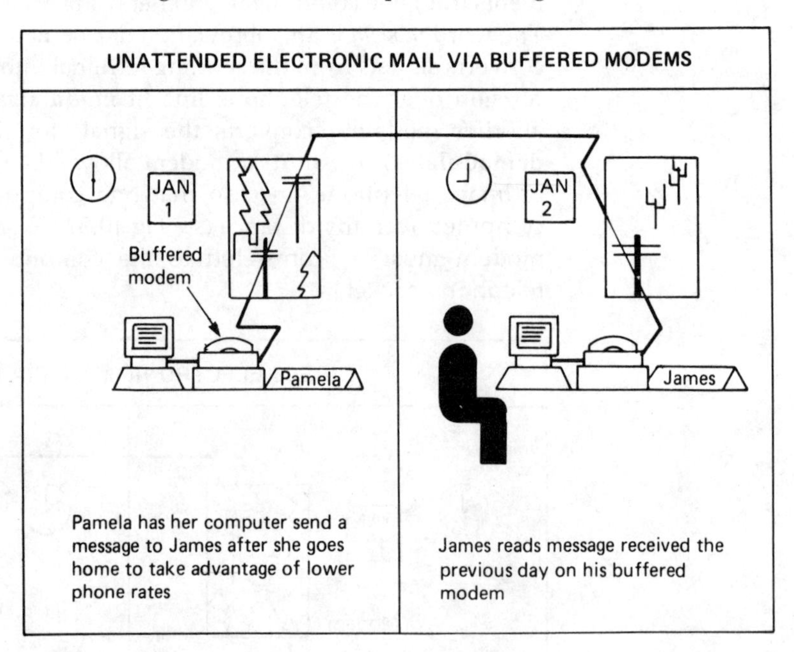

Fig 10.4
Unattended electronic mail via buffered modems

Facsimile

Facsimile is another service which can be placed under the heading of 'electronic mail'. It has been possible to transmit copies of documents electronically to worldwide locations for some years now. The technique is known as **facsimile**. Facsimile is particularly useful if copies of hand-written documents or graphics are required instantly at another location. The progress of this type of electronic mail was hampered early on by the lack of agreed protocols. Since the setting of international standards, when compatibility between different manufacturers' machines was assured, the growth of facsimile has escalated. Virtually every business now has at least one facsimile machine. As a means of business communication, the *fax* today is as important as the telephone.

Operation of a standard facsimile machine is very simple (*see* Fig 10.5). Documents are placed face down on the **document feeder** between the paper guides. The telephone system is used to make the initial connection with the recipient. Dialling can be done from the telephone set or by using the keypad on the machine. There is also a facility for abbreviated dialling. If the line is free, the document will be sent; if the line is busy, the machine will automatically redial the number for you twice after three-minute intervals. When transmission ends, the display shows the number of pages sent. Transmission time is usually around 20 seconds per A4 page. While the machine is transmitting, standard telephone charges apply. Other standard facilities are *multi-station transmission, polling, deferred transmission, confidential faxes* and *printout of reports*.

Fig 10.5
A plain paper facsimile (fax) machine

While the standard fax machine uses thermal paper for printout, the plain paper fax, incorporating laser printing and memory for storing and forwarding several pages, is making an impact on the market. A plain paper fax message will not curl or fade and a response can be written on the same sheet and faxed back to the sender. Plain paper is also cheaper than thermal and easier to obtain. These sophisticated facsimile machines also transmit faster than the standard fax.

Advantages

The advantages of a facsimile machine are:

1 It transmits and receives handwritten and/or printed data, text and graphics.

2 It transmits and receives in any alphabet, even Japanese or Arabic. This is most useful in international communication.
3 Documents can be received from anywhere in the world 24 hours a day.
4 High-quality exact copies of originals are received worldwide within a couple of minutes with immediate follow-up telephone discussion if required.
5 No special operator training is needed.
6 Fax communications are accepted in law.

Telex

Telex is one of the oldest forms of business electronic mail and has been in use for more than 30 years. In the UK it is a British Telecom service and links into a worldwide telecommunication network. Computerisation has given telex a new lease of life and the old-style telex terminal with floor-trailing paper tape has disappeared. New telex equipment is screen-based and provides the operator with editing facilities similar to those on a word processor. This is a great improvement on conventional telex, where editing facilities were crude and cumbersome. Message preparation can be carried out much more speedily on the new equipment, which generally includes additional features such as multi-destination addressing, automatic retries and pretimed and preselected batch transmission. These facilities mean that telexes are not only received when the machine is unattended, but also that telexes can be transmitted 24 hours a day without an operator being present all the time.

Teleconferencing

Teleconferencing in its basic form of speech only has been used in business for many years. This type of teleconferencing enables several people to hold a 'telephone conference' with each other from their own office. Each can contribute to the discussions and listen to the views of the others. Speech plus vision (**confravision**), a service offered by British Telecom which operates between regional centres in the UK, has also been available for some time. This service makes it possible for business executives in different cities to hold 'face-to-face' type meetings with each other without having to travel outside their city.

Videoconferencing is now also available between executives in the UK and others in the United States with the laying of a special trans-Atlantic cable. With new developments in telecommunication, and particularly in the field of image communication, videoconferencing could begin to play an important part in business communication. It could reduce the number of business meetings that executives are required to attend. A document could be discussed with a colleague in another part of the building or on another site without having to move from one's desk, as a close-up of the document can be projected on the screen. Any confidential mail can also be shown and discussed between parties, as direct contact is made first.

UNIT 37 Information retrieval systems

Another area which combines the technologies of computing and communication is that of information retrieval. All information which has to be saved must be stored or filed in such a way that it can be quickly and easily retrieved when needed. Information which is to be communicated to or accessed by several users will generally be held in a database in a computer system. A database is initially created by inputting all the data and storing it on-line in the system. The database is maintained by regularly updating the data. For example, it might be necessary to delete certain data items, add new data or alter data. This ensures that users who access the database will be given useful, accurate information. When a user requests information the computer searches the database, retrieves the information required and will even organise it so that it is presented to the user in the form wanted. The speed with which this is carried out depends on the power of the computer and the amount of data contained in the database. The ways in which the user is able to question (**interrogate**) the database depend on the capability of the software used. All this adds up to being able to retrieve what you want, when you want it and how you want it.

Teletext and Videotex are information retrieval systems. These systems enable subscribers to recall from databases a variety of information which is displayed on the screen of a computer terminal or an adapted television set.

Teletext

Teletext is a one-way communication system. This means that users can request information to be displayed on the television screen but they cannot send information back. Teletext is purely an information retrieval system. In the UK, Teletext is known as Ceefax (available on BBC) and Oracle (available on ITV). Teletext is an essentially free service, which gives the user access to an extensive range of information that can be displayed on the television screen as required. The user either purchases a television with Teletext included or an add-on Teletext facility for an existing television set. When accessing Teletext, the user is presented with an index on the screen and, with the aid of a hand-held digital unit, is able to request the pages or 'frames' of information required. Teletext provides information on subjects of general interest such as news, entertainment, sport, weather, business and religion (*see* Fig 10.6).

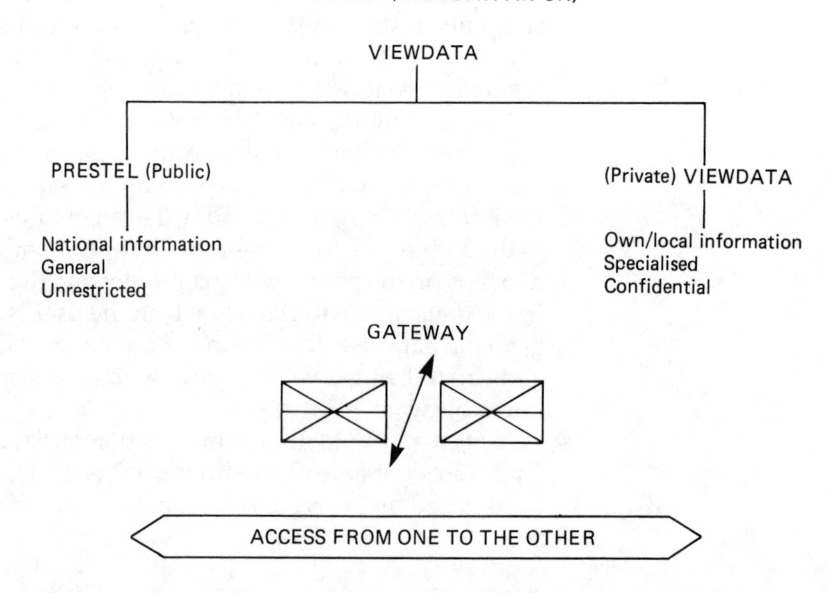

Fig 10.6
Information retrieval — Teletext/Viewdata

Videotex

Videotex, or Viewdata as it is usually called in the UK, is a two-way interactive communication system. This means that users can request particular pages of information to be displayed on a VDU and they can also send information back to the system. Viewdata equipment could be a dedicated Viewdata terminal, a computer or a television set with an adapter. A keyboard is required to enable the user to communicate with Viewdata and the Viewdata equipment is connected to a telephone line. Before discussing it any further, you need to know that there are two forms of Viewdata: one is a public service and the other is a private service.

Prestel

In the UK the public Viewdata service is known as Prestel. It is called by different names in other countries, for example Viditel in Holland and Telidon in Canada. To access the Prestel service, the subscriber dials a given number and then enters his/her identity and personal password. Prestel can be used at any time and offers subscribers over 320 000 pages of information on a wide variety of subjects, both general and specialist. (The organisations, companies and all those who supply information to the Prestel service are known as information providers.) Subscribers can use the index, that is first displayed on the screen, to assist in retrieving the information required or they can go direct to the particular frame needed. There is also a Prestel directory which can be consulted. Subscribers pay a small quarterly charge for the Prestel service, and in most cases the charge to access Prestel is that of a local telephone call. There is also a charge made for computer time during business hours. Prestel is a British Telecom service and access to information in Prestel's computers is not generally restricted. However, certain information is restricted to closed user groups, ie it is only available to specified users. For example, pages of information on a pharmaceutical company's products could be available only to members of the medical profession.

In addition to access to information, Prestel offers subscribers the following services:

1 Purchases may be ordered from a range of items offered for sale by information providers and payment arranged through the system. This is done by using the Viewdata keyboard to enter the appropriate details in a 'response frame' (a form displayed on the screen).
2 Messages can be sent and received (electronic mail) via the main Prestel computer by one subscriber to another. The sender calls Prestel and enters the mailbox number of the subscriber to whom the message is being sent. The computer will store the message until it is 'collected' by the recipient.
3 Prestel users can use the telex link service to send short telexes from their Prestel set to telex terminals in the UK (*see* Fig 10.7).
4 In business, Prestel can be used as a complete and confidential internal communications system.

Private Viewdata

Private Viewdata systems are those which are owned and operated by an organisation for private use. The system usually includes a computer, a number of Viewdata terminals and the Viewdata software. Viewdata is concerned with the input, storage and display of information and is ideal for certain applications. An organisation creates and maintains a private database, access usually being restricted to its staff and, in certain cases, extended to the organisation's clients. For example, in the travel industry a large tour operator would probably have a private Viewdata system which would be accessed not only by the operator's own staff but also by travel agents throughout the country. Very little training is required to use Viewdata and this is one of its attractions. Other advantages of private Viewdata are:

1 The provision of free communications on the user's own site.
2 The avoidance of an expensive telecommunications network as most Viewdata systems use the public telephone network.

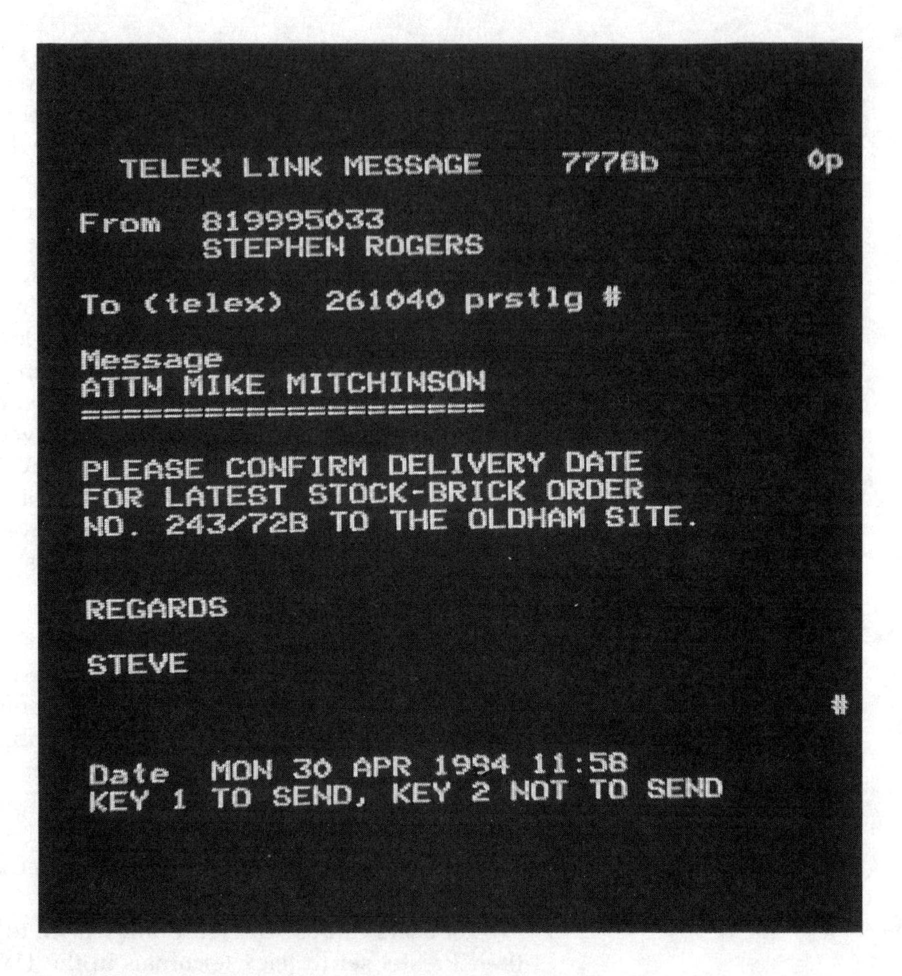

Fig 10.7
Prestel telex link message

3 The ease with which geographically scattered staff and clients can link into the user's computer for information.
4 The large number of terminals that a Viewdata computer can support, making the overall system relatively cheap.
5 The user organisation's complete control over the information supplied.
6 The provision of an electronic messaging system.
7 The provision of hard copy of Viewdata displays if required.

The information available on private Viewdata systems is very different from that available on Prestel. Prestel supplies information that is unrestricted and general, while the information supplied by private Viewdata systems is of a confidential and specialised nature. However, it is possible to have access to both. This is achieved through the Gateway system, which allows private Viewdata users to use the Prestel service. Similarly, Prestel subscribers can pass through the Gateway and link up to a private Viewdata computer, provided it is a system that does not restrict access. It is in the interests of certain companies to allow Prestel subscribers to browse through the information in their computer system. It is a cheap form of advertising (*see* Fig 10.6).

Private information services

Private Viewdata encompasses all private information services. These are services which provide instant on-line information, particularly for the financial sector, where quick decisions often have to be made. Banks, pension funds, investment trusts and fund managers need immediate access to the latest financial news, exchange rates, dealing prices, etc, in order to protect their financial interests and those of their clients.

Specialised information services are also available to the legal profession. Lawyers subscribing to these services can gain access to computerised law libraries. At the press of a button, they can summon up obscure judgments that may previously have taken them hours to track down in a conventional library.

Other information services collate, organise and store information on financial, business, political and other topics. They usually offer an extensive, full text or abstract coverage of top publications throughout the world. While access to such information is essential to the operation of some businesses, it would be impossible for any of them to process independently the vast quantities of information available to them as subscribers.

With so many companies subscribing to Viewdata services, there is every possibility that you may have to access one or more of these services regularly in your job. Learning to access and use an information retrieval service is not difficult. Whichever service you use, it is important to *first* define your aim, ie the precise information you want to retrieve, and then establish the quickest search route to it.

Microfilming

Microfilming, the miniaturisation of documents on film, is another method of recording and storing information. Documents are filmed and reduced in size on film to the point where the space required for storage is approximately 2 per cent of the space needed for the storage of the equivalent paper documents.

Computer output microfilm (COM)

A process called computer output microfilm (COM) enables users to store directly on microfilm the vast amount of information produced by computers without the need for this information to be output first in hard copy form. Storing directly from computer disk onto microfilm obviously represents a tremendous saving in paper, space, labour and time.

Computer-aided retrieval (CAR)

As you know, storage is only one part of any filing system; rapid retrieval is another. Traditional microfilm retrieval systems in the form of readers for the various types of microfilm are slow as they lack the facility to automatically and rapidly locate a particular document. Readers to magnify each frame on a roll of film or other microform and display it on a screen are, none the less, a necessary part of any microfilm retrieval system, as the user must be able to read and inspect the documents stored. What is needed is a speedy means of locating particular documents and this is provided by a system called computer-aided retrieval (CAR). This microprocessor-controlled system automatically finds, displays and copies one or more documents out of the vast number that might be stored on a roll of microfilm. This is possible because a computer database is created which contains the necessary information to identify each document. Each page is also indexed. Clearly, the more information the computer has, the easier it is to find a document.

'Office technologists'

We have discussed so far a wide range of equipment that is used in the electronic office. In the work environment it is important that you learn to operate such equipment and in this sense you should see yourself as an 'office technologist'. It is equally important that you use the equipment intelligently, which requires not just an understanding of how each unit operates, but an understanding of how they should function together. In the electronic office you will have at your disposal many machines which can fulfil many functions. You will need to think how you are going to use this capability to carry out specific tasks.

UNIT 38 Office systems

We have seen that computer technology has now been extended to general management and office administrative functions. The basic hardware requirements for the computerisation of these functions, such as a keyboard, VDU, printer and backing storage, are the same as those for word and data processing. The integration of all these functions into one system is therefore practical, providing clerical and administrative staff, secretaries and management with an office system capable of most or all of the following functions:

1 word processing for text communication
2 data processing for computation
3 personal computing for spreadsheets, databases, analysis
4 electronic filing and information retrieval
5 electronic mail, including telex and fax
6 business graphics
7 time management
8 security

There are several office systems on the market and not all offer the same functions or services. Once again an organisation should first analyse its needs and then select the office system with the services required. As these systems are not specialist systems but multifunction systems to be used by staff with different requirements, selection is not quite so simple. Greater gains are thought to be achieved if the system supports management and professional staff. For this group, internal and external communications, personal computing and time management providing diary, calendar and appointment scheduling services are probably the most useful functions. They might well use word processing for editing purposes, but not to the professional degree that it would be required by secretaries. Other facilities useful to secretarial staff would be electronic filing and information retrieval, time management (as they too need to keep diaries and calendars) and electronic mailing.

Office systems come in different sizes. There are mainframes with a large number of terminals. These systems are usually developed for large organisations. Multiterminal minicomputer systems are capturing a good share of the office systems market. These can be termed dedicated office systems, while local area networks and personal computers offer similar functions by means of various software packages.

As office systems embrace so wide a range of functions, support and training are vitally important. The numbers of staff to be trained can also be quite large and courses must be tailored to the level of use required for each function by different groups of staff.

While the office system is not the last word in computer technology — there is more to come — it does integrate data processing, word processing and communications. Thus all information processing can be handled on an office system.

Summary — Key Points

1. Electronic mail is the sending of information electronically from one machine to another.
2. Electronic mail can be incorporated in a LAN (local area network) by the addition of an electronic mail software package. The system will then collect, distribute and store mail.
3. Telecom Gold is a British Telecom electronic mail service whereby users can communicate with others externally, including internationally.
4. Some electronic mail systems use modems, buffered modems or electronic mailboxes.
5. A facsimile service transmits and receives handwritten and printed data, text, graphics and photographs electronically to and from worldwide locations.
6. New telex equipment is screen-based with editing facilities similar to those on word processors.
7. A teleconference call can connect several people worldwide to the same telephone call, while confravision makes it possible for people in different cities both to see each other on screen and to talk to each other.
8. Teletext provides information via television. It is known as Ceefax (BBC) and Oracle (ITV).

9 Videotex is a two-way communication system known as Viewdata in the UK. There is a public Viewdata system and private Viewdata.
10 Prestel is the public Viewdata system. It supplies users with information on a variety of subjects. It also provides other services such as electronic mail between users and a telex link.
11 Private Viewdata systems are set up and maintained by organisations generally for their own use or for the benefit of clients.
12 Microfilm is the miniaturisation of documents on film. COM (computer output microfilm) stores computer data output directly on to microfilm from disk or other media. CAR (computer-aided retrieval) uses a computer to quickly locate and display microfilmed documents.
13 An office system is capable of providing a variety of business services on one computer terminal. It is a multifunction system.
14 Computer technology has been extended to general management and office administrative functions.
15 An office system integrates such functions as word processing, data processing, personal computing, electronic filing and retrieval, electronic mail, business graphics, time management and security.

Knowledge Check on Section 10

Keywords (try to explain the meaning of these terms in your own words).

Baud rate	Facsimile (fax)	Open system
Computer-aided retrieval (CAR)	Gateway	Prestel
Computer output microfilm (COM)	Microfilming	Teletext
Confravision	Modem	Videotex
Electronic mail	Office system	Viewdata

Complete each of the following items and then check your responses either with your tutor or with the answers on page 194.

1 Match each term in the first column with its meaning from the second column:

a ____	*1* Telecom Gold	*a*	Transmits true copies of documents instantly to remote locations.
____	2 Confravision	*b*	Allows for speech plus vision communication between users in different UK regional centres.
____	3 Facsimile	*c*	Is a British Telecom electronic mail service which provides each subscriber with a unique mailbox number.

b

____	*1* Videotex	*a*	Is the British name for the public Viewdata service.
____	*2* Teletext	*b*	Is an information retrieval system, which is known in the UK as Viewdata.
____	*3* Viewdata	*c*	Is a two-way communication service which can be either public or private.
____	*4* Prestel	*d*	Gives users access to information as required via television (BBC and ITV).

2 Tick one or more of the following if appropriate. Microfilming is

a the miniaturisation of documents on film ____
b a method of recording and storing information ____
c a space-saving method of filing ____
d only possible from a hard copy original ____

3 Fill in the blanks:

a An office system is a ____ function system.
b ____ modems can be used to send mail electronically from one unattended terminal to another unattended terminal.
c Telecom Gold provides users with additional services, such as ____ and ____.
d The teletext service received via BBC is ______ and via ITV is ______

4 List five standard facilities that a fax machine provides:

____

____

____

____

____

Answers

1 **a** *1c* *2b* *3a*
  b *1b* *2d* *3c* *4a*
2 *a* *b* *c*
3 *a* multi *b* buffered *c* telemessages, telex *d* Ceefax, Oracle
4 Multistation transmission; polling; deferred transmission; confidential faxes; printout of reports.

Additional questions on Section 10

1 Compare the facilities and advantages offered by the Telecom Gold service and conventional mail. Which service do you think would be more useful to a medium-sized manufacturing company with regional branches in the UK and why?
2 Discuss the use of public and private Viewdata in business.
3 Discuss the part played by facsimile equipment in the electronic office.
4 Describe electronic mail:

a incorporated in a local area network
b using a modem
c using an electronic mailbox

Assignment 10

a Connect your computer, if possible, to another computer or device for the purpose of communicating, using whatever hardware and/or software is required to do so.
Transmit a message and request an answer back.
Take a printout of the response message.
b Access Prestel (or any other information retrieval system that you have access to).
Find out what today's rate of exchange is: Sterling £/$US.
With your objective in mind, work out the quickest route to obtaining the information.

Epilogue

While we are learning to live with information processors, computers which calculate and process information step by step, the birth of a new 'generation' of computers is taking place. These new machines are being endowed with artificial intelligence, which implies an ability to think and to reason. Instead of data they will process knowledge, and they will do this not in the serial fashion of present-day computers but more as the human mind during the thinking process.

Computers with knowledge bases are already being used for specific and intellectual tasks, as experts with a broad and deep knowledge of a particular subject would be. Not surprisingly, these systems are called 'expert' systems. In order to function intelligently, expert systems need two kinds of knowledge.

The first is the sort of knowledge that we acquire going through college, from textbooks and lectures. All these accepted facts are put into the system's knowledge base. But someone who has acquired textbook knowledge in a subject is not generally considered an expert in that field. The second, the expertise, comes with practical experience — what one finds out for oneself. Experimentation and intelligent guesswork (deduction) also enter into it. The same problem might be approached differently by two experts in the same field. Opinions, beliefs and intuition all play a part. In order to supply machines with this second type of knowledge, the brains of real live experts have to be picked. This is usually a difficult task, as experts are often not conscious of why they do things in a certain way. Special types of programs then have to be written to represent this 'expert' knowledge in the computer.

Clearly it is important to capture the knowledge of experts in machines when one considers that it takes a very long time for someone to become an expert in a subject. It also requires a special type of person to specialise to that extent — one who is capable, willing and keenly interested in the particular field. Once knowledge is captured in a computer, it can also be reproduced. It is also ongoing and can be added to or changed in the light of new knowledge. Many knowledge-based professions where experts are vital, such as the medical and engineering professions, are resorting to expert systems.

The ultimate object in developing the 'fifth generation' computer is to create a system which will 'learn'. Readers will hear much more of these intelligent machines in the future.

Past examination questions — Pitman Examinations Institute

Practical Spreadsheet Processing — Intermediate

Instructions to candidates

You are an administrative assistant at R K Smith Ltd, which produces sports equipment. One of your tasks is to work out the price to charge for orders which customers place weekly.

It has been decided that daily orders and charges will be kept on a spreadsheet package which you must set up. Perform the following tasks in the order in which they appear.

1 Construct a spreadsheet showing the product and price per unit. Today four orders have been received and you have copies of corresponding despatch notes showing the number of items sent out. On the spreadsheet show the cost of each of these orders along with its pre-discount and (if applicable) post-discount prices.
  Save this spreadsheet under an appropriate filename.

2 Using the spreadsheet, show the total value of sales for each product and for the week as a whole.
  Save this spreadsheet under a different filename.

3 Print out the spreadsheets.

R K SMITH LTD
PRICE LIST

PRODUCT	PRICE PER UNIT (£)
Tennis racquets	25.20
Leather football	5.80
Rubber football	3.00
Badminton racquets	11.60
Tennis balls (box)	19.20
Basket balls (each)	4.80
Baseball bat	6.00
Rounders bat	4.80

DISCOUNTS:

10% discount for orders of over £500

R K SMITH LTD

PRODUCT	NUMBER DESPATCHED
Tennis racquets	
Leather football	60
Rubber football	25
Badminton racquets	
Tennis balls (box)	25
Basket balls (each)	
Baseball bat	15
Rounders bat	

ORDER NUMBER 88/4/1

R K SMITH LTD

PRODUCT	NUMBER DESPATCHED
Tennis racquets	10
Leather football	20
Rubber football	50
Badminton racquets	25
Tennis balls (box)	25
Basket balls (each)	25
Baseball bat	15
Rounders bat	10

ORDER NUMBER 88/4/2

R K SMITH LTD

PRODUCT	NUMBER DESPATCHED
Tennis racquets	
Leather football	
Rubber football	5
Badminton racquets	5
Tennis balls (box)	
Basket balls (each)	
Baseball bat	10
Rounders bat	10

ORDER NUMBER 88/4/3

R K SMITH LTD

PRODUCT	NUMBER DESPATCHED
Tennis racquets	30
Leather football	5
Rubber football	25
Badminton racquets	25
Tennis balls (box)	10
Basket balls (each)	10
Baseball bat	10
Rounders bat	10

ORDER NUMBER 88/4/4

Understanding computers — selected questions

Part I

1 Which one of these is *only* an output device?
- a An optical character reader.
- b A terminal.
- c A teletypewriter.
- d A printer.
- e A magnetic disk drive. *(2 marks)*

2 Which of the following statements defines a mouse?
a an output device.
b an input device.
c a power switch.
d a security device.
e a backing store device. *(adapted) (2 marks)*

3 A spreadsheet is:
a a program for recovering specific information from stored data.
b a collection of words and phrases.
c a set of program documentation.
d an application package which is used to display financial or statistical information.
e a set of icons. *(2 marks)*

Part II

4 a Explain what is meant by *Word Processing*. *(2 marks)*
b List *three* typical uses. *(3 marks)*
c What are the hardware requirements for a word processing system? Distinguish between stand-alone and shared resource configurations. *(4 marks)*
d How does Word Processing affect the people in the organisation? *(3 marks)*
(Total 12 marks)

Disk Management — selected questions

Instructions to candidate

You work as an administrative assistant for a local surgery. Part of your job involves maintaining the computerised database. You have to update files based on information passed to you. You also have to ensure that the information contained in the system is accurate and safe from accidental corruption. It is also important that the data remains confidential and that only authorised personnel are able to access the data. Files are kept on patients, appointments and surgery staff.

Part II

Answer the following questions on lined paper and clearly number each answer.

One of the doctors has been asked to talk to some of his colleagues about the use of computers in a surgery. Since he knows very little about them, he has asked you to give him some information. Write down the answers you would give him to the following questions.

1 State the make and model of computer you are using.
Name the operating system used by this computer. *(3 marks)*

2 Briefly describe the purpose of an operating system. *(5 marks)*
3 State the amount of RAM available to the computer. *(1 mark)*
4 State the make, model and type of printer you are using. Briefly describe the method by which your printer produces printed output. *(5 marks)*
5 What purpose would a password system have in protecting computer files in a doctor's surgery? *(1 mark)*
6 What different levels of access may be required for doctors, reception staff and administration staff? *(5 marks)*
7 If the patients' files were kept on a hard disk, what procedures should be adopted to prevent data being lost? *(2 marks)*
8 What is the purpose of the write-protect tab/notch on a floppy disk? *(3 marks)*

Pitman Examinations Institute syllabuses

Office Technology and Information Processing

Word Processing — Elementary
Word Processing — Intermediate
Word Processing — Advanced
Masterclass Word Processing
Practical Word Processing
Keyboarding — Profile
Text Production Skills
Practical Data Processing — Elementary
Practical Data Processing — Intermediate
Practical Spreadsheet Processing — Elementary
Practical Spreadsheet Processing — Intermediate
Understanding Computers

Business Information Systems Diploma Levels 1, 2 and 3 Course Units

Computer-based Information Processing
Office Information Technology
Business Principles
Communications
Business Calculations
Planning and Problem-Solving
Personal Development

The RSA CLAIT Syllabus

This scheme provides both Stage I certification for those who fulfil the criteria specified on page 204 and profile certification for those who are unable, or do not wish, to fulfil full Stage I requirements.

Target population: anyone who wishes to be able to use computers and information technology. This scheme also provides a comprehensive basis for those intending to go on to specialised or more advanced studies.

Aim: to assess the candidate's ability to use computers and information technology effectively in common applications.

Topics	*Assessment Objectives* Candidates must be able to demonstrate ability to	*Profile Sentences*

1 Applications of computers and information technology

NB: For a profile certificate, candidates must attempt at least one of the following Applications; for award of a Stage I certificate candidates must meet all the Objectives on at least three of the Applications as well as all the Objectives in Section 2.

Topics	Assessment Objectives	Profile Sentences
a A Word Processing package	*01* **ENTER** text	
	02 **LOAD** text	**P1** Enter, load and save text
	03 **SAVE** text	
	04 **INSERT** words	
	05 **INSERT** paragraph	**P2** Insert/delete/replace words; insert/delete paragraphs
	06 **DELETE** words	
	07 **DELETE** paragraph	
	08 **REPLACE** words	
	09 **CHANGE** margins	**P3** Change margins
	FORMAT printout:	
	**010* line-spacing	***P4** Change layout
	**011* justification (on/off)	
b A Spreadsheet package	*012* **ENTER** text	
	013 **ENTER** numeric data	**P5** Enter and edit text and numeric data
	014 **DELETE** entries	
	015 **REPLACE** entries	
	016 **REPLICATE** entries	**P6** Replicate in a spreadsheet
	017 **CHANGE** the format	**P7** Change the format

Topics	*Assessment Objectives*		*Profile Sentences*	
	018	**USE** a formula	**P8**	Use formulae
	**019*	**ADD** a row or column	***P9**	Extend the spreadsheet
	**020*	**PROJECT** new values		
c A Database package	*021*	**SET UP** files containing alphabetic and numeric fields within the record	**P10**	Set up a database
	022	**ENTER** data		
	023	**ADD** records	**P11**	Enter data and edit the database
	024	**DELETE** records		
	025	**EDIT** records		
	026	**SORT** records by a keyfield	**P12**	Formulate selection procedures for target records
	027	**SEARCH** records by a keyfield		
	**028*	**PRINT** selected fields	***P13**	Print selected fields
	**029*	**SEARCH** on more than one criterion	***P14**	Search on more than one criterion
d A Videotex system	*030*	**LOG ON** to a Viewdata and/or teletext system	**P15**	Log on to a Videotex system
	031	**TRACE** pages on a specific topic	**P16**	Trace pages on a specific topic
	032	**AMEND** a directory of pages available	**P17**	Amend a directory of pages available
	033	**EDIT** a page	**P18**	Edit a page
	034	**CHANGE THE ROUTING** of a page	**P19**	Change the routing of a page
		COMPOSE a new page using techniques of:		
	**035*	coloured text	***P20**	Compose a new page using a variety of techniques
	**036*	double height characters		
	**037*	flashing		
	**038*	graphics		
	**039*	background filling		
e A Business/Accounting package	*040*	**ENTER** a variety of business information relevant to the package	**P21**	Enter information
(Packages most suitable for this are: General ledger; Purchase ledger; Sales ledger; Payroll; Stock control)	*041*	**SEARCH** the package for information	**P22**	Search the package for information
	042	**ADD** records		
	043	**DELETE** records	**P23**	Change file details
	044	**CHANGE** records		
	**045*	**PRODUCE** a report on specified information	***P24**	Produce a report on specified information
f A Graphics/Plotting package (It *may* be necessary to use more than one package for this section.)				
i a drawing system	*046*	**DRAW** shapes/symbols	**P25**	Draw, change, label and store shapes/symbols
	047	**CHANGE** shapes/symbols		
	048	**STORE** shapes/symbols		
	049	**COLOUR OR SHADE** sections		
	050	**USE** text to label drawings		

Topics	*Assessment Objectives*	*Profile Sentences*
ii graphical representation	**USE** a variety of prepared data to produce:	
	051 pie charts	**P26** Produce graphical outputs from numeric data
	052 histograms	
	053 graphs	
	054 **USE** text to label graphs/charts	
	055* **USE a formula to produce a graph	***P27** Use a formula to produce a graph

2 Computers and information technology

Topics	*Assessment Objectives*	*Profile Sentences*
a Using the computer system	*056* **POWER UP** in correct sequence	**P24** Start up a computer system; load the program and data; close down the system
	057 **LOAD** a program	
	058 **LOAD** data into the system	
	059 **CLOSE DOWN** the system in correct sequence	
b Using components of the computer system		
i Input device	*060* **USE** the keyboard or other input device to enter data	**P29** Use an input device
ii Output device	**USE** the printer to output information:	
	061 **LOAD** paper into printer, set paper and printer to the top of a form	**P30** Use a printer
	062 **CHECK** printer is on-line	
	063 **OUTPUT** hard copy	
iii Storage media	*Either*	
	064 **FORMAT** a blank disk or select an empty user area	
	065 **COPY** a file from one disk to another or copy a file from one user area to another	**P31** Use a disk storage system
	066 **LIST** the directory of files available	
	067 **ERASE** a file from disk or user area	
	or	*or*
	068 **LOAD** a file from tape	**P32** Use a tape storage system
	069 **SAVE** a program on tape	
	070 **OPERATE** a simple system to ensure the backing of data	**P33** Operate a simple system to ensure the backing of data

Topics	*Assessment Objectives*	*Profile Sentences*
c Using a computer as a communicating device	*071* **CONNECT** the computer, using appropriate hardware and software to *a* send information to, OR *b* receive or retrieve information from, another source (eg another computer) locally through a network or remotely through an external communications system.	**P34** Use a computer as a communicating device

Scheme of assessment

Assignments set in the *contexts* of the six Applications (1(a)–(f)) will also test all the Objectives of Section 2 in integrative tasks. Centres have the option of using Assignments set by the RSA or of devising their own Assignments. Assessment will be carried out locally, by marking against an RSA checklist, and a sample of the assessed work from each centre will be checked by the RSA.

Criteria of assessment

To quality for any Profile Sentence candidates must satisfy the Assessor in all the Assessment Objectives specified for it in the syllabus above.

Objectives relating to the entry of data must be carried out to a level of accuracy equivalent to no more than 3 errors per Assignment.

Objectives relating to the manipulation and alteration of data must be carried out with complete accuracy.

Objectives in Section 2 (eg relating to the use of software instructions to carry out tasks such as copying, printing, loading data) are either carried out correctly (in which case the candidate has met the criteria) or not carried out correctly (in which case the criteria have not been met).

Certification

Certificates will be awarded as follows:

a Candidates who qualify for one or more of the Profile Sentences will be awarded a profile listing of all the sentences in which they have demonstrated competence.

b Candidates who qualify for all the Profile Sentences, except those marked with an asterisk, in at least *three* of the Applications of Section 1 and all the Objectives in Section 2 will be awarded a Certificate denoting a Pass at Stage I.

c Those who further qualify for all the asterisked Profile Sentences in three Applications of Section 1 will be awarded an endorsement for a Distinction at Stage I.

Glossary

Append	To join one file to another file
Application program	A program to carry out a specific business task, eg stock control
Archive	Store files off-line to make room for new input and to keep the system running efficiently
Back-up copy	An additional copy of a file stored on another disk or a duplicate of a complete disk
BASIC	A programming language
Batch processing	Processing documents in a batch at the end of a working period
Baud rate	The speed at which data are transmitted and received
Bidirectional	Ability of the printhead to move from left to right and then from right to left across a page while printing
Bitstream fonts	Fonts generated by software
Boilerplate	The technique of combining into a document blocks of previously created text
Boldface	Printing head prints twice over the same word(s)
Byte	A group of 8 'bits' (*b*inary dig*its*) strung together to represent a number or character
Central processing unit (CPU)	The part of the computer which performs computations, reads, interprets and processes information, oversees the use of the main memory and controls the input and output operations of the system
Computer-aided retrieval (CAR)	The use of a computer to locate quickly and display microfilmed documents
Computer output microfilm (COM)	The storage of computer data output directly onto microfilm from disk or other media
Concaved keys	Keyboard keys sunken in the middle to prevent the operator's fingers from slipping off
Concurrent operation	Simultaneous operation. For example, two or more workstations inputting data at the same time when sharing a CPU and hard disk
Configuration	An arrangement of system components
Confravision	A British Telecom service which enables groups of people in different cities to hold a conference (speech plus vision)
CP/M	Control Program for Microcomputers — a popular operating system
Cursor	A flashing or solid rectangle or horizontal line which indicates on the VDU the position of the next typed character
Data	Raw facts and figures
Database	An organised pool of data
Default drive	The disk drive currently in use
Desktop publishing	Using a computer to replace all the stages of producing a published document previously done by hand
Destination disk	The disk to which a file is being copied from another disk
Directory	A section of the disk with a unique name in which a group of related files are stored

Disk drive	The mechanism which spins the disk at a high speed and rapidly reads information from the disk or writes information to it
DOS	Short for Disk Operating System. DOS is a program that gives you control over what your computer does and how it does it
Dot matrix	Characters on the screen are made of dots and the number of dots in a given area is called the dot matrix. The more dots in a dot matrix the clearer the character or picture
Down time	The period during which the system is inoperable
Edit	To change text in some way — by overtyping, deleting, inserting or rearranging
Electronic mail	The electronic transmission of documents from one device to another
Ergonomics	The study of fitting the equipment to the operator with emphasis on safety, comfort and efficiency
Facsimile/fax	The transmission of a copy of a document over a telephone line
Feasibility study	A study carried out to establish whether or not computerisation is a practicable solution
Field	In data organisation a field is an item of data. Several fields or items of related data make up a record
File	A group of similar records kept together is a file
Floppy disk	Recording medium on which information is stored (often called a diskette)
Footer	Text which is to appear at the foot of each page of a document
Font	A set of characters (all the letters, numbers and other characters) in a particular typeface
Foreground/background	A facility which allows the operator to edit text on the screen (foreground) while outputting another document on the printer (background)
Format	In word processing the format is the layout of the document, covering margins, page design, tabs etc
Formatted disk	A disk which has been prepared to accept (store) files
Function keys	Keys which perform different functions according to the application program in use
Gateway	The link between private Viewdata and Prestel
Gigabytes	One billion bytes, ie 1 billion characters
Glare	Strong fierce light, unwanted and unpleasant
Global search	Search through the entire document/file
Glossary	This word has two meanings in computing: **1** it is a function which allows previously created text or data to be stored under a few easily remembered keystrokes for quick recall and insertion into another document; **2** a list of terms and their explanations
Hard copy	The paper copy of a processed document
Hard return	A 'return' entered manually by the operator, eg at the end of a paragraph
Hardware	The tangible (or physical) parts of a computer system, ie all input and output devices
Header	A standard heading to be printed at the top of each page of a multipage document
Highlight	Identify and emphasise text by brightening or deepening the words or background
Icons	Pictures or symbols used on the screen to represent files, documents, in/out trays, etc
Index	This is a list of all the files on a particular disk and is sometimes called 'directory'. The disk operating system sets up an index for each disk used and as a new file is opened it is automatically added to the index/directory of the disk

Information industries	Industries whose actual business is handling information, such as education and banking
Initialised	This is another word for a formatted disk, ie a disk which has been prepared to accept files
Input	Data or text entered into the system
Integrated software	Software which allows the operator to perform complicated tasks involving the use of more than one application without the need to stop and change software
Interpreter	Translates programs written in a high-level language such as BASIC into machine code
In-use light	A light located below the disk drive opening which comes on when the system is performing reading or writing operations on the disk in the drive. Also known as 'indicator light'
Justified	Text printed out with an even right-hand margin
Kerning	Adjusting the space between characters, ie moving a character closer to the previous character
Kilobytes	One thousand bytes, ie 1000 characters
Leading	The vertical space between two lines of print, measured from the tops of the capital letters in one line to the tops of the capital letters in the next line
Legend	Explanatory note on a graph indicating which colour or symbol corresponds to each set of data
Load	The transference of a program into the computer's memory
Light pen	A device which the user points at the screen to select an activity or draw the input
Macro	A simple keyboard command, which automatically repeats a particular string of keystrokes and/or commands previously entered and saved (sometimes called a Glossary)
Megabytes	One million bytes, ie 1 million characters
Menu	A list of facilities displayed on the VDU from which the operator makes a choice
Merge	This is a function which allows variable data items to be incorporated into a standard letter
Microfilming	The miniaturisation of documents on film for the purpose of storing the information
Mnemonic	The use of ordinary letters or words on the keyboard to give instructions to the system
Modem	An abbreviation of *mo*dulator/*dem*odulator. It enables data to be transmitted across ordinary telephone lines so that one computer can 'talk' to another computer
Monitor	A VDU (screen)
Mouse	A hand-held pointing device which is used to input commands and quickly move the cursor around the screen
Multitasking	Working with more than one application program at a time
Multi-user system	A system where a number of terminals share a powerful CPU, hard disk and printers
Natural language	Language as spoken by people
Network	A facility which interconnects all the electronic equipment in a building, so that communication and sharing of information and equipment can take place
Numeric keypad	An extra set of figure keys grouped in rows like a calculator on the right of the keyboard
Office system	A multifunction system which provides a variety of business services covering also management and administrative functions

Off-line storage	Storage of files on disks or tapes which are not under the direct control of the CPU. For example, those work disks stored on the operator's desk
On-line storage	Disks, tapes, etc under the direct control of the CPU (ie in the disk drive)
Operating system	A collection of programs which controls the operation of other programs
Optical character reader	A machine which reads and processes typed or printed pages and automatically transfers the contents into word processors, computers or other devices
Originator	Writer or author of text
Output	The end product of a computer operation
Overwrite	To save an amended version of a file on the same disk as the original file, under the same filename, thus substituting the amended file for the original
Pen Windows	An operating system for pen-based computers
Pitch	The number of characters typed (or printed) per inch
Plotter	An electromechanical device which reproduces on paper, with a pen, the images produced on the VDU
Prestel	This is the public viewdata system. It supplies subscribers with information on a variety of subjects via a television or other VDU. It also provides a host of other services
Primary sort	Sorting in the first order of priority
Printout	The printed copy of the information processed by the system
Procedures manual	A manual clearly outlining the procedures to be followed when undertaking a specific task
Program	A set of instructions which tells the computer what to do, step by step
Prompt	The system's way of telling the operator that information is required. A question or symbol appears on the screen
Proofread	Check for errors
Protocols	Rules and conventions for transmitting data
Purge	Erase files from disks
Query languages	Languages which have been compiled especially for management to question a system's database
QWERTY keys	Standard typewriter keys. The name QWERTY comes from the arrangement of the letters on the left-hand side of the third row
RAM	Short for Random Access Memory. The memory that DOS uses for temporarily storing programs and data
Read/write head	The part of the disk drive which floats a minute distance above the disk and which reads information from and writes information to the disk
Reformat	Change the layout of a document
Repagination	This is a word processing function which allows existing page breaks to be changed
Required space	This is a word processing facility which ensures that groups of words such as names and dates are not separated by the word wraparound feature and placed on two separate lines
Response time	The time required to retrieve or process data or text
ROM	Short for Read Only Memory. The portion of the computer's memory that is permanently recorded
Root directory	The main directory that DOS creates on the disk
Scalable fonts	Fonts in varying sizes, from very small to very large
Scanner	A device to capture text and graphic images and directly input these into a computer
Scrolled	Applies to text moved up, down or across on the screen, the purpose being to bring other text into view
Search and replace	This is a word processing function which allows a document to be searched for a specified string of characters and to replace this with another character string

Shared mode	Graph and data from which it was generated displayed on the screen simultaneously
Shared resources	A configuration whereby a group of workstations share peripherals such as the printer
Soft hyphen	This type of hyphen is inserted at an appropriate point in a word at the end of a line either manually or automatically to keep a tidy right-hand margin. If the format is changed later, and the position of the word is such that hyphenation is no longer required, the soft hyphen will be deleted automatically
Soft programmable keys	Keys which can be programmed to generate different characters, commands or functions
Software	Programs (instructions to the computer)
Software house	A company which produces and markets packaged software (programs)
Source disk	The disk on which a file to be copied is stored
Spooling	The queueing of documents for a printer when the printer is shared between several workstations
Spreadsheet	A worksheet for calculation and analysis of business data
Stand-alone	A single independent data/word processing system
Status line	A line of information on the file being worked on which appears either across the top or the bottom of the screen
Strikeover	This is a method of correcting by simply typing over the incorrect character
Subscript	The character is printed below the line. Sometimes referred to as 'inferior'
Superscript	The character is printed above the line. Also called 'superior'
System	A group of interacting parts that operate together to achieve a common goal
System disk	The disk on which the operating system is stored
System software	Programs which control the performance of the computer system
Systems analyst	A computer professional whose job is to analyse the existing business system or function and design an efficient computerised system for the job
Systems furniture	Furniture designed to accommodate computer equipment and users
Tape streamer	A drive unit into which a data cartridge is inserted for the purpose of backing up the files on a hard disk
Teletext	An information retrieval system available via television known as Ceefax on BBC and Oracle on ITV. Users receive information but cannot respond
Terminal language	The labels or words used on the keyboards of different microcomputer systems
Terminology	The words and terms used in connection with specialist occupations, eg computing
Text	Words (as opposed to data)
Topology	Term used to define the shape of a network
Touch tablet	An input device. Anything drawn on the touch tablet with the finger appears on the screen. An electric stylus can be used instead of a finger
Turnaround time	Time taken to produce a completed document from receipt of original draft
User interface technology	Devices and methods incorporated in hardware and software which allow the user to think and act intuitively, thus making computers easier to use
Videotex	This is known as Viewdata in the UK
Viewdata	The Viewdata service is divided into Prestel and private Viewdata. Private Viewdata is set up by organisations for their own use and for the benefit of special groups of users
Visual display unit (VDU)	A screen on which the stored information is displayed
Widow and orphan lines	Widow line: the first line of a new paragraph on its own at the bottom of a page. Orphan line: the last line of a paragraph at the start of a fresh page
Windows	The display of more than one document on the screen at the same time, allowing the user to take information from one document and insert it into another. Provides the facility to work with more than one document or program at the same time

Wordspace	The space between words. All word processors accept the space following a word as part of that word
Word wraparound	This is a word processing feature. When text is being entered, the cursor, when it reaches the right margin, will automatically return to the left of the next line, taking with it any word or portion of a word which does not fit onto the typed line above
Work disk	A disk used to store documents/data being worked on, and also completed files
Workflow	The stages of production through which a document (or any job) passes
Work measurement	Measuring over a period of time the pattern, quantity and type of work done by an employee and the time it takes the employee to carry out each task
Workstation	A computer connected to a network
Write protect	When a diskette is write-protected, no information can be written to the diskette, thereby protecting existing files on the disk from being overwritten
WYSIWYG	Short for What You See Is What You Get, ie what you see on the screen will be produced exactly in the printout

Index